P9-CFX-140

FOUNDATIONS

in PERSONAL FINANCE®

college edition

DAVE RAMSEY

Notice of Copyright Protection

It is unlawful to copy or reproduce any part of the working textbook without the written consent of the publisher.

Permissions

Requests for permission to make copies of any part of the work should be mailed to:
Permissions - Curriculum Department
Ramsey Solutions
1011 Reams Fleming Blvd
Franklin, TN 37064

Note to the Reader

This publication is designed to provide accurate and authoritative information in regard to the subject matter covered. It is sold with the understanding that the publisher is not engaged in rendering legal, accounting, or other professional advice or services. If legal advice or other expert assistance is required, the service of a competent professional person should be sought.

7 8 9 10 jst 24 23 22 21

978-1-936948-00-0

Acknowledgments

The Lampo Group, Inc. would like to give special thanks to the following people for their assistance with this project. This input was essential for creating a financial literacy curriculum that meets the needs of college students and empowers them in the area of personal finance.

Curriculum Development

Cheryl Brehm

Editing

Allen Harris
Amber Dillon
Dana Owen
Darcie Clemen
Grace Clausing
Jennifer Gingerich
Jim King
Kajsa White
Michelle Grooms
Rachel Cruze
Richard Speight
Robert Bruce

Video and Print Development

Bobby Marko
Brian Williams
Cam Cornelius
Collin Fatke
Daniel Bell
Dave Oglesby
David Wilkinson
Diana Key
Hannah Cook
Jason Miller
Jennifer Sievertsen
Jessalynn Whyte
Jessica Sloan
Jon Acuff
Jon Melton
Josh Hancock
Katie Crenshaw
Megan Hill

Website Development

Aaron Fleckenstein
Andrew Kallemeyn
Brett Kozimor
Corey Robertson
David Leeds
Dino Evangelista
Jon Fouss
KC Jones
Kelli Hansbauer
Kevin Powell
Luke LeFevre
Phil Thomas
Scott Chaney

Academic Curriculum Review Committee

Adele Harrison PhD
Associate Professor of Finance and Accounting
Azusa Pacific University, California

Bob Garner MBA
Assistant Professor of Business
Flager College, Florida

Brad Barnett MS, AFC
Senior Associate Director of Financial Aid
James Madison University, Virginia

Jeff Guernsey MS
Assistant Professor of Finance
Cedarville University, Ohio

Kent Ford MAEcon
Professor of Economics
Onondaga Community College, New York

Robert Ford DMin
Professor of Business
Kentucky Christian University, Kentucky

Roger Bingham MBA
Vice Chancellor for Student Affairs
Ivy Tech Community College, Indiana

Ron Beckman MBA
Professor of Business
Arkansas Community College, Arkansas

Steve Neilsen MEd
Director of Student Retention
California Baptist University, California

Professional Contributors

Dave Ramsey
Financial Expert, Best-selling Author, and National Radio Personality

Jeffrey Zander CIC
President
Brokerage Insurance Agency

Jeffrey Dobyns CFP®, CLU, ChFC
President and Founding Partner
Investment Agency

Chris Hogan FMC, LCT
Director, Wealth Coach Program
Dave Ramsey's Team

Lisa Barber
Personal Financial Coach
Dave Ramsey's Team

Eddie White
Director of Financial Aid
Higher Education Institution

Kim York
Vice President of Marketing
Credit Union

Terry DeSelms CRS, GRI
Owner
Real Estate Agency

Jennifer Sievertsen MBA
Chief Marketing Officer
Dave Ramsey's Team

Rick Perry
Director of HR
Dave Ramsey's Team

L.H. "Mike" Hardwick, III
Founder, Owner and President
Mortgage Company

Norman D. Rollins
Attorney, Owner and Partner
Private Law Firm

Chris LoCurto
Vice President
Dave Ramsey's Team

Jon Acuff
Author and Speaker
Dave Ramsey's Team

Dave Ramsey

America's trusted voice on money and business, Dave Ramsey is a personal money-management expert and extremely popular national radio personality. His company, Ramsey Solutions, offers a message of hope, through various means, to anyone who wants to better understand the principles of proper money management. Dave has authored seven best-selling books. *The Dave Ramsey Show* is heard by more than 11 million listeners each week on more than 550 radio stations and digitally through podcasts, online audio streaming, and a 24-hour online streaming video channel.

Rachel Cruze

As a seasoned communicator and Ramsey Personality, Rachel Cruze has been speaking to groups as large as 10,000 for more than a decade. The daughter of Dave Ramsey, she joined Ramsey Solutions in 2010 and uses the knowledge and experiences from growing up in the Ramsey household to educate others on the proper way to handle their money wisely and stay out of debt. Rachel co-authored the #1 *New York Times* best-selling book *Smart Money Smart Kids* with her dad. Her new book, *Love Your Life, Not Theirs*, releases October 2016. You can follow Rachel on Twitter at @RachelCruze and online at rachelcruze.com or at facebook.com/rachelramseycruze.

Curriculum Overview

DVD Library

- Exposes students to the knowledge of 14 field experts covering topics from investments and insurance to marketing and banking
- Incorporates humor and relevant application, taking in-depth personal finance topics to a practical level for college students
- Averages 80 minutes of video material per chapter, broken into segments 10–20 minutes long

Working Textbook

- Excerpts from Dave Ramsey's *New York Times* best-seller, *The Total Money Makeover* and *Dave Ramsey's Complete Guide to Money*
- Excerpts from Jon Acuff's book, *Gazelles, Baby Steps And 37 Other Things Dave Ramsey Taught Me About Debt*
- Corresponding notes for video material
- Objectives
- Key terms
- Discussion questions
- Graphs
- Chapter reviews
- Money facts
- Case studies
- Glossary

Student Website: www.foundationsU.com

- Budgeting tools
- "Ask Dave" radio calls
- Various calculators (investment, mortgage, retirement, cost of living, etc.)
- Articles relating to college life
- Goal Tracker tool

Instructor's Guide

- Lesson plans for up to 75 contact hours
- Sample syllabus
- Chapter assessments including quizzes and tests
- Three to five activities per chapter (online, individual and group)
- Three case studies per chapter
- Answer keys
- Blank financial forms

Table of Contents

UNIT 1

MASTERING THE BASICS

CHAPTERS 1–5

1: Savings

2: Budgets

3: Debt

4: College Student Essentials

5: Family, Friends and Philanthropy

GETTING STARTED

Introduction

The reading excerpt below is taken from the *New York Times* best-selling book, *The Total Money Makeover*, by Dave Ramsey. With more than 17 years of experience counseling people on how to manage their money, Dave knows what it takes to get control of your cash. He designed the seven Baby Steps as a way to save for emergencies, get rid of debt, and plan for the future.

More than 20 years ago, my wife, Sharon, and I went broke. We lost everything due to my stupidity in handling money, or not handling it, as the case may be. Hitting bottom and hitting it hard was the worst thing that ever happened to me and the best thing that ever happened to me.

We started with nothing, but by the time I was twenty-six years old, we held real estate worth over $4 million. I was good at real estate, but I was better at borrowing money. Even though I had become a millionaire, I had built a house of cards. The short version of the story is that we went through financial hell and lost everything over a three-year period of time. We were sued, foreclosed on, and, finally, with a brand-new baby and a toddler, we were bankrupt. Scared doesn't begin to cover it. Crushed comes close, but we held on to each other and decided we needed a change.

So after losing everything, I went on a quest, a quest to find out how money really works, how I could get control of it, and how I could have confidence in handling it. I read everything I could get my hands on. I interviewed older rich people, people who made money and kept it. That quest led to a really, really uncomfortable place—my mirror. I came to realize that my money problems, worries, and shortages largely began and ended with the person in my mirror. I realized also that if I could learn to manage the character I shaved with every morning, I could win at money. That quest, the one that ended with me staring at myself in the mirror, led me on a new journey over the last fifteen years: the journey of helping others, literally millions of others, take that same quest to the mirror.[1]

The stuff we teach in this class represents everything I've learned about money since then, from savings and debt to insurance and investing. And I'm excited that my daughter, Rachel, has joined me to get this information to you before you graduate college. Trust me, knowing this stuff then would have saved me a whole lot of trouble!

Together, Rachel and I will teach you practical, relevant skills. Our message is different. We simply challenge the way you view money and empower you to graduate on a solid foundation. I think we can all agree this class is needed. The numbers speak for themselves:

- Nearly 70 percent of college students believe that their colleges and universities need to increase financial literacy initiatives and expand programs that teach students the skills they need to successfully manage their money.[2]
- Only 46.4 percent of college students reported that they had adequate financial resources to finish college.[3]
- 84 percent of college students have at least one credit card. Sadly, 68 percent of college students have charged items to their credit cards knowing they didn't have the money to pay the bill.[4]
- The average student loan debt has now surpassed $20,000 for an undergraduate degree—a figure that excludes popular "private" loans that may have much higher interest rates.[5]

During this class, we'll cover a number of topics on the videos. As you watch, follow along by filling in the blanks listed in your textbook. The answers to the fill-ins always appear on the left side of the video screen.

The videos include a mixture of Dave teaching on stage and answering student questions, Rachel emphasizing information that is specific to young adults, experts in the financial profession being interviewed, college students answering common financial questions, and various other interviews.

1. *The Total Money Makeover*, pgs 2–4
2. Higher One Survey, 2010
3. Noel Levitz, 2009
4. Sallie Mae, 2009
5. U.S. Dept. of Education National Center for Education Statistics, 2007

Topics Presented in the Videos

UNIT 1: MASTERING THE BASICS

1. Savings

- Describe emergencies that can happen during college and prepare a financial plan for them.
- Explain the three basic reasons for saving money (emergency fund, purchases and wealth building).

2. Budgets

- Design and apply a zero-based budget based on students' income and expenses.
- List ways to earn money while attending college.
- Calculate tax withdrawals and fill out tax forms.

3. Debt

- Describe reasons for avoiding debt.
- Demonstrate how to reduce debt by applying the debt snowball.

4. College Student Essentials

- Summarize how to apply for financial aid.
- Explain effective job-search tools, such as cover letters, résumés and interviews.

5. Family, Friends and Philanthropy

- Compare different personality traits in relation to money management.
- Integrate healthy communication about money with parents, roommates and others.

UNIT 2: DEVELOPING YOUR SKILLS

6. Consumer Awareness

- Identify marketing strategies that encourage college students to go into debt.
- Summarize and apply the five basic rules for making large purchases.

7. Bargains

- List the seven guidelines of negotiation.
- Discuss ways to save money while attending college.

8. Credit Bureaus

- Describe the value of credit reports and credit scores.
- Communicate effectively with credit bureaus and other agencies about collection issues.

9. Insurance

- Identify the types of insurance coverage needed during and after college.
- Explain why insurance is an essential part of a healthy financial plan.

UNIT 3: CONSIDERING THE FUTURE

10. Investments

- Compare and contrast various types of investments.
- Define the relationship between diversification and risk.

11. Retirement and Savings Plans

- Classify various types of retirement savings options.
- Describe savings plans for a child's college fund.

12. Real Estate

- Explain helpful tips for buying and selling homes and properties.
- Compare different types of mortgages.

This is one of the most important classes you will ever take. We're excited you are joining us. Now let's begin!

Directions:

Please watch the *Introduction* video clip and then discuss the questions below.

Discussion Questions: Introduction

- When you think about the phrase "managing money," what thoughts and feelings arise? Are they positive or negative? How do your pre-existing thoughts and feelings about money affect your ability to learn?
- "If you will live like no one else now, later you can LIVE like no one else." What do you think this means? Is it worth the effort? Why/why not?

CHAPTER 1

Savings

UNIT 1: MASTERING THE BASICS

The first step to becoming wealthy is committing to **save money**. This simple habit can change your life in the years to come. In fact, it's the only foolproof way to becoming a millionaire. The best part is, anyone can do it! The earlier you start changing your behavior, the wealthier you can become—it's as simple as that.

Learning Outcomes

List the Baby Steps:

1. Save $1,000 in an emergency fund (or $500 if you make less than $20,000 per year)
2. Pay off all debt except the house
3. Save three to six months of expenses
4. Invest 15% of your household income into Roth IRAs and pre-tax retirement plans
5. Begin children's college fund
6. Pay off your home early
7. Build wealth and give

Explain the three basic reasons for saving money:

- Emergencies
- Large purchases
- Wealth building

Identify the benefits of an emergency fund:

- Reduces stress
- Covers unexpected expenses
- Provides a rainy-day umbrella
- Prevents borrowing money in a financial crisis

Calculate the power of compound interest and describe the impact of rate of return:

- Compound interest is earning interest on the interest you've previously earned. Over time, this really adds up.
- Rate of return (the interest rate) will also make a difference in how large investments grow over time.

Evaluate emergencies that can happen during college and prepare a plan for them.

Key Terms

Baby Steps: the seven steps to a healthy financial plan

Compound Interest: Interest paid on interest previously earned; credited daily, monthly, quarterly, semiannually on both principal and previously credited interest

Emergency Fund: Three to six months of expenses in readily available cash to be used only in the event of an emergency; Baby Step 1 begins the process, and Baby Step 3 is the completed amount

Interest Rate: Percentage paid to a lender for the use of borrowed money

Money Market Mutual Fund: Mutual fund that seeks to maintain a stable share price and to earn current income by investing in interest-bearing instruments with short-term (usually 90 days or less) maturities

Sinking Fund: Saving money for a specific purpose to allow interest to work for you rather than against you

CHAPTER 1

Reading

The following excerpts are taken from Dave Ramsey's *New York Times* best-selling book *The Total Money Makeover*. With over 17 years of experience counseling people on how to manage their money, Dave Ramsey knows what it takes to get control of your cash. He designed the seven Baby Steps as a way to save for emergencies, get rid of debt, and plan for the future. In the passages below, Dave details the importance of the first baby step—the emergency fund.

The Baby Steps

In my first book, *Financial Peace*, there is a chapter entitled "Baby Steps," the premise of which is that we can do anything financially if we do it one little step at a time. I have developed the Baby Steps over years of counseling one on one, in small group discussions, and by answering questions on our radio show. Tens of thousands have followed this tried-and-true system to achieve their Total Money Makeover. The term "baby steps" comes from the comedy *What About Bob?* starring Bill Murray. Bill plays a crazy guy who drives his psychiatrist crazy. The therapist has written a book called *Baby Steps*. The statement, "You can get anywhere if you simply go one step at a time," is the framework for the movie. We will use the Baby Steps to walk through our Total Money Makeover.[1]

Baby Step One: Save $1,000 Cash as a Starter Emergency Fund

It *is* going to rain. You need a rainy-day fund. You need an umbrella. *Money* magazine says that 78 percent of us will have a major negative event in a given ten-year period of time. The job is downsized, right-sized, reorganized, or you plain get fired. There's an unexpected pregnancy: "We weren't going to have kids yet/another one." Car blows up. Transmission goes out. You bury a loved one. Grown kids move home again. Life happens, so be ready. This is not a surprise. You need an emergency fund, an old-fashioned Grandma's rainy-day fund. Sometimes people tell me I should be more positive. Well, I *am* positive; it *is* going to rain, so you need a rainy-day fund. Now, obviously, $1,000 isn't going to catch all these big things, but it will catch the little ones until the emergency fund is fully funded. (If you have a household income under $20,000 per year, use $500 for your beginner fund.)

This emergency fund is not for buying things or for vacation; it is for emergencies only. No cheating. Do you know who Murphy is? Murphy is that guy with all those negative laws, such as, "If it can go wrong, it will." For years, I have worked with people who felt that Murphy was a member of their families. They have spent so much time with trouble that they think trouble is a first cousin. Interesting enough, when we have had a Total Money Makeover, Murphy leaves. A Total Money Makeover is no guarantee of a trouble-free life, but my observation has been that trouble, Murphy, is not as welcome in homes that have an emergency fund. Saving money for emergencies is Murphy repellent! Being broke all the time seems to attract ol' Murphy to set up residence.

Whether the emergency is real or just poor planning, the cycle of dependence on credit cards has to be broken. A well-planned budget for anticipated things and an emergency fund for the truly unexpected can end dependence on credit cards.

> **"Whether the emergency is real or just poor planning, the cycle of dependence on credit cards has to be broken."**

The first major Baby Step to your Total Money Makeover is to begin the emergency fund. A small start is to save $1,000 in cash *fast!* If you have a household income under $20,000 per year, use $500 for your beginner fund. Those who earn more than $20,000 should get together $1,000 fast! Stop everything and focus.

Since I hate debt so much, people often ask why we don't start with the debt. I used to do that when I first started teaching and counseling, but I discovered that people would stop their whole Total Money Makeover because of an emergency—they felt guilty that they had to stop debt-reducing to survive. It's like stopping your whole fitness program because you get a sore knee from a fall when running; you'll find any excuse will do. The alternator on the car would go out, and that $300 repair ruined the whole plan because the purchase had to go on a credit card since there was no emergency fund. If you use debt after swearing it off, you lose the momentum to keep going. It is like eating seven pounds of ice cream on Friday after losing two pounds that week. You feel sick, like a failure.

So start with a little fund to catch the little things before beginning to dump the debt. It is like drinking a light protein shake to fortify your body so you can work out, which enables you to lose weight. The beginner fund will keep life's little Murphies from turning into new debt while you work off the old debt. If a real emergency happens, you have to handle it with your emergency fund. No more borrowing! You have to break the cycle.

Hide It

When you get the $1,000, hide it. You can't keep the money handy, because it will get spent. If your $1,000 from Baby Step 1 is in the underwear drawer, the pizza man will get it. No, the pizza man isn't in your underwear drawer, but you will impulse-buy something if the money is easily accessible. You can put it in the bank savings account, but it cannot become overdraft protection. Don't attach the savings account to your checking to protect you from overdrafting, because then your emergency fund will get spent on impulse. I have had to learn to protect myself from me. We are not putting money in the bank to earn money, but rather to make it hard to get. Since $1,000 at 4 percent earns only $40 per year, you aren't getting rich here, just finding a safe place to park money.

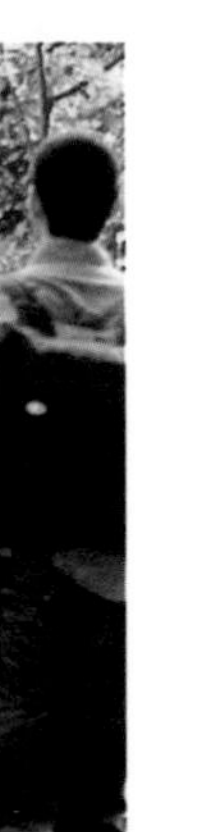

I know some of you think this step is very simplistic. For some this is an instantaneous step, and for others this is the first time they have ever had enough control over their money to save it. For some readers, this is an easy step. For others, this is the step that will be the spiritual and emotional basis for the entire Total Money Makeover.

Lilly was such a case. A single mom with two kids, she has been divorced for eight years; struggle has been a way of life for some time. Lilly had survival debt, not stupid spoiled-brat debt. She had been ripped off with a super-high-interest car loan, check-advance debt, and lots of credit card debt. She had a take-home pay of only $1,200 per month with two baby birds to feed, along with a host of greedy rip-off lenders. Saving seemed like such a fairy tale to her that she had long ago lost hope of ever being able to save money. When I met her, she had already begun her Total Money Makeover. After hearing me teach the Baby Steps at an event, weeks later she dropped by a book signing to give me an unsolicited report.

As she moved through the book line, I looked up and saw a huge grin. She asked if she could give me a big hug to say thanks. How could I turn that down? As I looked at her, tears began to run down her cheeks as she gleefully told of fighting through a budget, her first ever. She told me of years of struggle. Then she laughed, and everyone in line (now fully engaged) cheered when she said she now has $500 in cash saved. This is the first $500 in her adult life that is earmarked for her emergency fund. This is the first time she has had money between her and Murphy. Her friend Amy, who was with Lilly that day, told me that Lilly is a different person already. Amy said, "Even her face has changed, now that she has peace." Don't be confused; it wasn't $500 that did all that. What caused Lilly's liberation was her newfound hope. She has hope that she never had before. She has hope because she has a sense of power and control over money. Money has been an enemy her whole life, and now that she has tamed it, money is going to be Lilly's new lifelong companion.

How about you? Now is the time to decide. Is this theory, or is it real? Am I a simpleton kook, or have I found something that works?[2]

---

1. *The Total Money Makeover*, pg 93.
2. Ibid, pgs 102–108.

The Seven Baby Steps

THE STEPS YOU SHOULD TAKE TO REACH FINANCIAL SUCCESS

Even if you are not in debt, these steps will serve as your compass or framework for financial security. You will find the seven Baby Steps explained in detail throughout this course.

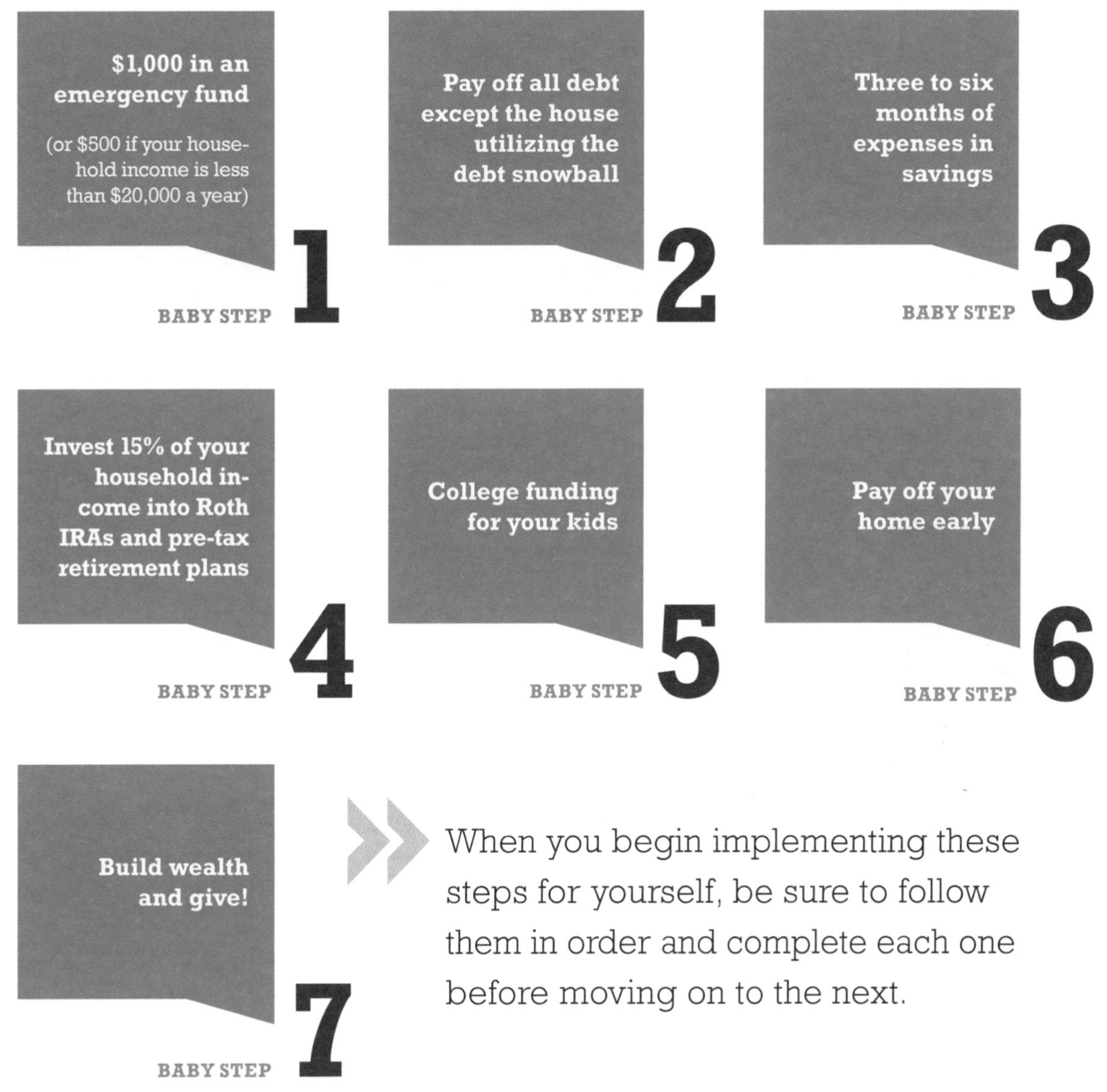

When you begin implementing these steps for yourself, be sure to follow them in order and complete each one before moving on to the next.

CHAPTER
1
Video: Sections 1–4

SECTION 1

Take The First Step: Baby Step 1

Refer to the graphic on page 16 as Dave begins the chapter by explaining the Seven Baby Steps. Once Dave completes the explanation of the Baby Steps and you see a graphic appear on the left hand side of the screen, you will know the fill-in-the-blank section below has started.

Baby Step 1 is ________________ (1) in an emergency fund (or if you make less than $20,000 per year in your household, put ________________ (2) in an emergency fund).

____________________ (3) must become a priority. Decide to pay

____________________ (4) first.

Many Americans have a ____________________ (5) savings rate.

Saving money is about ____________________ (6)

and ______________________________ (7).

Money is ____________________ (8).

Discussion Questions: Section 1

- What is keeping you from saving? How can you change this?
- Dave explained that money is amoral. Have you ever thought of money as being "good" or "bad"?

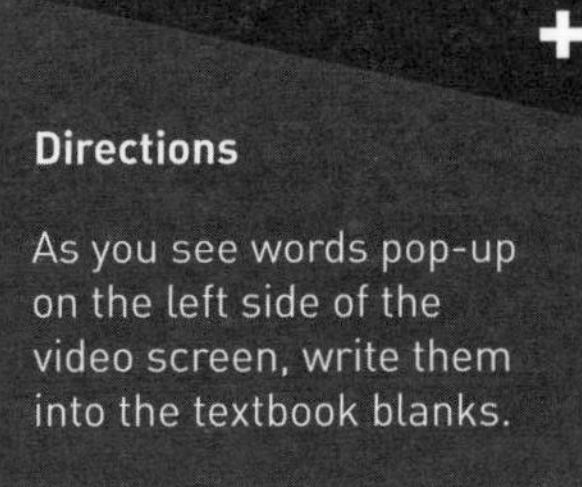

"Today there are three kinds of people: the haves, the have-nots, and the have-not-paid-for-what-they-have's."

EARL WILSON
American Columnist

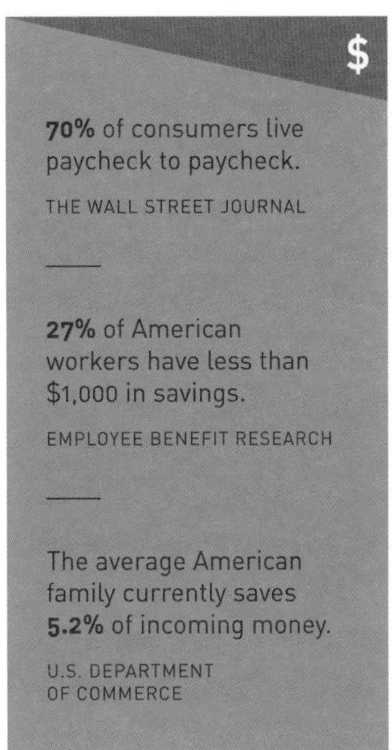

?

"I want to buy a car in a couple of years. How much money will it take to get a good one?"

DAVE'S ANSWER: You can buy a good used car for around $3,000. This may seem like a lot right now, but let me show you how easy it can be. Let's say you work a part-time job during school and on weekends. If you make $100 a week and save it all, you'll have enough for a car in only eight months. Not bad, right?

If you've got a little more time or a little less money, you could save $3,000 in 15 months with just $50 a week. Even without a regular job, you could come up with $50 a week just by cutting one or two yards on Saturday mornings!

$

25% of Americans have no savings at all. No retirement. No investments. Nothing.

CNN MONEY

"When you have that moment of commitment, you'll change your life. It's absolutely incredible what happens as this stuff starts to unfold for you."

DAVE RAMSEY
Financial Expert

+

You should have an emergency fund because unexpected things are going to happen. Smart people have known this for centuries and used to say, "In the house of the wise are stores of choice food and oil, but a foolish man devours all he has" (Proverbs 21:20). In other words, having some money saved back can turn a crisis into an inconvenience.

SECTION 2

You Should Save Money for Three Basic Reasons:

1. ____________ ____________ 9

2. ____________ 10

3. ____________ ____________ 11

Emergency Fund

____________ 12 are going to happen. Count on it.

Baby Step 1, a beginner emergency fund, is ____________ 13 in the bank (or $500 if you make less than $20,000 per year in your household).

Baby Step 3

Baby Step 3 is a fully funded emergency fund of 3–6 months of expenses.

A great place to keep your emergency fund is in a ____________ ____________ 14 mutual fund from a mutual fund company.

Elroy & Angela: $51,531 in Debt

We want to be financially secure, and we often talk about our dreams of Angela being a stay-at-home mother and adopting children into our family. We assumed that we would be better off financially than our parents because we had more education and we're on good career tracks. But unfortunately, we still ended up with $51,531 in debt. I (Elroy) am in grad school and Angela works at a local college. I'm scheduled to graduate with my doctorate degree next May, which is a huge accomplishment; I'm the first person in my family to go to college.

Our debt included a personal loan, student loans, car payments, credit cards and store cards. Every month, we always paid more than the minimum payment on our debt, but a dent never seemed to be made. We also lived in a tiny apartment and were frugal livers compared to our peers. To make things worse, we didn't have savings or an emergency fund. Plus our friends and family members often called on us when an emergency arose or they needed extra cash. What we were doing didn't seem to work if we ever wanted to move into a home and start our family.

That was until we started the Baby Steps. Since then, we have paid off over $12,000, and our current debt only includes student loans and $4,000 on our car. This is huge to us. We have a plan that works, and we are doing it one baby step at a time.

Your emergency fund is not an ________________ (15). It is insurance.

Do not ________________ (16) this fund for purchases.

The emergency fund is your ____________ (17) savings priority. Do it quickly.

Purchases

The second thing to save money for is ________________ (18).

Instead of ________________ (19) to buy something, pay cash by using the ______________ ______________ (20) approach.

$

60% of American retirees say using a credit card is a roadblock to saving.

SCOTT TRADE STUDY

43% of American workers have less than $10,000 in savings.

EMPLOYEE BENEFIT RESEARCH

"Discipline yourself to do the things you need to do when you need to do them, and the day will come when you will be able to do the things you want to do when you want to do them."

ZIG ZIGLAR

Famous Businessman and Motivational Speaker

Discussion Questions: Section 2

- Has Murphy visited you recently? If you had more savings, do you think you'd have fewer emergencies?
- What is the "sinking fund" approach? When have you seen "paying in Benjamins" create a better deal?

Compound Interest Is Powerful

Take a one-time investment of $1,000 and earn 10% on it. Your interest at the end of the year is $100. Add that to your original $1,000, and you have $1,100. At the end of the next year, your $1,100 is compounded at 10% interest, so your return on investment is $110. Add that to the $1,100, and you now have $1,210. Your interest on $1,210 is $121.

So as time passes, the amount you earn from interest grows. That is why it is so important that you start now. You have more time for your interest to snowball and pick up more and more snow!

How to Calculate Compound Interest

Use this simple formula to figure out the future value of a deposit once compound interest has worked its magic. (When calculating this formula, remember to use the mathematical order of operations.)

$$FV = PV(1 + r/m)^{mt}$$

FV: the future value
PV: the present value
r: the annual rate of interest as a decimal (5% is expressed as the decimal .05)
m: the number of times per year the interest is compounded (monthly, annually, etc.)
t: the number of years you leave it invested

$ Only **16%** of Americans have confidence in their ability to save enough for a comfortable retirement.

EMPLOYEE BENEFIT RESEARCH

SECTION 3

Wealth Building

The third thing to save money for is __________ __________. 21

__________ 22 is a key ingredient when it comes to wealth building.

Building wealth is a __________ 23, not a sprint.

__________ __________ 24 (PACs) withdrawals are a good way to build discipline.

__________ __________ 25 creates a mathematical explosion.

You must start right __________ 26.

"This class has taught me to be wise with money, because the money I would be spending on something I don't need could be going into a savings account."

COLLEGE STUDENT

Compound interest: Paid on interest previously earned. It can be awarded daily, monthly, quarterly, semiannually or annually on both principal and previously credited interest.

+ See what your investment will be worth in 40 years! Check out the **Investing Calculator** at www.foundationsU.com.

Discussion Questions: Section 3

- How is saving an exercise of your character? Of emotion? Of contentment? Is all of this exercising worth it?
- Why don't more people save for the future? Which reasons can be fixed by having a plan? Which cannot?

The Story of Ben & Arthur

THE POWER OF COMPOUND INTEREST

AGE	BEN INVESTS:		ARTHUR INVESTS:	
19	2,000	2,240	0	0
20	2,000	4,749	0	0
21	2,000	7,558	0	0
22	2,000	10,706	0	0
23	2,000	14,230	0	0
24	2,000	18,178	0	0
25	2,000	22,599	0	0
26	2,000	27,551	0	0
27	0	30,857	2,000	2,240
28	0	34,560	2,000	4,749
29	0	38,708	2,000	7,558
30	0	43,352	2,000	10,706
31	0	48,554	2,000	14,230
32	0	54,381	2,000	18,178
33	0	60,907	2,000	22,599
34	0	68,216	2,000	27,551
35	0	76,802	2,000	33,097
36	0	85,570	2,000	39,309
37	0	95,383	2,000	46,266
38	0	107,339	2,000	54,058
39	0	120,220	2,000	62,785
40	0	134,646	2,000	72,559
41	0	150,804	2,000	83,506
42	0	168,900	2,000	95,767
43	0	189,168	2,000	109,499
44	0	211,869	2,000	124,879
45	0	237,293	2,000	142,104
46	0	265,768	2,000	161,396
47	0	297,660	2,000	183,004
48	0	333,379	2,000	207,204
49	0	373,385	2,000	234,308
50	0	418,191	2,000	264,665
51	0	468,374	2,000	298,665
52	0	524,579	2,000	336,745
53	0	587,528	2,000	379,394
54	0	658,032	2,000	427,161
55	0	736,995	2,000	480,660
56	0	825,435	2,000	540,579
57	0	924,487	2,000	607,688
58	0	1,035,425	2,000	682,851
59	0	1,159,676	2,000	767,033
60	0	1,298,837	2,000	861,317
61	0	1,454,698	2,000	966,915
62	0	1,629,261	2,000	1,085,185
63	0	1,824,773	2,000	1,217,647
64	0	2,043,746	2,000	1,366,005
65	0	**2,288,996**	2,000	**1,532,166**

Both save $2,000 per year at 12%. Ben starts at age 19 and stops at age 26, while Arthur starts at age 27 and stops at age 65.

Ben stops investing; Arthur starts investing

$2,000	ANNUAL SAVING
÷ 12	MONTHS
$167	

Saving $2,000 a year works out to only $167 per month!

Ben invested ONLY $16,000.

Arthur invested $78,000 and NEVER CAUGHT UP!

80% of America's millionaires are first-generation rich. That means they started with nothing, did smart stuff, and became millionaires.

THE MILLIONAIRE NEXT DOOR

College students receive an average of **four phone calls** and **five mailings** each month encouraging them to apply for credit cards.

HIGHER ONE STUDY

Only **22%** of those age 18 to 24 have enough savings to get them through three months without income.

BANKRATE.COM

"Most people have the will to win, few have the will to prepare to win."

BOBBY KNIGHT
NCAA Basketball Coach

Want to know more about investing? You will see more about this in **Chapter 10, Investments**.

Rate of return, or the ______________ rate, is important to consider.
27

$1,000 One-Time Investment

No withdrawals, age 25–65 (40 years)

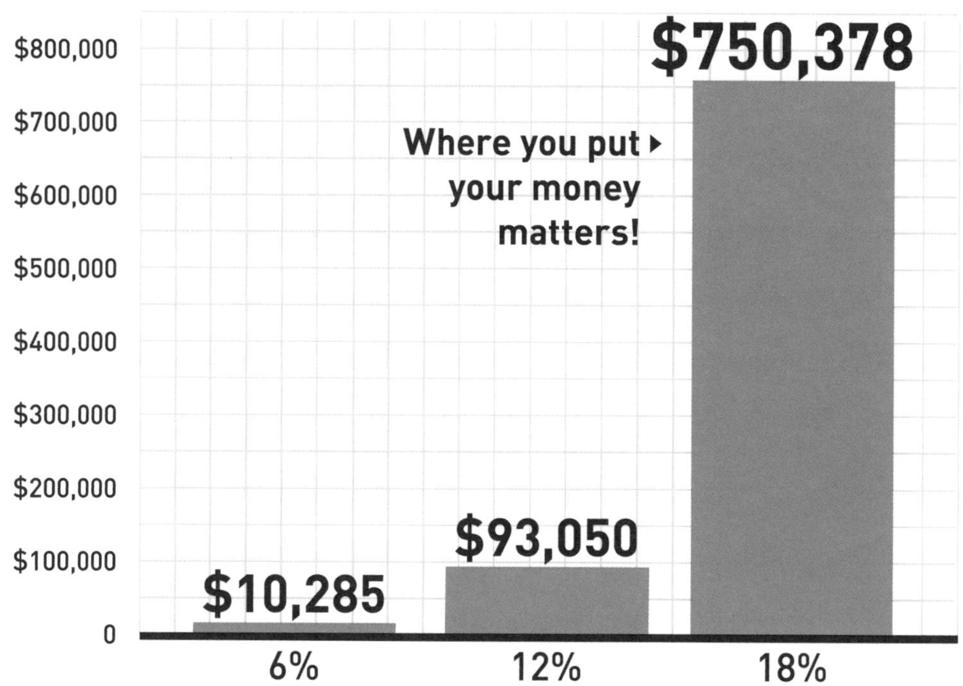

Discussion Questions: Section 4

- Why do people feel pressured to spend money they don't have?
- There is an old proverb that says, "Dishonest money dwindles away, but he who gathers money little by little makes it grow." What does this mean?

Recap & Review

Not Everything Is An Emergency

Jon Acuff has plenty of experience making people laugh. With a popular blog and three books under his belt, Jon has a vision to help people learn how to say no when it comes to gaining respect and self-control over their hard-earned cash. The reading below is from his book, *Gazelles, Baby Steps And 37 Other Things Dave Ramsey Taught Me About Debt*. His funny yet brutally honest take on what qualifies as an emergency will help you put Baby Step 1 into perspective.

When you start working through the Dave Ramsey materials, one of the first things you'll do is build up your beginner emergency fund. That's when you put $1,000 in the bank as fast as you can to cover those little emergencies that used to hit your credit cards. It's a simple step, but this little account is foundational to your long-term success with money.

But something funny happens once you realize you've got money in the bank. A lot of people have never had that kind of cash lying around. Even though you know it's only there for emergencies, even though you might have fought and clawed to pile up that money, your definition of "emergency" may start to get a bit...liberal.

You'll find yourself dipping into the emergency fund for things that aren't really emergencies. That's why we came up with this convenient checklist to help you identify an actual emergency.

10 Ways To Spot An Emergency-Fund-Worthy Emergency

1. If the emergency is that your car won't run unless you fix it, that's a real emergency.
2. If the emergency is that your car won't bling unless you get some shiny rims, that's not an emergency.
3. If you've got an open wound, a femur bone jutting out at a disconcerting angle, or you can't see straight, that's a real emergency.
4. If you've got skin that could be more bronze, that could glimmer with a deeper shade of awesome if you went to the tanning salon, that's not an emergency.
5. If there are small, woodland creatures that are able to get into your house because of a gaping hole caused by a tree limb, that's an emergency.
6. If you feel like the tile on the bottom of the pool could be a deeper shade of coral if you redid it, that's not an emergency.
7. If the concern is that unless you buy this purse right now, you'll miss the two-for-one deal the store has running, that's not an emergency.
8. If the emergency is that you won't be released from jail until you pay bail, go ahead and dip into that fund. You've got an emergency on your hands, my friend.
9. If in describing the emergency, you use the phrase "out of style" to describe the item you want to replace, that's not an emergency.
10. If the item you want to buy is some sort of clothing for a car or dog, that's probably not an emergency.

I, unfortunately, was able to write this list based on my own life. I once spent months explaining to my wife the emergency status of my need to buy a new laptop. (It will make me a better writer, the old one doesn't work well, etc.) When a new version would come out, I would raise the threat level to orange status and let her know our emergency was getting critical. I'd barter with her, "If I get a laptop, you can get ________." For some reason, she felt like buying two things we didn't need was twice as dumb as buying just one. Go figure.

A laptop is rarely an emergency. Fishing rods often don't reach emergency status. Leave the emergency fund alone.

Chapter 1 Key Concepts

- Make savings a priority. Start now!
- Compound interest works over time and the rate of return will make a difference in how large your investment grows. Remember Ben and Arthur.
- An emergency fund is your backup strategy when unexpected financial events happen. Baby Step 1 is $1,000 in your emergency fund (or $500 if you earn less than $20,000 per year in your household).
- Discipline and focused emotion is the key to saving.
- Use the 80/20 rule. Handling money is 80% behavior and only 20% head knowledge. Anyone can learn to save!

Video Section Answers

1. $1,000
2. $500
3. Savings
4. Yourself
5. Negative
6. Emotion
7. Contentment
8. Amoral
9. Emergency Fund
10. Purchases
11. Wealth Building
12. Emergencies
13. $1,000
14. Money Market
15. Investment
16. Touch
17. First
18. Purchases
19. Borrowing
20. Sinking Fund
21. Wealth Building
22. Discipline
23. Marathon
24. Pre-Authorized Checking
25. Compound Interest
26. Now
27. Interest

CHAPTER 1

Case Studies

Jeremy and Student Loan Debt

Jeremy graduated from college two years ago with a degree in communications. He has a good job as a Communications Specialist making $50,000 a year. Because he took a basic financial class during his sophomore year of college, he understands the importance of creating a plan for his money. So he made it a priority to start saving, and he currently has a savings account of $5,000 built up. He's motivated to continue putting away money for the future. However, he has $6,500 in school loans left to pay. He's already paid off $8,500 since finishing college. Just like with his savings, he's being aggressive and paying more than the minimum payments each month. Jeremy plans to be debt-free in 15 months.

1. Should he continue to pay extra on the student loan and get it paid off in his desired time frame? If he does this, he plans to continue contributing to his savings account at the same time.
2. Or, should he stop putting money into savings and put all of his extra cash toward the student loan? If he does this, how much more quickly will he have the student loan paid off?
3. Compare and contrast other options that Jeremy has available to him.

Latisha and New Furniture

Latisha works as a graphic designer and just got a raise of $100 each month. She wants to buy a new television and furniture and thinks this raise is enough to pay for those purchases. Tired of her hand-me-down furniture from her parents and her 10-year-old television that she got from a garage sale, she plans to use her credit card to buy the new things. Currently, she has $500 in her savings account, and she figures that with her raise she can easily do payment plans toward the television and furniture. To make the situation even more tempting, her credit limit still has $1,000 before it is maxed out. She plans to use the card toward the purchases so she can buy everything now.

1. Does her plan sound like a smart one? Why or why not?
2. Create a list of pros and cons that you see about Latisha's plan to purchase a new television and furniture. Make sure you are able to justify your answer.
3. Are there any other ideas you can think of as a way for her to get the new stuff without spending all of her savings?
4. Is there something better she could do with her $1,000 credit on her credit card?

Jorge and Transportation

Jorge is a junior at a state university. He's lived in the dorm for two years but is ready to move off campus for his remaining college time. After searching online, he found a house with a room for rent for $400 a month. The only downside is that the house is two miles from campus and Jorge doesn't have a car, although he's wanted one for a long time. He decides that moving off campus is the perfect reason to buy a car. Jorge has $3,000 in student loans but doesn't have to start paying them back until after he graduates in another two years. He decides that he can afford a car payment of $200 a month. Jorge begins to search for a car and finds a good used one for $5,000. He buys the car and moves off campus.

1. Did Jorge make the best decision by moving off campus and buying a car that he pays for with monthly payments?
2. If yes, justify your answer. If no, develop an alternative plan for Jorge.
3. What other options could Jorge have chosen for his living and transportation?

CHAPTER 1

Money in Review

Matching

Match each term to its definition below.

a. Money market mutual fund
b. $500/$1,000 in an emergency fund
c. 3–6 months of expenses
d. Pay off debt
e. Amoral
f. Discipline
g. Compound interest
h. Murphy's Law
i. Sinking fund
j. Savings account

1 _____ Saving money for a purchase and letting the interest work for you rather than against you

2 _____ Money is neither good nor bad

3 _____ Completed emergency fund goes here

4 _____ Interest on interest

5 _____ If it can go wrong, it will

6 _____ Baby Step 1

7 _____ Baby Step 3

8 _____ Key to wealth building

True or False

Determine whether these statements are true or false. Change the false statements to read true.

9 **T / F :** The saving habits of Ben and Arthur help to illustrate the principle of compound interest.

10 **T / F :** Dave's 80/20 rule says when it comes to money, 80% is head knowledge and 20% is behavior.

11 **T / F :** Your income level is the biggest factor in your ability to save money.

12 **T / F :** Interest payments can go in both directions: from a person to the financial institution and from the financial institution to a person.

13 **T / F :** The correct order for using your money is pay bills, save, then invest.

Multiple Choice

14 For most families, a fully funded emergency fund will be approximately:

a. $500
b. $1,000
c. $5,000
d. $8,000 or more

15 Ben and Arthur illustrate which principle of saving?

a. rule of 72
b. compound interest
c. simple interest
d. none of the above

16 Baby Steps 1 and 3 have to do with:

a. saving
b. emergency fund
c. getting out of debt
d. all of the above

17 You should save for the following:

a. emergency fund
b. purchases
c. wealth building
d. all of the above

18 How many Baby Steps are there?

a. 4
b. 5
c. 6
d. 7

19 Saving is about contentment and:

a. emotion
b. greed
c. having money
d. pride

20 The following is true about PACs:

a. stands for Personal Account Coordinator
b. stands for Pre-Authorized Checking
c. helps build discipline when saving
d. both b and c

Short Answer

21 Why do you think many Americans have a negative savings rate? How does this relate to your saving habits?

22 List the Baby Steps. Why do you think Dave skips Baby Step 2 in this lesson?

23 Explain the relationship between having an emergency fund and Murphy's Law.

24 Calculate the compound interest for each problem below:

- $1,000 at 6% interest for 3 years
- $500 at 18% interest for 4 years
- $1,500 at 12% interest for 2 years

25 What are the three primary savings goals?

26 What changes can you make now in your own life, based on what you saw in the video, and how will they help?

27 Why do you need an emergency fund at your age?

28 Why do you need to have $500 in the bank before paying off debt?

29 How does compound interest differ from simple interest?

30 What was the most important concept you learned from this lesson, and how will you apply it to your life?

CHAPTER 1

Notes

CHAPTER 2

Budgets

UNIT 1: MASTERING THE BASICS

Becoming wealthy doesn't happen accidentally. You need a game plan that works, and a budget is the perfect solution. It's simple—just write down a plan for your money and intentionally follow it every day. Surprisingly, when you put boundaries on your spending, you will end up with more freedom!

Learning Outcomes

Explain how money is active.

- Money is in a constant state of motion, moving from one place to another

Describe reasons why people do not do a budget.

- They feel it has a straitjacket connotation
- They feel abused by a budget
- They've never had a budget that worked
- They have paralysis from fear of what they will find

List common problems associated with budget failures.

- Items are left out
- The plan is overcomplicated
- People don't actually do it
- People don't actually live on it

Summarize the benefits of a budget.

- Removes the "management by crisis" from your finances
- Makes your money go further
- Removes many of the money fights from your marriage
- Removes guilt, shame and fear
- Removes many of the overdrafts from your life and reduces stress
- Shows overspending on certain areas

Design and apply a zero-based budget based on income and expenses.

- A zero-based budget is a cash flow plan that assigns an expense to every dollar of your income. The total income minus the total expenses equals zero.

Identify ways to earn money while attending college.

Calculate tax withdrawals and demonstrate how to fill out tax forms.

Key Terms

Budget: written cash flow plan; assigns every dollar to a specific category/expense at the beginning of each month

Carbon Check: a copy of each check you write; the check has a piece of carbon paper underneath that duplicates it

Envelope System: series of envelopes that are divided into categories (food, entertainment, gas, etc.) and are used to store cash for planned monthly expenses

Impulse Purchase: an item that is bought without your consideration of the long-term effects

Reconcile: to match your bank statement with your checkbook, preferably within 72 hours of receiving the statement

Zero-Based Budget: cash flow plan that assigns an expense to every dollar of your income, wherein the total income minus the total expenses equals zero

CHAPTER 2

Reading

This excerpt is from *Dave Ramsey's Complete Guide to Money: The Handbook of Financial Peace University.* In this passage, Dave discusses the dreaded "B word"—the *budget.* Hopefully you'll discover that budgeting is a lot easier than you think. It just takes a little practice and a little time to give yourself room for error.

Budgeting is crucial to your success. Your income is your responsibility. If you get to retirement with a mountain of debt and nothing to live on, it's no one else's fault. But beyond the obvious financial benefits to taking control of your money, there are a ton of other reasons to pull out the budget forms every month.

First Things First: The Four Walls

A written plan removes the "management by crisis" from your finances. You know what I'm talking about, right? We've already said that 70% of Americans are living paycheck to paycheck, just one missed payday away from disaster. When you're living on the razor's edge like that, with no plan at all for your money and no savings in the bank, it doesn't take much to qualify as a crisis. You could make $100,000 a year and still go into crisis mode if you need an unexpected $500 car repair!

No matter how blessed or distressed you are financially, your first priority every month is to cover what I call the Four Walls. Think of it as the four walls that hold your house together. They are food, shelter, clothing and transportation. If you have food in your belly, a roof over your head, clothes on your back and a way to get to work tomorrow, you'll live to fight another day.

Starting today, make a commitment to never allow anything or anyone to prevent you from covering these basics every month. You've got to take care of your family before you do anything else. Your family comes first.

It's sad, but about a quarter of the people who come into our office for financial counseling are current with their credit cards but behind on their mortgage. How backwards is that? I understand the reason, though. The credit card collectors start yelling at you if they even think you're going to be late with a payment. Mortgage companies act a little more dignified (at first, anyway), so they don't seem as intimidating. So what happens is that people put their house in jeopardy in order to keep Visa and MasterCard off their backs. Never again! We'll cover this more later when we deal with collection practices.

"You could make $100,000 a year and still go into crisis mode if you need an unexpected $500 car repair!"

The Money Stretcher

Managed money goes further. It's the weirdest thing, but practically everyone who has gone through the Baby Steps comes into our office for counseling and says almost the same thing: "The first time we did a budget, it felt like we got a huge raise!" How does that happen? It's because when you write up a budget, you're accounting for every single dollar of your income. You know exactly what's coming in and exactly what needs to go out. You cut out all of those little expenses that fly into your wallet like moths and eat away at your money.

When you run your money through a budget, it just works harder. It has more muscle. It's like the guy who discovered he was spending $1,200 on restaurants every month. Once you cut out all the "spending by accident" stuff that most people never think about, you'll find money you never knew was there. You'll hear this from me a lot: Your income is your most powerful wealth-building tool. But you'll only build that wealth and security if you free your income from accidental, careless spending and an endless cycle of debt payments.

The Best Method

When you sit down to do your budget, there's one crucial thing to remember: Every month is different. There is no such thing as "the perfect month." That means you've got to do a fresh budget every single month. You can't just do a template of all your income and expenses and expect it to work every month. It won't. You've got to plan for each month, one month at a time.

Counting To Zero

One of my all-time favorite scenes of any movie is in *Jerry McGuire*. Remember the scene where Jerry is on the phone with his client, and he's about to lose him, and he's willing to do anything it takes to keep that one client happy? What does Cuba Gooding Jr.'s character tell Jerry to do? What's the one thing he needed to hear? It's four simple words: "Show me the money!"

I make people stand up and shout that during my live events, and they all start out as hesitant and quiet as Jerry did in the movie. I tell them to shout it, and they just kind of whisper it and look down as they shuffle their feet. That's not good enough! I'll yell, "Say it again!" and they'll pick it up a little bit. I'll come back with, "Say it like you mean it!" and they'll start to scream. After four or five times, I'll hear up to 10,000 men and women yelling in unison, "SHOW ME THE MONEY!"

"This is your wealth we're talking about here! Get excited! Make those dollars dance!"

When you sit down to do a budget, that's what you're telling the paper. It should not be some calm, casual, half-thought-out, quiet discussion. You should sit down with your budget, calculator and pencil and literally scream, "SHOW ME THE MONEY!" That's what your budget does; it shows you exactly where your money is, where it's going, what it's doing, and everything else. This is your wealth we're talking about here! Get excited! Make those dollars dance!

The best, easiest and most powerful method is the zero-based budget. [There are forms in this chapter that show you how to do it.] Whether you do it on paper or online, the point is to be intentional about where every dime of your income is going.

The forms and online tools have instructions to walk you through the budget, but I'll cover the basics quickly here. With a zero-based budget, your goal is to spend your income all the way down to zero before you ever even get paid. You'll write your income at the top of the page, and then you'll write every single expense for the month under it, including giving and saving. By the time you get to the bottom of the page, your income minus expenses should equal zero. If it doesn't, go back and adjust some numbers. Maybe you have some extra that could go toward clothing, or maybe it'd be nice to go out for a fancy meal at a restaurant. Again, it's your money; I don't care what you do with it, as long as you do it on purpose!

But if you're working the Baby Steps like we teach, then you know every cent of any extra money you have goes to saving up the $1,000 Baby Step 1 emergency fund first. After that, all the extra money goes toward attacking your Baby Step 2 debt snowball. After that, everything you can squeeze out of the budget goes to filling up your full Baby Step 3 emergency fund of three to six months of expenses. If you're working through these first three Baby Steps, you already know where any "extra" money is going, so go back to the budget, adjust those categories, and write a zero at the bottom of the page.

Ready to start budgeting? What are you waiting for? Make your budgeting plan today, understanding that you won't come up with a perfect budget right out of the gate. But, a few months from now, you'll have it down.

---

1. *Dave Ramsey's Complete Guide to Money: The Handbook of Financial Peace University*, Chapter 3

CHAPTER 2

Video: Sections 1–5

SECTION 1

Money is ________________.
1

You must do a written ____________ ________________ plan every
2

______________________.
3

Reasons We Don't Do a Cash Flow Plan

Most people hate the word "budget" for four reasons:

1. It has a ____________ ___________ connotation.
   4
2. It has been used to ________________ them.
   5
3. They've never had a budget that ________________.
   6
4. They have paralysis from __________ of what they will find.
   7

Discussion Questions: Section 1

- How is money active? How have you seen this in your life? How can you control the activity?
- What are the benefits of a written cash flow plan? How can this impact you as a college student?

SECTION 2

You must also keep your checkbook ________________.
8

________________ are a sign of crisis living and sloppy,
9
lazy ______________ habits.
10

Use ________________ checks if necessary.
11

If not managed and made to behave, the ____________ card and
12
the ____________ card are certain to become budget busters.
13

+

Your budget will only work if you follow it. Here are three tips to help you stick to a budget.

1. Write It Down: A budget is not a form of medieval torture! It is YOUR game plan, where YOU tell YOUR money what YOU want it to do. This isn't rocket science! Just give every dollar a name on paper.

2. Stay Away From Places That Tempt You To Spend: If you have a problem sticking to a budget, you may not yet be disciplined. If that's the case, stay out of the mall or wherever your spending weakness occurs. Think of it like this: it's not smart for an alcoholic to hang out at a bar.

3. Use The Envelope System: Take some envelopes, write the budget categories on the envelopes, and use only that money to purchase those items. Try only a couple of categories at first until you get the hang of it. If the money is not in there, you can't spend it. Easy as pie. And remember, it takes practice; you won't get it right the first time.

$

42% of college students who leave school do so for financial reasons. A budget can alleviate many of these money problems.

NATIONAL CENTER FOR EDUCATION STATISTICS

Budget: The Essential Planning Tool

As a college student, you probably find yourself doing a lot of planning—planning your schedule to make sure you graduate on time, planning your assignments, planning for club meetings, and, of course, planning for lots of fun. But, one area that you must make sure to plan is your money. I know it may sound nerdy or old fashioned, but it isn't. It really is helpful for everyone. A simple, written plan can actually give you more money to enjoy!

I know doing a budget or cash flow plan doesn't sound like much fun. But I bet going out on a date, to Cancun for spring break, or on a shopping spree at the mall sounds like fun. You can do all of those without coming home to face debt or credit card bills. That is what a proper plan will do for you because you can begin to formulate debt-free fun as a part of your plan today. If you don't "put your money on paper" and have a plan, you will look up one day and realize that it is all gone and you don't even know what you spent it on.

So how do you get started? First, figure out how much money you have to work with for the month. This amount should include anything your parents give you to live on as well as your income from a job. You should be setting up a new budget EVERY month. If your parents pay for everything except for when you go out with your friends, then you just need to budget for how often you go out to eat, to the movies or to concerts.

Don't try to have the perfect budget for the perfect month because you'll never have one. Spend every dollar on paper before the month begins. Give every dollar a name before the month begins. This is called a zero-based budget. Income minus outgo equals zero every month. Look at this month's income and what you'll be putting your money toward (like food, entertainment, savings and debts), and match them up until you have given every income dollar an outgo name. You shouldn't have any money left over.

A good plan lives and moves—it is dynamic—and changes as your life changes. You will need to review your budget throughout the month to make adjustments. You may have budgeted too little for some areas and feel strained, so you will need to adjust. Some areas you will have budgeted too much and you'll have a surplus. You will need to adjust there as well. If you have lived on an ill-prepared budget or no budget at all, it will take you a few minor adjustments to get the plan to a realistic level. The plan is not to complicate your life. However, when you begin to know where your cash is going, it will make life a whole lot easier.

"People don't plan to fail, they fail to plan."

ANONYMOUS

"There are plenty of ways to get ahead. The first is so basic I'm almost embarrassed to say it: spend less than you earn."

PAUL CLITHEROE
Australian Financial Advisor

Cash flow plans do not work when you:

1. ________________ [14] things ________________ [15].
2. ________________________________ [16] your plan.
3. Don't actually ____________ ______________ [17].
4. Don't actually ________________ [18] on it.

$

Only 58% of young adults pay their monthly bills on time.

NATIONAL FOUNDATION FOR CREDIT COUNSELING

\+

Need help creating a budget? Check out the budgeting tool at **www.foundationsU.com**

Why Balance Your Checking Account?

KEEPING TRACK OF THE SMALL DETAILS CAN MAKE A BIG DIFFERENCE.

At first, keeping track of your transactions may seem tedious and unnecessary. But once you get the hang of it, balancing a checking account is actually easy. By keeping track, you can avoid a bunch of headaches, like bouncing a check, the bank making mistakes with your account, or not knowing your actual balance. Remember, when you take responsibility for your money, you'll have more of it!

What You'll Need to Balance Your Checking Account:

1. **Your Check Register**
2. **Your Last Bank Statement** (in print or online)
3. **A Reconciliation Sheet** (on the back of most bank statements)

Things to Remember:

- If you were diligent with recording transactions in your check register every time money went in or out, your check register has the most current balance.
- Remember, the account balance from the bank statement or ATM is not as current as your register's balance, because they don't account for transactions that haven't gone through yet.
- Contact the bank if you feel they made an error. It happens more than you may think.
- Don't be discouraged on the first few tries. It takes practice. The more you do it, the easier it becomes.

How to Do It:

- Throughout the month, write down every deposit or withdrawal in your register. Your transactions might include ATM withdrawals, checks you've written, debit card purchases, bank fees and paychecks.
- Each time you make an entry in your register, add or subtract that amount from the current balance.
- When you receive your monthly bank statement, record any interest accrual and bank fees in the check register.

Compare your check register with the bank statement side by side:

- ↳ Compare each transaction one by one. As you do this, make check marks on both lists.
- ↳ On the reconciliation sheet, list any debits or deposits that are present in the register but not present in the bank statement. Then calculate those into your bank statement balance.
- ↳ Compare your register balance to the statement balance. They should be the same. If not, look for discrepancies like outstanding checks, unrecorded bank fees or transactions, or bank errors.

Check Register

✓	Check #	Date	Transaction Description	Payment (-)	Deposit (+)	Balance
	5671	8/12	One Stop Grocery	57.40		507.06
	5672	8/14	Electric Company	101.00		406.06
		8/14	Paycheck		700.00	1106.06
	5673	8/16	Telephone Company	50.00		1056.06
	5674	8/19	One Stop Grocery	66.00		990.06
		8/16	Bank Service Charge	2.50		$987.56

◂Starting balance of $564.46

Bank Statement

Statement of Account No. 09876 — NB NATIONAL BANK — FDIC Insured

Joe Q. Public
1234 Main Street
Anytown, ST 98765

Statement Period: FROM 7/21 THRU 8/22

Overdraft Limit: $400.00
SUBJECT TO A PER-ITEM TRANSACTION CHARGE

Beginning Balance	Total Withdrawals	Total Deposits	Ending Balance
$ 492.09	$ 129.89	$ 142.36	$ 504.56

DATE	WITHDRAWALS	DEPOSITS	TRANSACTION DESCRIPTION
7/24	20.00		ATM Trns #76543

To reconcile your register with your bank statement, start with the ending balance from your statement.

Reconciliation Sheet

Transaction Description	Check #	Date	Payment
Electric Company	5672	8/14	101.00
Telephone Company	5673	8/16	50.00
One Stop Grocery	5674	8/19	66.00

List the withdrawal amounts in your register that aren't on your statement. Then total these transactions. **$217.00**

Transaction Description	Check #	Date	Deposit
Paycheck		8/14	700.00

List the deposit amounts in your register that aren't on your statement. Then total these transactions. **$700.00**

This should be the same as your register balance.

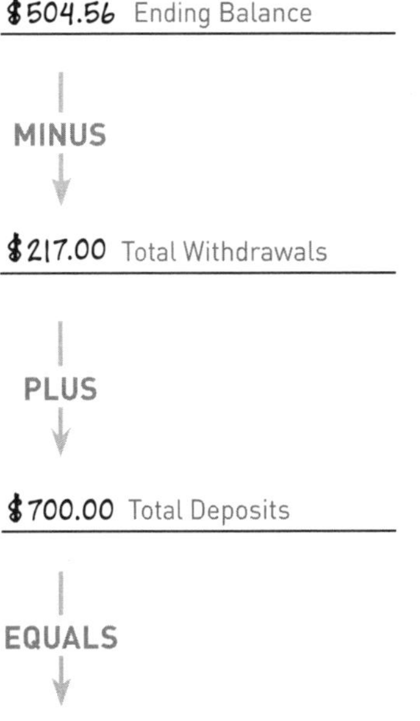

Patricia: $60,000 in Debt

Great news: I am about to graduate as a Doctor of Physical Therapy. The last three years have been tough to say the least, and I can't believe the end is within sight! Unfortunately, when I receive my degree, I will owe nearly $60,000 in student loans.

About a year ago my husband and I realized that we needed to figure out a plan for managing our money. After reading the *The Total Money Makeover*, my husband paid off his truck, we had a written budget, and we were paying for everything in cash. We also have a plan for tackling my student loans, and we estimate we can have them paid off in three years. My husband is planning on returning to school next year for his nursing degree, and we already have one year of tuition saved.

We both wish we didn't have my student loans looming over our heads and that we had applied these principles earlier. But since we can't change the past, we are so grateful for the peace you have helped us have for our future.

It's important to know how much things cost before you buy.

Whether it's a vacation, a car with all the options, or a house, you need to know the total price. A wise man once wrote, "Suppose one of you wants to build a tower. What is the first thing you will do? Won't you sit down and figure out how much it will cost and if you have enough money to pay for it? Otherwise, you will start building the tower, but not be able to finish. Then everyone who sees what is happening will laugh at you. They will say, 'You started building, but could not finish the job.'" (Luke 14:28-30, CEV)

"Since we have had to keep track of all our incoming and outgoing expenses this month, I have realized how much money I spend on food."

COLLEGE STUDENT

Reasons We Should Do a Cash Flow Plan

- A written plan removes the "management by ________[19]" from your finances.
- ________[20] money goes farther.
- A written plan, if actually lived and agreed on, will remove many of the ________ ________[21] from your marriage.
- A written plan, if actually lived and agreed on, will remove much of the ________[22], ________[23] and ________[24] that may be part of buying necessities such as food or clothing.
- A written plan, if actually lived and agreed on, will remove many of the ________[25] from your life, consequently removing a lot of ________[26].
- A written plan, if actually lived and agreed on, will show if you are ________[27] in a certain area.

?

I just got a part-time job and I want to make sure I save money in case something bad happens to my car. Do I need a checking account AND a savings account?

DAVE'S ANSWER: First, congratulations on the new job! You've taken a big first step toward financial independence.

Second, I think it's a great idea to keep your checking and savings accounts separate, and here's why. If you put all your money in one place, it becomes too easy to dip into your savings or emergency fund when you're writing checks. This defeats the original purpose of saving money.

This separation acts as a mental note and barrier. It's a way of telling you that you're reaching your spending limit!

Discussion Questions: Section 2

- What are reasons why some college students hate the idea of a budget? What are your initial reactions to budgeting?
- How can the concept of the Four Walls (food, shelter, clothing and transportation) empower you to prioritize your spending? How does this create freedom?

SECTION 3

- The easiest and most powerful plan is a ____________ [28] -based plan using the ____________________ [29] system.

See pages 40–43 for corresponding forms.

Discussion Questions: Section 3

- How could the envelope system be an effective tool for you during college? What envelope categories would you use?
- How is a zero-based budget better than other types of budgets? How is a written budget better than a budget that exists only in your mind?

SECTION 4

There are no fill-in-the-blank statements for this section.

See pages 44–55 for corresponding forms.

Discussion Questions: Section 4

- Based on your lifestyle, what would you add or subtract from the Monthly Cash Flow Plan explained on the video?
- How can you use the budgeting principle in other parts of your life?

$

Percentage of College Students Who Were Able to Save Money By:

- Reduced Spending **73%**
- More work/earnings **48%**
- Tax credits / deductions **43%**
- Living at home **43%**
- Accelerated class schedule **30%**
- Early Loan payments **23%**
- Less expensive classes **23%**
- Part-time classes **16%**
- Military **4%**.

SALLIE MAE

\+

Want to learn more about finding great bargains? Check out **Chapter 7, Bargains**.

Major Components of a Healthy Financial Plan

	ACTION NEEDED	ACTION DATE
Written Cash Flow Plan	Complete first budget	NOW!
Will and/or Estate Plan	Make an appt. with lawyer	June 6
Debt Reduction Plan	Begin debt snowball	July 1
Tax Reduction Plan	NA	NA
Emergency Funding	On hold until Baby Step 3	NA
Retirement Funding	On hold until Baby Step 4	NA
College Funding for Kids	On hold until Baby Step 5	NA
Charitable Giving	Start giving	June 15
Teach My Children	Get Financial Peace Jr.	August
Life Insurance	Done	NA
Health Insurance	Done	NA
Disability Insurance	Check company options	This week
Auto Insurance	Check current policy details	July 1
Homeowner's Insurance	Check replacement cost	This week

I Joe & Suzie Public, a responsible adult, do hereby promise to take the above stated actions by the above stated dates to financially secure the well-being of my (our) family and myself (ourselves).

Signed: Joe Q. Public Date: June 2

Signed: Suzie Q. Public Date: June 2

Consumer Equity Sheet

ITEM / DESCRIBE	VALUE	-	DEBT	=	EQUITY
Real Estate ________	$180,000		$149,000		$31,000
Real Estate ________					
Car ________	$2,500				$2,500
Car ________	$3,000				$3,000
Cash On Hand					
Checking Account					
Checking Account					
Savings Account	$1,600				$1,600
Money Market Account					
Mutual Funds					
Retirement Plan 1	$400				$400
Retirement Plan 2	$8,000				$8,000
Cash Value (Insurance)					
Household Items	$30,000				$30,000
Jewelry					
Antiques					
Boat					
Unsecured Debt (Neg)					
Credit Card Debt (Neg)					
Other ________					
Other ________					
Other ________					
TOTAL	$225,500		$149,000		$76,500

Income Sources

SOURCE	AMOUNT	PERIOD / DESCRIBE
Salary 1	$2,716	1st of Month
Salary 2	$945	1st & 15th - $472.50
Salary 3		
Bonus		
Self-Employment		
Interest Income		
Dividend Income		
Royalty Income		
Rents		
Notes		
Alimony		
Child Support		
AFDC		
Unemployment		
Social Security		
Pension		
Annuity		
Disability Income		
Cash Gifts		
Trust Fund		
Other________		
Other________		
Other________		
TOTAL	$3,661	

Lump-Sum Payment Planning

Payments you make on a non-monthly basis, such as insurance premiums and taxes, can be budget busters if you do not plan for them every month. Therefore, you must annualize the cost and convert these to monthly budget items. That way, you can save the money each month and will not be caught offguard when your bimonthly, quarterly, semiannual, or annual bills come due. Simply divide the annual cost by 12 to determine the monthly amount you should save for each item.

ITEM NEEDED	ANNUAL AMOUNT		MONTHLY AMOUNT
Real Estate Taxes	______	/ 12 =	______
Homeowner's Insurance	______	/ 12 =	______
Home Repairs	$1,800	/ 12 =	$150
Replace Furniture	______	/ 12 =	______
Medical Bills	$600	/ 12 =	$50
Health Insurance	______	/ 12 =	______
Life Insurance	______	/ 12 =	______
Disability Insurance	______	/ 12 =	______
Car Insurance	______	/ 12 =	______
Car Repair/Tags	______	/ 12 =	______
Replace Car	______	/ 12 =	______
Clothing	______	/ 12 =	______
Tuition	______	/ 12 =	______
Bank Note	______	/ 12 =	______
IRS (Self-Employed)	______	/ 12 =	______
Vacation	$1,200	/ 12 =	$100
Gifts (including Christmas)	______	/ 12 =	______
Other ______	______	/ 12 =	______

Monthly Cash Flow Plan

Every single dollar of your income should be allocated to some category on this form. When you're done, your total income minus expenses should equal zero. If it doesn't, then you need to adjust some categories (such as debt reduction, giving or saving) so that it does equal zero. Use some common sense here, too. Do not leave things like clothes, car repairs or home improvements off this list. If you don't plan for these things, then you're only setting yourself up for failure later.

Yes, this budget form is long. It's *really* long. (Pages 44–47.) We do that so that we can list practically every expense imaginable on this form to prevent you from forgetting something. Don't expect to put something on every line item. Just use the ones that are relevant to your specific situation.

Every main category on this form has subcategories. Fill in the monthly expense for each subcategory, and then write down the grand total for that category. Later, as you actually pay the bills and work through the month, use the "Actually Spent" column to record what you really spent in each area. If there is a substantial difference between what you budgeted and what you spent, then you'll need to readjust the budget to make up for the difference. If one category continually goes over or comes up short for two or three months, then you need to adjust the budgeted amount accordingly.

Use the "% Of Take-Home Pay" column to record what percentage of your income actually goes to each category. Then, use the "Recommended Percentages" form to see if your percentages are in line with what we recommend.

Notes:

- An asterisk (*) beside an item indicates an area for which you should use the envelope system.
- The emergency fund should get all the savings until you've completed your full emergency fund of three to six months of expenses (Baby Step 3).
- Don't forget to include your annualized items from the "Lump-Sum Payment Planning" form, including your Christmas-gift planning.

Monthly Cash Flow Plan *(Continued)*

BUDGETED ITEM	SUB TOTAL	TOTAL	ACTUALLY SPENT	% OF TAKE HOME PAY
CHARITABLE GIFTS		$366	______	10%
SAVING				
Emergency Fund	$224		______	
Retirement Fund	______		______	
College Fund	______	$224	______	6%
HOUSING				
First Mortgage	$915		______	
Second Mortgage	______		______	
Real Estate Taxes	______		______	
Homeowner's Ins.	______		______	
Repairs or Mn. Fee	______		______	
Replace Furniture	$50		______	
Other ______	______	$965	______	27%
UTILITIES				
Electricity	$100		______	
Water	$55		______	
Gas	$75		______	
Phone	$45		______	
Trash	______		______	
Cable	$21	$296	______	8%
***FOOD**				
*Groceries	$360		______	
*Restaurants	$50	$410	______	12%
TRANSPORTATION				
Car Payment	______		______	
Car Payment	______		______	
*Gas and Oil	$150		______	
*Repairs and Tires	______		______	
Car Insurance	$80		______	
License and Taxes	______		______	
Car Replacement	______	$230	______	5%
PAGE 1 TOTAL		$2,491	______	

Monthly Cash Flow Plan *(Continued)*

BUDGETED ITEM	SUB TOTAL	TOTAL	ACTUALLY SPENT	% OF TAKE HOME PAY
***CLOTHING**				
*Children				
*Adults	$100			
*Cleaning/Laundry		$100		3%
MEDICAL/HEALTH				
Disability Insurance				
Health Insurance	$300			
Doctor Bills	$50			
Dentist	$20			
Optometrist				
Medications		$370		10%
PERSONAL				
Life Insurance	$65			
Child Care				
*Baby Sitter				
*Toiletries				
*Cosmetics				
*Hair Care	$60			
Education/Adult				
School Tuition				
School Supplies				
Child Support				
Alimony				
Subscriptions				
Organization Dues	$25			
Gifts (incl. Christmas)				
Miscellaneous	$50			
*Blow Money	$100	$300		8%
PAGE 2 TOTAL		$770		

Monthly Cash Flow Plan *(Continued)*

BUDGETED ITEM	SUB TOTAL	TOTAL	ACTUALLY SPENT	% OF TAKE HOME PAY
RECREATION				
*Entertainment	$50			
Vacation	$25	$75		2%
DEBTS (Hopefully None)				
Visa 1	$100			
Visa 2				
MasterCard 1	$75			
MasterCard 2				
American Express	$50			
Discover Card				
Gas Card 1				
Gas Card 2				
Dept. Store Card 1				
Dept. Store Card 2				
Finance Co. 1				
Finance Co. 2				
Credit Line				
Student Loan 1	$100			
Student Loan 2				
Other ______				
Other ______				
Other ______				
Other ______				
Other ______		$325		9%
PAGE 3 TOTAL		$400		
PAGE 2 TOTAL		$770		
PAGE 1 TOTAL		$2,491		
GRAND TOTAL		$3,661		
TOTAL HOUSEHOLD INCOME		$3,661		
		ZERO		

Recommended Percentages

How much of your income should be spent on housing, giving, food, etc.? Through experience and research, we recommend the following percentages. However, you should remember that these are only recommended percentages. If you have an unusually high or low income, then these numbers could change dramatically. For example, if you have a high income, the percentage that is spent on food will be much lower than someone who earns half of that.

If you find that you spend much more in one category than we recommend, however, it may be necessary to adjust your lifestyle in that area in order to enjoy more freedom and flexibility across the board.

ITEM	ACTUAL %	RECOMMENDED %
Charitable Gifts	10%	10–15%
Saving	6%	5–10%
Housing	27%	25–35%
Utilities	8%	5–10%
Food	12%	5–15%
Transportation	5%	10–15%
Clothing	3%	2–7%
Medical/Health	10%	5–10%
Personal	8%	5–10%
Recreation	2%	5–10%
Debts	9%	5–10%

Allocated Spending Plan

Now that you've planned out the entire month on the "Monthly Cash Flow Plan," let's get just a little bit more precise. On this form, you will allocate—or spend—all of your money from each individual pay period.

There are four columns on this form, representing the four weeks in a given month. You will use one column for each week you get paid. If you are married and your spouse earns an income, then you will both use this same form. For weeks in which you both receive a paycheck, simply add those two incomes together and use a single column. Be sure to write the pay date at the top of the column.

Now, go down the list and allocate each expense to a specific payday, using your bills' due dates as a guide. For example, if your phone bill is due on the 22nd and you get paid on the 15th and 30th, then you know that you would probably pay that bill from your income on the 15th. Some things like utility bills will be paid monthly, while other items, such as food and gasoline, could be paid weekly. The point here is to anticipate both your upcoming expenses and your upcoming income and plan accordingly.

Beside each line item, you'll see two blanks separated by a slash (/). Put the expense to the left of the slash and the remaining income from that pay period to the right of the slash. As you work your way down the column, the income remaining should diminish until you reach a perfect zero at the bottom of the list. If you have money left over at the end of the column, go back and adjust an area, such as savings or giving, so that you spend every single dollar.

This level of detail may be uncomfortable to you at first, but the payoff is worth it. By specifically "naming" every dollar before you actually get it in your hands, you will remove an incredible amount of stress and curb your overspending.

Notes:

- If you have an irregular income, such as self-employment or commissions, you should use the "Irregular Income Planning" form instead of the "Allocated Spending Plan."
- If you know that you have an impulse spending problem, then you may want to allocate more money to the "Blow" category. That way, you are at least planning for it and setting up some boundaries for yourself.
- An asterisk (*) beside an item indicates an area for which you should use the envelope system.

Allocated Spending Plan *(Continued)*

PAY PERIOD:	7 / 1	7 / 8	7 / 15	7 / 22
ITEM:				
INCOME	$3,188	0	$472	0
CHARITABLE	366 / 2,822	/	/	/
SAVING				
Emergency Fund	224 / 2,598	/	/	/
Retirement Fund	/	/	/	/
College Fund	/	/	/	/
HOUSING				
First Mortgage	915 / 1,683	/	/	/
Second Mortgage	/	/	/	/
Real Estate Taxes	/	/	/	/
Homeowner's Ins.	/	/	/	/
Repairs or Mn. Fees	/	/	/	/
Replace Furniture	/	/	50 / 422	/
Other ________	/	/	/	/
UTILITIES				
Electricity	100 / 1,583	/	/	/
Water	/	/	55 / 367	/
Gas	/	/	75 / 292	/
Phone	45 / 1,538	/	/	/
Trash	/	/	/	/
Cable	21 / 1,517	/	/	/
*FOOD				
*Groceries	200 / 1,317	/	160 / 132	/
*Restaurants	25 / 1,292	/	25 / 107	/

Allocated Spending Plan *(Continued)*

TRANSPORTATION				
Car Payment	___/___	___/___	___/___	___/___
Car Payment	___/___	___/___	___/___	___/___
*Gas and Oil	75 / 1,217	___/___	75 / 32	___/___
*Repairs and Tires	___/___	___/___	___/___	___/___
Car Insurance	80 / 1,137	___/___	___/___	___/___
License and Taxes	___/___	___/___	___/___	___/___
Car Replacement	___/___	___/___	___/___	___/___
***CLOTHING**				
*Children	___/___	___/___	___/___	___/___
*Adults	100 / 1,037	___/___	___/___	___/___
*Cleaning/Laundry	___/___	___/___	___/___	___/___
MEDICAL/HEALTH				
Disability Insurance	___/___	___/___	___/___	___/___
Health Insurance	300 / 737	___/___	___/___	___/___
Doctor	50 / 687	___/___	___/___	___/___
Dentist	___/___	___/___	20 / 12	___/___
Optometrist	___/___	___/___	___/___	___/___
Medications	___/___	___/___	___/___	___/___
PERSONAL				
Life Insurance	65 / 622	___/___	___/___	___/___
Child Care	___/___	___/___	___/___	___/___
*Babysitter	___/___	___/___	___/___	___/___
*Toiletries	___/___	___/___	___/___	___/___
*Cosmetics	___/___	___/___	___/___	___/___
*Hair Care	___/___	___/___	___/___	___/___
Education/Adult	60 / 562	___/___	___/___	___/___
School Tuition	___/___	___/___	___/___	___/___
School Supplies	___/___	___/___	___/___	___/___
Child Support	___/___	___/___	___/___	___/___

Allocated Spending Plan *(Continued)*

Alimony	____/____	____/____	____/____	____/____
Subscriptions	____/____	____/____	____/____	____/____
Organization Dues	25 / 537	____/____	____/____	____/____
Gifts (including Christmas)	____/____	____/____	____/____	____/____
Miscellaneous	50 / 487	____/____	____/____	____/____
***BLOW MONEY**	100 / 387	____/____	____/____	____/____
RECREATION				
*Entertainment	50 / 337	____/____	____/____	____/____
Vacation	25 / 312	____/____	____/____	____/____
DEBTS (Hopefully None)				
Visa 1	100 / 212	____/____	____/____	____/____
Visa 2	____/____	____/____	____/____	____/____
MasterCard 1	75 / 137	____/____	____/____	____/____
MasterCard 2	____/____	____/____	____/____	____/____
American Express	50 / 87	____/____	____/____	____/____
Discover Card	____/____	____/____	____/____	____/____
Gas Card 1	____/____	____/____	____/____	____/____
Gas Card 2	____/____	____/____	____/____	____/____
Dept. Store Card 1	____/____	____/____	____/____	____/____
Dept. Store Card 2	____/____	____/____	____/____	____/____
Finance Co. 1	____/____	____/____	____/____	____/____
Finance Co. 2	____/____	____/____	____/____	____/____
Credit Line	____/____	____/____	____/____	____/____
Student Loan 1	87 / 0	____/____	12 / 0	____/____
Student Loan 2	____/____	____/____	____/____	____/____
Other ________	____/____	____/____	____/____	____/____
Other ________	____/____	____/____	____/____	____/____

Irregular Income Planning

Many people have an "irregular" income, which simply means that their compensation fluctuates from month to month. This is especially common for the self-employed, as well as commission-based salespeople. While this makes it more difficult to predict your income, you are still responsible for doing a monthly budget!

The "Monthly Cash Flow Plan" should remain a crucial part of your plan, as it lays out exactly how much money you need to bring home each month to survive and prosper. However, instead of doing the "Allocated Spending Plan," you will use this "Irregular Income Planning" sheet.

On this form, simply look at the individual items from your "Monthly Cash Flow Plan" sheet and prioritize them by importance. Ask yourself, "If I only have enough money to pay one thing, what would that be?" Put that at the top of your list. Then, ask yourself, "If I only have enough money to pay one more thing, what would that be?" That's number two. Keep this up all the way down the list.

With your list in place, you're ready to get paid. If you get a $1,500 paycheck, you will spend that $1,500 right down the list until it is gone, recording the cumulative amount spent in the "Cumulative Amount" column. At that point, you're finished spending, no matter what remains unpaid on the list. That's why the most important things are at the top of the list, right?

Be prepared to stand your ground. Things usually have a way of seeming important when they are only urgent. For example, a once-in-a-lifetime opportunity to see your favorite band perform live may seem important, but in reality, it is only urgent, meaning that it is time-sensitive. Urgency alone should not move an item to the top of this list!

ITEM	AMOUNT	CUMULATIVE AMOUNT
JC Penney	$150	$150
Sears	$250	$400
Visa	$500	$900
Vacation - part	$200	$1,100
Christmas	$400	$1,500

Breakdown of Savings

After you have fully funded your emergency fund, you can start to save for other items, such as furniture, car replacement, home maintenance or a vacation. This sheet will remind you that every dollar in your savings account is already committed to something. For example, it's a bad idea to take money away from car repairs to pay for an impulse Hawaiian vacation, even if you pay cash for it. What would you do if the car broke down the week you got back home? However, it can be okay to re-assign the dollars to another category, as long as you do it on purpose and it doesn't put you in a pinch in another category. Keep up with your breakdown of savings every month.

ITEM	**BALANCE BY MONTH**		
	October	November	December
Emergency Fund (1) $1,000			
Emergency Fund (2) 3–6 months			
Retirement Fund			
College Fund			
Real Estate Taxes			
Homeowner's Insurance			
Repairs or Mn. Fee			
Replace Furniture			
Car Insurance			
Car Replacement	$600	$700	$800
Disability Insurance			
Health Insurance	$500	$500	$500
Doctor			
Dentist			
Optometrist			
Life Insurance			
School Tuition			
School Supplies			
Gifts (incl. Christmas)	$500	$650	$800
Vacation			
Other ______			
Other ______			
TOTAL	$1,600	$1,850	$2,100

Basic Student Budget

ITEM	MONTHLY TOTAL	ACCOUNT
GIVING	________	________
SAVING		
General Savings	________	________
Emergency Fund	________	________
Next Semester: Tuition, Books, Fees	________	________
HOUSING		
Rent / Rental Insurance	________	________
UTILITIES		
Cell Phone	________	________
Electric	________	________
Cable / Internet	________	________
Water / Trash	________	________
FOOD		
Groceries / Meal Plan	________	________
Eating Out	________	________
TRANSPORTATION		
Car Payment	________	________
Gas / Oil Change / Repairs & Tires	________	________
Registration & Insurance	________	________
Public Transportation	________	________
Trips & Traveling	________	________
PERSONAL		
Clothing / Laundry	________	________
Personal Hygiene / Toiletries	________	________
Entertainment	________	________
Blow Money	________	________
Health / Medical	________	________
OTHER MISC.	________	________
TOTAL MONTHLY NECESSITIES	________	

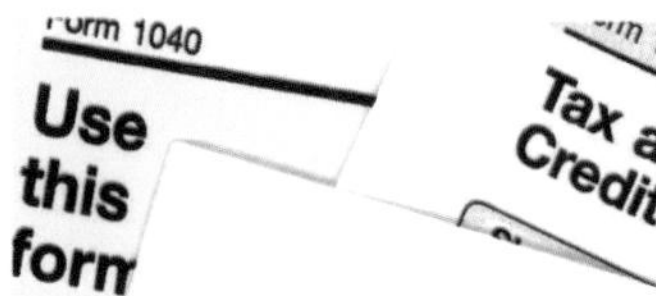

"That man is richest whose pleasures are cheapest."

HENRY DAVID THOREAU
American Author and Poet

Important Tax Information

- Gather your information: tax return forms, bank statements, bills and any other paperwork you might need.
- If a professional will do your tax return for you, see them in February because March and April are very busy.
- If you are a student who is 24 years old or younger, your parents can still claim you as a dependent. This is usually the best way to go, and they can take full advantage of the tuition credits.
- December 31st is an important date because it determines your tax status for the year (single, married or divorced).
- April 15th is when your individual tax returns are due. If you can't meet the April 15th deadline, you can file an extension. Extensions are good up to six months, until October 15. However, you don't want to file late. There is a penalty of 5% per month, up to 25% of your tax liability.

The Types Of Forms

- If you are doing your own tax return and you have only wages (no other side job or side income), use the 1040EZ form. You should have received a W-2 in the mail.
- If you own a business (like a landscaping business in the summer), this falls under a sole proprietorship. If your business makes more than $600, you will use the 1099 form. You have to pay income tax and the employer portion of FICA and Medicare tax, as well as your own portion of FICA and Medicare tax. You need to have a parent or professional help you with this.
- Additional income, interest, dividends and sale of stock will go to a 1040A form.
- If you have itemized deductions, credits or tuition credits, then use the full version of the 1040 form. You need to have a parent or professional help you with this.

$

How college students spend their money:

- **40%** blow money (**6%** entertainment, **7%** apparel, **5%** vacation, **22%** other)
- **26%** room and board
- **19%** tuition
- **7%** miscellaneous
- **4%** books and supplies
- **3%** transportation
- **1%** health care

COLLEGE STUDENT SPENDING BEHAVIOR SURVEY

SECTION 5

Earning Income and Tax Information

There are no fill-in-the-blank statements for this section.

Managing how your money is spent is only part of the budget equation. The other half is managing how your money comes in. Your income and taxes play important roles in balancing your budget.

Discussion Questions: Section 5

- How do you feel about working part time while in school? What are the advantages? What are the disadvantages?
- Based on your working situation, how will you file your taxes? How is help from a parent or professional beneficial to you in this process?

Recap & Review

Dave Doesn't Want You to Wear a Barrel With Suspenders

BY JON ACUFF

One of my favorite myths about following Dave Ramsey's theories is that if you subscribe to the theories, you'll have to get rid of all your stuff and wear a barrel instead of clothes. Each day, you'll eat stone soup with a group of drifters you meet while riding the rails to work since you no longer own a car. You'll have to do your own health care, too, since it's expensive, but you can always Google® how to set a broken bone. From the library, of course, because you'll no longer have the internet. Or power.

These are lean times ahead of you, my friend, lean times indeed.

What's funniest about that is where that belief comes from. Often, when we realize that we need to cut back on an area of our lives in order to really attack a huge debt snowball, we simply overreact. A spouse or friend mildly challenges our $50 weekly Starbucks® habit, and we instantly respond, "Great! So now you want me to sell my car and make all my clothes by hand! I'm so mad!"

That's not what Dave is saying at all. Not even a little bit. When I started going through the Baby Steps, I didn't trade in my Mac® laptop and start writing on brown paper grocery bags instead. Stuff is part of our lives, and *managing* it does not mean *eliminating* it.

Sometimes, people go to extreme (and illegal) measures to save money. I heard someone call in on a radio station once and say that they wash out soda cups they find in the trash at the movies so they can get a free refill they didn't actually pay for.

If they called Dave with that story, I promise you he wouldn't say, "Great!"

He'd say, "Gross!"

Put the barrel down. Stop stealing apples from Old Man Johnson's farm. It's going to be all right. Dave doesn't want you to drive a burro.

Chapter 2 Key Concepts

- Do a written budget! You have to tell your money what to do.
- Spend every dollar on paper before the month begins.
- Use the envelope system and fill each envelope with the money allotted to that category. When it's gone, you are done spending for that category—no ATM visits! Give it time. It takes three to four months to get it right.
- Working part time will keep you away from debt and enrich your life.
- Complete your tax forms on time every April.

RECAP & REVIEW

Video Section Answers

1. Active
2. Cash Flow
3. Month
4. Straight jacket
5. Abuse
6. Worked
7. Fear
8. Balanced
9. Overdrafts
10. Money
11. Duplicate
12. ATM
13. Debit
14. Leave
15. Out
16. Overcomplicate
17. Do It
18. Live
19. Crisis
20. Managed
21. Money Fights
22. Guilt
23. Shame
24. Fear
25. Overdrafts
26. Stress
27. Overspending
28. Zero
29. Envelope

CHAPTER 2

Case Studies

Waverly and Disappearing Dollars

Waverly believes that it's a great idea to give every dollar a name. So every month she does this, without fail. She writes down everything she spends, including every last penny, and enters it into a spreadsheet. As the month progresses, she updates her spreadsheet every time she makes a purchase. Then, at the end of the month, Waverly reviews her spreadsheet to see where her money has gone. Unfortunately, every month she somehow manages to spend more than she should. She tries to figure out what went wrong, but it just doesn't make sense to her.

1. How would you solve Waverly's budgeting issue?
2. Is Waverly right in giving every penny a name? Why or why not?
3. Instead of updating her spreadsheet every time she makes a purchase, is there a better way for her to keep track of her money? If so, how?

Tyler and Brittany's New Expenses

Tyler and Brittany got married six months ago, and they both have good jobs coming out of college. Tyler landed a marketing job with a communications company making a starting salary of $40,000 take-home pay per year. Brittany began her career as a first grade teacher's aide for the local school district making $10.00 per hour after taxes for 30 hours a week. After their wedding, they each purchased new vehicles, complete with car loans. Tyler's payments on his new truck are $488 per month, and Brittany is leasing her new compact car for nothing down and $239 per month for the next three years. They are also thinking about buying a new home with a monthly mortgage payment of $1,850. After figuring in monthly expenses, they realize that there isn't much left over at the end of the month.

1. If they continue their spending habits, predict what their financial state will be in two years from now.
2. Should Tyler and Brittany make any changes to their budget? If so, what?
3. If they didn't purchase a home right now, how would their financial life look in two years?
4. Are there other options that Tyler and Brittany have for transportation instead of making payments on two new vehicles?

Sofia and Variable Income

Sofia is a full-time student and works part time as a babysitter for three families in her college town. She consistently works five hours a week, but some weeks she is able to work more hours. She has a $7,500 student loan but doesn't plan on making payments toward that until she graduates. Sofia has basic living expenses like rent, utilities, gas, car insurance, etc. She wants to start investing her money for the future. She also wants to purchase a new laptop for school. Unfortunately she never knows what her monthly income will be due to her irregular work schedule.

1. What advice can you give her to help her meet her goals?
2. Should Sofia purchase a new laptop? Why or why not?
3. Should she pay off her student loan first or start investing?

RECAP & REVIEW

CHAPTER 2

Money in Review

Matching

Match each term to its definition below.

a. budget
b. irregular income form
c. monthly cash flow form
d. duplicate (carbon) checks
e. reconciliation
f. currency

1 _____ Used to do a budget

2 _____ Used by persons earning an inconsistent monthly income

3 _____ Process used to determine if the balance in your checking registry matches the balance reported on the bank statement

4 _____ Another name for cash flow plan

5 _____ Helps people who forget to record checks in their register after writing them

True or False

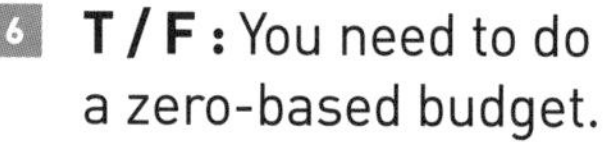

Determine whether these statements are true or false. Change the false statements to read true.

6 **T / F :** You need to do a zero-based budget.

7 **T / F :** You will pay interest on debit card purchases.

8 **T / F :** A budget will be the same each and every month.

9 **T / F :** You need to reconcile your bank statement once every year.

10 **T / F :** People who don't earn a consistent monthly salary do not have to do a budget.

Multiple Choice

11 Bounced checks are a sign of _________ living.

a. normal
b. crisis
c. comfortable
d. both a and b

12 A written budget should be done every

a. month
b. week
c. 3 months
d. 6 months

13 Your budget should include

a. fixed expenses
b. variable expenses
c. money to blow
d. all of the above

14 What would account for a difference in balances in your checkbook registry and bank statement after reconciling the two?

a. an error or omission
b. outstanding checks that didn't clear
c. deposits that did not post
d. all of the above

15 Doing a budget does not

a. lead to an increase in arguments
b. make your money go farther
c. show if you are overspending in an area
d. remove guilt and shame sometimes associated with purchases

Short Answer

16 Explain how to complete a zero-based budget.

17 What are some reasons why the balance in your checkbook registry might not match the balance on your bank statement?

18 Why do you need a written budget even when you know you can afford your expenses?

19 How does a budget differ when you have an irregular income vs. a predictable income?

20 How can a budget help when you are working on Baby Step 2?

CHAPTER 2

Notes

CHAPTER 3

Debt

UNIT 1: MASTERING THE BASICS

We've all been taught that we "need to build a good credit score." Sadly, borrowing money is so ingrained in our culture, we can't imagine life without it. The truth is, "building a good credit score" causes more harm than good. Debt forces us to become slaves financially and it limits how we spend our money.

Learning Outcomes

Summarize the history and evolution of credit.

Describe reasons for avoiding debt.

- Debt causes people to be "slave to the lender." In other words, when people make debt payments, they are limited in how they can spend and invest their money. They watch their money go out the door, which prevents them from winning financially.
- The best way to beat debt is to quit borrowing money and live on less than you make.

Demonstrate how to reduce debt by applying the debt snowball.

- The debt snowball is an effective way of paying off debt quickly. Start making minimum payments on all of the debts except for the smallest one. At the same time, attack the smallest one with intensity until it is gone. Then attack the next smallest one, then the next—until all of the debts are paid off.

Compare and contrast credit cards and debit cards.

- Credit cards are used when a person wants to borrow money to make purchases. Unfortunately, the person gets further into debt and spends their money on unnecessary interest payments. People often spend more when using a credit card, which is the opposite of building wealth.
- Debit cards are linked directly to a person's bank account. When they make purchases, that money is taken from their savings or checking account, which keeps them accountable to spend less money. Everything you "need" a credit card for can be done with a debit card instead. If you don't have money in your bank account to cover a purchase, don't buy it.

Evaluate and refute the myths associated with debt.

Key Terms

Annual Percentage Rate (APR): cost of borrowing money on an annual basis; takes into account the interest rate and other related fees on a loan

Credit: an amount of money placed at a person's disposal by a bank; money owed

Credit Card: type of card issued by a bank that allows users to finance a purchase

Debt Snowball: preferred method of debt repayment; includes a list of all debts organized from smallest to largest balance; minimum payments are made to all debts except for the smallest, which is attacked with the largest possible payments

Introductory Rate: an interest rate charged to a customer during the early stages of a loan; the rate often goes up after a specified period of time

Loan Term: time frame that a loan agreement is in force, and before or at the end of which the loan should either be repaid or renegotiated for another term

Reading

In the following excerpt from *The Total Money Makeover*, Dave Ramsey explains the history of credit and its effect on our country over the decades. He also refutes the myth that debt is a necessary part of winning financially.

Red-faced and fists clenched, the toddler yells with murder in his voice, "I want it! I want it! I want it!" We have all watched this scene unfold in the grocery store. We may even have watched our own children do this (once). Now that I'm older and more mellow, I sometimes grin a little as a young mom tries without success to stifle the out-of-control screams of a child who is denied something.

It is human nature to want it and want it now; it is also a sign of immaturity. Being willing to delay pleasure for a greater result is a sign of maturity. However, our culture teaches us to live for the now. "I want it!" we scream, and we can get it if we are willing to go into debt. Debt is a means to obtain the "I want its" before we can afford them.

Joining The Lie

I have heard it said that if you tell a lie often enough, loudly enough, and long enough, the myth will become accepted as a fact. Repetition, volume, and longevity will twist and turn a myth, or a lie, into a commonly accepted way of doing things. Entire populations have been lulled into the approval of ghastly deeds and even participation in them by gradually moving from the truth to a lie. Throughout history, twisted logic, rationalization, and incremental changes have allowed normally intelligent people to be party to ridiculous things. Propaganda, in particular, played a big part in allowing these things to happen.

We have propaganda in our culture today. I'm not speaking in a political sense, but rather recognizing that there are people out there who want us to think their way and who will go to great lengths to accomplish that. The financial and banking industries, in particular, are very good at teaching us their way of handling money, which, of course, leads us to buy their products. If I see an ad again and again that tells me I will be cool and sharp looking if I drive a certain car, I can fall under the illusion that with the purchase of that car, those good things will happen to me. We may not really believe that we will become a model just from purchasing a car, but notice that ugly people aren't used in the TV spots to sell cars. We aren't really falling for that lie, or are we? I'm just asking. After all, we do buy the car and then justify our purchase on the basis of something academic like gas mileage.

"When we participate in what the crowd identifies as normal, even if it is stupid, we gain acceptance into the club."

When we participate in what the crowd identifies as normal, even if it is stupid, we gain acceptance into the club. Sometimes we don't even realize what we are doing is stupid because we have been taught that it's just "the way you do it," and so we never ask why. As we participate in the myth, we learn to spout the principles of the myth. After the years go by and we have invested more money and time into the myth, we become great disciples and can preach the points of the myth with great fervor and volume. We become such experts on the myth that we can sell others on joining the lie. I once joined in the lie, but no more.

Don't Let the Monkeys Pull You Down!

Debt has been sold to us so aggressively, so loudly, and so often that to imagine living without debt requires myth-busting. We have to systematically destroy the inner workings of the myths. Debt is so ingrained into our culture that most Americans can't even envision a car without payment, a house without a mortgage, a student without a loan, and credit without a card. We have been sold debt with such repetition and with such fervor that most folks cannot conceive what it would be like to have no payments. Just as slaves born into slavery can't visualize freedom, we Americans don't know what it would be like to wake up to no debt. According to the Federal Reserve, the total revolving debt in America is currently $796 billion. We can't do without debt, or can we?

Working with tens of thousands of people in the last several years, I have found that a major barrier to winning is our view of debt. Most people who have made the decision to stop borrowing money have experienced something weird, ridicule. Friends and family who are disciples of the myth that debt is good have ridiculed those on the path to freedom.

John Maxwell tells of a study done on monkeys. A group of monkeys were locked in a room with a pole at the center. Some luscious, ripe bananas were placed on the top of the pole. When a monkey would begin to climb the pole, the experimenters would knock him off with a blast of water from a fire hose. Each time a monkey would climb, off he would go, until all the monkeys had been knocked off repeatedly, thus learning that the climb was hopeless. The experimenters then observed that the other primates would pull down any monkey trying to climb. They replaced a single monkey with one who didn't know the system. As soon as the new guy tried to climb, the others would pull him down and punish him for trying. One by one, each monkey was replaced and the scene repeated until there were no monkeys left in the room that had experienced the fire hoses. Still, none of the new guys were allowed to climb. The other monkeys pulled them down. Not one monkey in the room knew why, but none were allowed to get the bananas.

We aren't monkeys, but sometimes we exhibit behavior that seems rather chip-like. We don't remember why; we just know that debt is needed to win. So when a loved one decides to get a Total Money Makeover, we laugh, get angry, and pull him down. We Americans are like the last set of monkeys. With rolled eyes we spout the pat lines associated with the myth as if anyone not wanting to have debt is unintelligent. That person must be a simpleton, a fanatic, or worst of all, "uneducated in finance."[1]

> **"We have been sold debt with such repetition and with such fervor that most folks cannot conceive what it would be like to have no payments."**

Bottom line: You don't need debt to make it in today's world. In fact, you'll be much better off without it.

---

1. *The Total Money Makeover*, pp. 17-20

CHAPTER 3

Video: Sections 1–7

SECTION 1

Debt is Everywhere

According to *The Wall Street Journal*, ________ of Americans are living paycheck to paycheck.
1

When it comes to debt, if you tell a lie or spread a ____________ long enough, eventually it becomes accepted as the ______________.
2 3

Debt has been _________________ to us with such intensity for so long that to imagine living without it requires a complete ____________ shift, a completely new way of looking at things.
4 5

Paradigm: Your belief system; the way you see or perceive things

History of Credit

- **1910:** In the Sears catalog, credit was called "folly."
- J.C. Penney didn't believe in debt and would not allow credit to be given in his stores. It wasn't until after his death in 1971 that credit was widely accepted in the J.C. Penney stores.
- Henry Ford of Ford Motor Company hated debt and would not offer credit on cars for 10 years after General Motors began offering credit.
- **1950:** This was the birth of what is now known as the credit card; Frank McNamara established partnerships with several New York City restaurants. His goal was to allow patrons the ability to pay for meals with a single payment card—the first credit card. McNamara's company, Diners Club, is still in business today.

$

The total consumer debt in America is **$2.4 trillion,** which is close to the Gross Domestic Product of England!

FEDERAL RESERVE

"I realized that sometimes I let my emotions rule over all else with my credit card purchases. When I feel upset and somehow reason to myself that 'stuff' will help, I don't struggle swiping the card. I think it would be different if I paid cash."

COLLEGE STUDENT

+

When someone borrows money from another person, we understand they have an obligation to repay. A study in the dictionary will show you what this really means. A definition of obligation is "bound," which is defined as "tied; in bonds: a bound prisoner." Like Proverbs says, "The rich rules over the poor, and the borrower is the slave of the lender" (Proverbs 22:7, NRSV).

Don't become a prisoner or slave to debt!

Liberty: $16,473 in Debt

My name is Liberty and I'm 34 years old. While I was in college, my parents lived two states away and were unable to help financially. As a result, I have $16,473 in student loans that I am currently repaying. During school, I earned my associate's degree while working full time on the side. My meager income was eaten up by insurance, books, rent, utilities, food and gas. After I finished my associate's degree in medical laboratory technology, I returned to school for my bachelor's degree. I finally graduated at the ripe old age of 29.

My husband and I discovered Dave Ramsey's plan about a month ago and we are on Baby Step 2. We've got that debt snowball going, and we love the progress we're making. I'm so glad that we're both on board with this. It's much easier to do the Baby Steps proactively rather than out of desperation. I want to be financially secure for all the years to come.

- **1958:** A West Coast bank, Bank of America, issued a little piece of plastic called the BankAmericard to its customers. Later that year, American Express was born.
- **1970:** Only 15% of Americans owned credit cards.
- **1976:** BankAmericard changed its name to Visa.
- **1986:** Sears gets into a dispute with Visa over the fee structure. As a result, Sears created their own brand, the Discover Card. This quickly became the most profitable division of Sears.

$

There are nearly **1.5 billion** credit cards in use in the United States. A stack of all those credit cards would reach more than **70** miles into space and be almost as tall as **13** Mount Everests.

U.S. CENSUS BUREAU

84% of undergraduates have at least one credit card.

SALLIE MAE

Discussion Questions: Section 1

- Do you view credit differently than your parents view it? Differently than your grandparents view it? What has changed over the generations?
- If you do not own a credit card, why did you decide against one? How do you plan to succeed financially without using debt along the way?

"Rather go to bed supperless, than rise in debt."

BENJAMIN FRANKLIN

A Founding Father of the United States

"Before borrowing money from a friend, decide which you need the most."

OLD PROVERB

The National Economy, in Household Budget Terms

DR Whenever the talking heads on TV start ranting about the national economy, most of our eyes start to glaze over. The gigantic numbers that they throw out there are ridiculous; most Americans have no idea what those numbers mean in practical terms. So, I thought it'd be fun to turn those figures into something we can understand a little better—like a household budget.

The federal government will take in $2.173 trillion this year. That's their income, and it sounds pretty good. Until, that is, you factor in that the federal government will spend $3.818 trillion during the year. So, just like many families, the government's outgo exceeds their income—to the tune of **$1.645 trillion in overspending.** That's called the deficit. Altogether, the government has $14.2 trillion in debt.

What would happen if Joe Q. Public and his wife called my show with these kinds of numbers? Here's how their financial situation would stack up:

If their household income was $55,000 per year, they'd actually be spending $96,500—*$41,500 more than they made!* **That means they're spending 175% of their annual income! So, in 2011 they'd add $41,500 of debt to their current credit card debt of $366,000!**

What's the first step to getting out of debt? *Stop overspending!* But that means a family that is used to spending $96,500 a year has to learn how to live on $55,000. That's a tough pill to swallow. Those kinds of spending cuts seriously hurt, but it's the only way out of debt for Joe Q. Public.

If I ever got a call from a family that was spending $41,500 more than they made every year, you would definitely expect me to yell at them for their dumb behavior, right? Kids, no more McDonald's four times a week. Snacks come from the grocery store now. And we're not going to the movies for a while, so break out the board games and *TV Guide*. This family has a problem, so it's time to amputate the lifestyle!

It works the same way for the government. **You can't borrow your way out of debt**, whether you're a typical American family or the entire U.S. government. At some point, you've got to say, "Enough is enough!" and make the hard cuts necessary to win over the long haul.

Want to know more about how to relate to your friends and family around the subject of money? You will see more of this in **Chapter 5, Family, Friends and Philanthropy.**

SECTION 2

Debunking the Myths

Myth 1

MYTH: If I ____________ money to a friend or relative, I will be helping them.
6

TRUTH: The relationship will be strained or ____________.
7

Myth 2

MYTH: By ____________ a loan, I am helping out a friend or relative.
8

TRUTH: The bank requires a cosigner because the person isn't likely to ____________. Be ready to pay the loan and have your credit damaged.
9

Myth 3

MYTH: ____________ ____________ (10), payday-lending, rent-to-own, title pawning and tote-the-note lots are needed ____________ (11) for lower income people to help them get ahead.

TRUTH: These are horrible, greedy ripoffs that aren't needed and benefit no one but the owners of these companies.

80% of ____________ (12) in America are first-generation rich. That means they started out with nothing, did smart stuff, and became millionaires. That's the opposite of what we're talking about here.

$

76% of consumers in their twenties are in debt. For consumers in their thirties, that number jumps to **90%**.

FEDERAL RESERVE'S SURVEY OF CONSUMER FINANCES

"The only man who sticks closer to you in adversity than a friend is a creditor."

AUTHOR UNKNOWN

Myth 4

MYTH: The ____________ (13) and other forms of gambling will make me ____________ (14).

TRUTH: The lottery is a ____________ (15) on the poor and on people who can't do math.

Texas Tech University did a study on the Texas lottery and found that people without a high school diploma spent an average of ____________ (16) a month playing the lottery. College graduates spend ____________ (17) a month on average.

When studies are done on the lottery, it's always the lower-income ZIP codes that generate the highest revenue or sales.

Discussion Questions: Section 2

- What is your reaction to the phrase, "The borrower is the slave of the lender"? How have you seen this in your life?
- Have you ever borrowed money from a friend or family member? Has anyone ever borrowed money from you? How did it affect the relationship?

Myth 5

MYTH: ______________ [18] payments are a way of life and you'll always have a car payment.

TRUTH: Staying away from car payments by driving reliable used cars is what the typical ______________________________ [19] does. This is how they became millionaires.

The average car payment today is $464 per month over 64 months.

Myth 6

MYTH: ___________________________ [20] your car is what sophisticated financial people do. You should always lease things that go down in value. There are tax advantages.

TRUTH: *Consumer Reports, Smart Money* magazine, and a good calculator will tell you that the car ________________ [21] is the most _________________________ [22] way to finance and operate a vehicle.

If you own a business, you can ______________ ____________ [23] your paid-for car on taxes without paying payments for the privilege.

The way to __________________________ [24] the money lost on things that go down in value is to buy slightly __________________ [25].

Lease: A long-term rental agreement; a form of secured long-term debt

Tax Deduction: Expense that a taxpayer is allowed to deduct from taxable income; examples include money paid as home mortgage interest and charitable donations

$

On an inflation-adjusted basis, the average cost of owning a car has declined from a generation ago. But auto-related expenses jumped **52%** because the typical family now owns at least two vehicles.

USA TODAY

Of those who lease cars, **75%** say it's because leasing allows them to upgrade, **25%** say it's because it's the only way they can afford something decent.

BANKRATE.COM

"Your largest wealth-building tool is your INCOME, and when it's not all going out the door with someone else's name on it, you can make it grow."

DAVE RAMSEY
Financial Expert

Dannie: $30,000 in debt

My name is Dannie and I've already acquired $30,000 in debt during my 21 years of living. I discovered Dave last year while flipping through my local radio stations, and I was caught offguard when he said, "Don't give a toot about your credit score!" Even though my parents make $100,000 a year, they live paycheck to paycheck and can't help me pay for school.

During my senior year of high school, my parents co-signed on a $20,000 car which I pay for myself. I also took out about $17,000 in student loans during my first three semesters of school. But I recently decided that I am done being dumb! This last semester I moved back home and transferred to a local university that will cost me about half the amount. My cost of living is now zero. I have paid off $2,000 on my car by working part time, and I've also saved money for the next two semesters so I don't need loans! I am so glad that I found Dave. I love my parents, but I am so glad I will not make the same financial mistakes they have made. Even though I am not living like my friends and racking up the loans, I am looking forward to the day that I will live like no one else!

Myth 7

MYTH: You can get a good deal on a ________ (26) car.

> **Depreciation:** A decline in the value of property; the opposite of appreciation

TRUTH: A new car loses ________ (27) of its value in the first four years. This is the largest purchase most consumers make that goes down in value.

- On average, a $28,000 car will be worth $8,400 in four years.

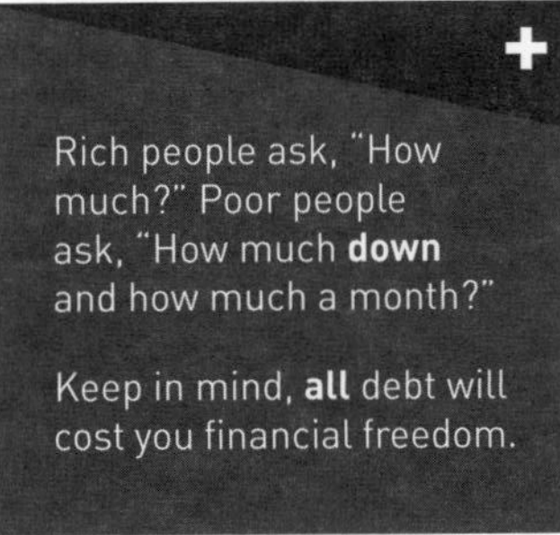

Discussion Questions: Section 3

- If you had to live without a car during college, how would you get around? Are other methods of transportation cheaper than having a car?
- Over the next 50 years, how much could you save if you didn't make car payments of $464 every month? What else could you do with this money?

"Modern man drives a mortgaged car over a bond-financed highway on credit-card gas."

EARL WILSON
American Columnist

"Another way to solve the traffic problems of this country is to pass a law that only paid-for cars be allowed to use the highways."

WILL ROGERS
American Cowboy and Comedian

American families have different views about which debts are okay. Mortgages were considered to be a very acceptable type of debt by the most number of families (**34%**), followed by student loans (**29%**) and car loans (**17%**). Credit card debt is considered not acceptable by over half of all the families (**52%**), followed by cash advance and personal loans (**46%**) and retail purchases on credit (**44%**).

SALLIE MAE

Want to know more about mortgages? Check out **Chapter 12, Real Estate.**

Myth 8

MYTH: I'll take out a 30-year mortgage and pay ________________[28].

TRUTH: Life happens and something else will always seem more important. Never take out more than a __________[29] - year fixed-rate mortgage.

Myth 9

MYTH: It's wise to take out an ____________[30] or a ____________________[31] mortgage if "I know I'll be moving."

TRUTH: You *will* be moving when they ______________________[32].

- The adjustable-rate mortgage is here to keep the ____________[33] from losing money. It transfers the __________[34] of higher interest rates to you.

Adjustable Rate Mortgage (ARM): Home loan secured by a deed of trust or mortgage in which the interest rate will change periodically

Balloon Mortgage: Home loan in which the sum of the monthly payments is insufficient to repay the entire loan; as a result, a final payment comes due, which is a lump sum of the remaining principal balance

Foreclosure: The holder of a mortgage sells the property of a homeowner who has not made payments on time

Discussion Questions: Section 4

- Do you believe it is possible to pay cash for a house? Is this something you would consider doing if it meant you could save $100,000 or more?
- Do you know anyone who has a paid-off house? How did they manage to pay it off? What do they do with their money that families with monthly mortgages cannot do?

The Secret Alliance

BETWEEN COLLEGES AND CREDIT CARDS

For years, the quickest way to get a free T-shirt or pizza on most college campuses was to sign up for a credit card. At most schools, credit card booths were as easy to find as a game of ultimate frisbee.

That's because credit card companies know what they are doing. Their research shows that people are the **most loyal to their first credit card**—it's the one they'll have the hardest time cutting up. Credit card companies know that if they can get college students early—even with a co-signer, then they have a great chance of keeping them for life.

Recent credit card legislation nixed some of these aggressive marketing practices. But there are still plenty of problems, because the credit card issuers won't back down. **Many schools are still aligned with credit card companies, and these companies can still pay colleges to receive access to students.** According to the Huffington Post Investigative Fund, some of the nation's biggest and most well-known schools sell students' personal information to credit card companies, earn royalties when students open a card and maintain a balance, make money when students use their cards, and even use their own marketing to promote these credit cards.

Now that students must be 21 (or have a co-signer) to receive a credit card, these companies have changed their tactics. **Instead of credit cards, many students now use a student ID that is linked to their loan accounts.** With the swipe of a card, a student can easily access that money and use it for any purpose.

Is this disturbing? Absolutely! But we've known for years that credit card companies and schools have a special relationship. Why else has it always been so easy—until the recent legislation passed—to find a credit card booth on every corner of the campus?

Sallie Mae says that 33% of college students graduate with more than $10,000 in credit card debt. Not only that, but **60% of first-year students max out their credit card within the first year.** It's pretty easy to see that students are pros at spending money, and credit cards will only increase that activity to more outrageous levels! If you think that having your parents or friends cosign will change your habits, think again.

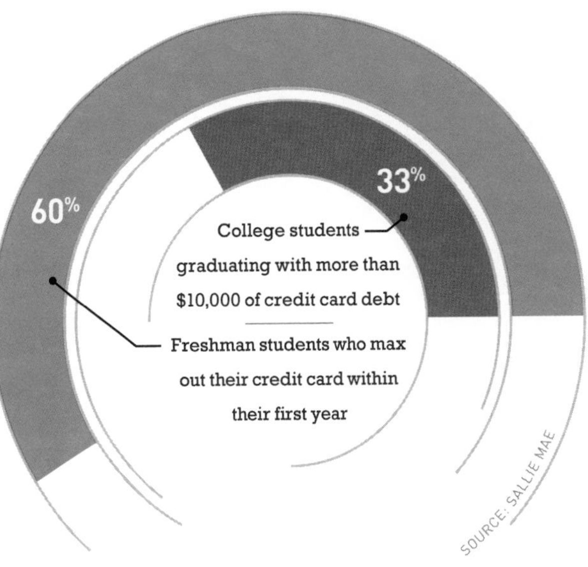

The core of this is a behavior issue. If you'll learn how to manage money responsibly (i.e. live below your means without credit), then you won't have to worry about the college sharing your information with these companies. You won't have to worry about credit card legislation or ridiculous interest rates. Credit cards simply won't be an issue, because you have already decided to not play the tricky credit game.

You'll sleep better at night knowing that you won't have to deal with all of this credit card nonsense and can actually focus on your education and making your hard-earned money work *for* you.

82% of college students carry credit card balances each month and incur finance charges.

SALLIE MAE

College students receive an average of **four phone calls** and **five mailings** each month encouraging them to apply for credit cards.

STUDY BY HIGHER ONE

Young adults who have credit cards will spend nearly **30%** of their income on debt payments over their lifetime.

STUDY BY DEMOS RESEARCH

College seniors graduate with an average of **$4,100** in credit card debt.

SALLIE MAE

Want to know more about credit? You will see more of this in **Chapter 8, Credit Bureaus.**

Myth 10

MYTH: You need a __________ ______________ (35) to rent a car or make a ______________ (36) online or by phone.

TRUTH: A ______________ (37) card does all of that.

Debit Card: A card that often bears the seal of a major credit card company, issued by a bank and used to make purchases; unlike a credit card, the money comes directly out of a checking account; also called a check card

Myth 11

MYTH: I pay my __________ ______________ (38) off every month with no annual payment or fee. I get brownie points, air miles and a free hat.

TRUTH: A recent Dunn and Bradstreet study found that when you use cash instead of plastic, you spend ______________________ (39) less because spending cash hurts.

Grace Period: Time period during which a borrower can pay the full balance of credit due with no finance charges

Myth 12

MYTH: I'll make sure my ______________________ (40) gets a credit card so he or she can learn to be responsible with money.

TRUTH: Teens are a huge ______________________ (41) of credit card companies today.

Discussion Questions: Section 5

- Students ages 18–25 are the number-one target for credit card offers. Why do credit card companies target you? What is your reaction to being a target?
- Why does Dave approve of the debit card but not the credit card? How has using a debit card benefited you personally?

Beating the Odds

WRITTEN BY A RECENT COLLEGE GRADUATE

Fresh out of business school, I was filled with ambition and courage. I confidently opened the doors of a new fitness center in my small home town in Idaho. Two years later, I closed those doors, shaken and discouraged.

For the next seven years, I carried $50,000 of debt from that experience. Although I never earned more than $48,000 per year during those days, I also never missed a payment to a creditor. My moral convictions just wouldn't let me. So I slogged along, making no headway while trying to raise my young family.

Then one day, I got the news: **My youngest son was diagnosed with a severe form of debilitating epilepsy.** I knew immediately that things would have to change. I would never be able to carry the costs that would surely come with his disease while continuing to service my failed-business debt.

So with **renewed determination** to free myself of the burden, I got a second full-time job (and my wife's blessing to disappear each day for as long as necessary) and got to work.

For the next two years, I worked around the clock, frequently logging more than a hundred hours a week, chipping away at the mountain at the rate of $13 per hour.

Finally, in 2005, I paid off the final creditor and declared myself *debt free!* Amazingly, as Dave frequently hints, I have been additionally blessed with a significantly increased income, so my current salary now exceeds the combined salaries of those two years. I now have the resources to ensure the best care for my son and a comfortable life for my family.

Oh, and my youthful ambition and courage have returned full strength. This is how life is supposed to be lived!

SECTION 6

Myth 13

MYTH: The home equity loan is good for ______________ (42) and is a substitute for the emergency fund.

Home Equity Loan (HEL): Credit line offered by mortgage lenders that allows a homeowner to borrow money against the equity in their home

TRUTH: You don't go into ______________ (43) for emergencies.

$

60% of retirees believe credit card use is an impediment to saving.

SCOTT TRADE RETIREMENT STUDY

+

"Give no sleep to your eyes, nor slumber to your eyelids. **Deliver yourself like a gazelle** from the hand of the hunter, and like a bird from the hand of the fowler" (Proverbs 6:4-5, NKJV).

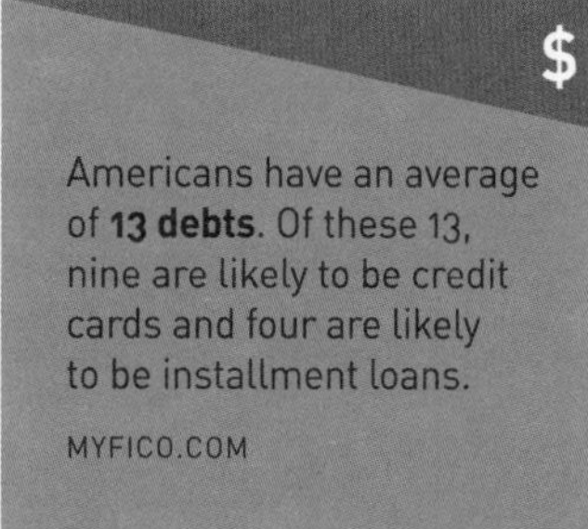

Americans have an average of **13 debts**. Of these 13, nine are likely to be credit cards and four are likely to be installment loans.

MYFICO.COM

Go In Debt So You Can Build Up Your Credit?

The FICO score is an I-LOVE-DEBT SCORE. It's not a measure of winning financially. You can inherit $10 million or get a $1-million-a-year-raise, and your FICO score won't change ONE POINT.

Myth 14

MYTH: Debt ______________ (44) saves interest and you get a smaller ______________ (45).

TRUTH: Debt consolidation is a ______________ (46).

> **Debt Consolidation:** Act of combining all debts into one monthly payment, typically extending the terms and the length of time required to repay the debt

- Debt consolidation saves little or no ______________ (47) because you will throw your low-interest loans into the deal.
- You cannot ______________ (48) your way out of debt!
- ______________ (49) payments equal more ______________ (50) in debt.

Myth 15

MYTH: Debt is a ______________ (51). It should be used to create prosperity.

TRUTH: The ______________ (52) is slave to the lender.

- When surveyed, the Forbes 400 were asked, "What is the most important key to building wealth?" ______________ (53) replied that becoming and staying ______________ (54) free was the number-one key to wealth building.

Discussion Questions: Section 6

- If you had to convince someone that getting into debt to "build a credit score" would hurt them long term, what would you say? How would you persuade them?
- Have you ever believed any of the 15 myths we've covered? Why are some of them hard to overcome?

SECTION 7

Steps Out of Debt

1. Quit ____________ (55) more ____________ (56)!

2. You must ____________ (57) money.

3. ____________ (58) something.

4. Part-time ____________ (59) or ____________ (60) (temporarily).

5. Use the ____________ ____________ (61).

› **Baby Step 2:** Pay off all debt using the debt snowball.

Discussion Questions: Section 7

- In your life, how have you seen debt hurt people's lives? What would it feel like to have absolutely no debt for the rest of your life?
- Why is "gazelle intensity" so important when avoiding debt? How can you use that intensity in your life today?

$

76% of undergraduates carry credit cards with an average balance of more than $2,000.

SALLIE MAE

Half of college undergraduates have **four or more** credit cards.

SALLIE MAE

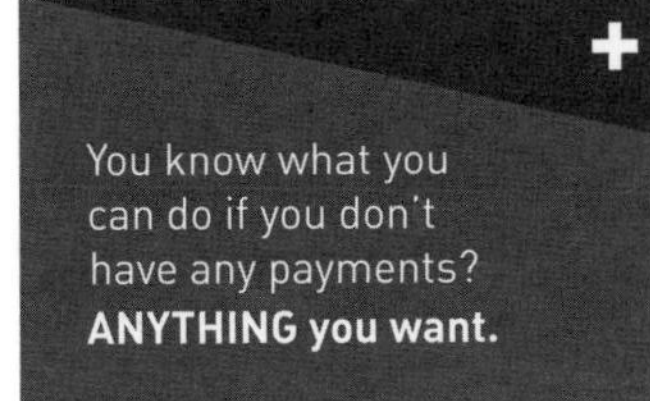

Debt Snowball

Now it's time to knock out that debt! List your debts in order, from the smallest balance to the largest. Don't be concerned with interest rates, unless two debts have a similar payoff balance. In that case, list the one with the higher interest rate first. As you start eliminating debts, you'll start to build some serious momentum. These quick wins will keep you motivated, so you'll be able to stay on track.

The idea of the snowball is simple: pay minimum payments on all your debts except for the smallest one. Then, attack that one with gazelle intensity! Every extra dollar you can get your hands on should be thrown at the smallest debt until it is gone. Then, you attack the second one. Every time you pay off a debt, you add its old minimum payment to your next debt payment. So, as the snowball rolls over, it picks up more snow. Get it?

Redo this sheet every time you pay off a debt so that you can see how close you're getting to total debt freedom. The "New Payment" is the total of the previous debt's payment PLUS the current debt's minimum. As these payments compound, you'll start making huge payments as you work down the list.

ITEM	TOTAL PAYOFF	MINIMUM PAYMENT	NEW PAYMENT
JC Penney	$150	$15	(Garage Sale)
Sears	$250	$10	$25
Visa	$500	$75	$100
MasterCard	$1,500	$90	$190
Car	$4,000	$210	$400
Student Loan	$4,000	$65	$465

Recap & Review

A Credit Card is a Credit Card is a Credit Card

BY JON ACUFF

Dave Ramsey has ruined me for credit cards. Not just using credit cards. He's certainly changed that part of my life. Even when I pull out my debit card, I feel a little weird. I don't exactly feel crazy, but at least a smidge odd.

He's even ruined my ability to see credit card advertisements and not laugh out loud. I blame him for that. I used to be able to watch television, see an ad for a credit card, and not think twice about it. Now? What happens when I see them? I really watch them. I don't casually let them float by the screen—I listen to what they're saying and then talk back to the television like an over-excited crowd watching a horror movie.

I see a spot in which a couple talks about booking a vacation with a credit card so that they can earn miles, and in my chair at home I yell, "Don't do it! Don't go on that vacation. Don't open that door! There are killer fees waiting inside. You'll never be able to redeem those miles. Noooo!"

And when I'm not yelling at the television, I'm picking apart what's being said in the ad. One of my favorite things credit card companies do is criticize other credit card companies.

There's an ad I've seen recently where the commercial talks about how horrible the customer service is if you do business with their competitor. Other commercials warn you about the high fees and jacked-up rates their competitors offer. "We're the good guys, not like our competitors. They just want your money. We're not about that. We're different. We're not like everyone else."

If you've spent seven seconds with Dave Ramsey's materials, though, you know that a credit card is a credit card is a credit card. In the world of credit card marketing, there are not good guys and bad guys. There's not one credit card company who wants your money and another who wants your hugs and just hopes to see you follow your dreams with everything you've got.

Put in even simpler terms: A credit card company criticizing another credit card company is like a hammerhead shark talking trash about a great white shark. In that scenario, you still get bitten.

There's not a shark victim on the planet who says, "You know, a shark took my leg. Ripped it clean off my body, but I'm not mad. It was a tiger shark, not a mako, and that makes all the difference in the world."

A shark is a shark. A credit card is a credit card. When they're telling you they're not, be very careful. At that point, they're already circling.

Chapter 3 Key Concepts

- Remember, debt is heavily marketed to young people. You will receive a lot of offers from credit card companies.
- Avoid car payments—they do not have to be a way of life.
- Do not build your credit score by using a credit card.
- Quit borrowing money and live on less than you make.

RECAP & REVIEW

Video Section Answers

1. 70%
2. Myth
3. Truth
4. Marketed
5. Paradigm
6. Loan
7. Destroyed
8. Cosigning
9. Repay
10. Cash Advance
11. Services
12. Millionaires
13. Lottery
14. Rich
15. Tax
16. $173
17. $49
18. Car
19. Millionaire
20. Leasing
21. Lease
22. Expensive
23. Write off
24. Minimize
25. Used
26. New
27. 70%
28. Extra
29. 15
30. ARM
31. Balloon
32. Foreclose
33. Bank
34. Risk
35. Credit Card
36. Purchase
37. Debit
38. Credit Card
39. 12–18%
40. Teenager
41. Target
42. Consolidation
43. Debt
44. Consolidation
45. Payment
46. Con
47. Interest
48. Borrow
49. Smaller
50. Time
51. Tool
52. Borrower
53. 75%
54. Debt
55. Borrowing
56. Money
57. Save
58. Sell
59. Job
60. Overtime
61. Debt Snowball

CHAPTER 3

Case Studies

Jerome and Money for College

During his summers, Jerome volunteers at the Red Cross, works 10 hours a week at social service organizations, and saves some money for college. He is about to start his junior year of college, and unfortunately he's out of money. The two-year tab for tuition, room, board and books is nearly $20,000. He has the option to borrow the money through low-interest student loan programs. As a result, Jerome is thinking about taking out student loans so he can finish school and get a job to pay them off quickly.

1. Should Jerome take out the student loans to pay for the last two years of college? Why or why not?

2. If he doesn't take out the loans, what other options does he have to pay for tuition, room, board and books?

3. Is it reasonable for Jerome to believe he can find a good job to help him pay off the student loans quickly? Why or why not?

4. Is there another way he could save up the $20,000 he needs for the last two years of college?

Austin and Paying Debts

Austin is a junior in college and recently returned from a spring- break trip to Panama City with his friends. However, the vacation followed Austin home. He ended up putting the entire trip on his credit card, including airfare, a two-night hotel stay, entertainment, food and other expenses. He already had a $1,750 balance on the credit card prior to the trip and added $2,000 of spring-break expenses to that. Austin now has almost $4,000 to pay off. Between the large credit card payments and his other monthly bills, he's having trouble paying all of his bills. This month Austin found himself $275 short of paying his bills. On top of all that, he's stressed because his employer is considering cutting his 20 hour/week job down to 10 hours a week. Austin is trying to find a way to fairly pay his debts, knowing that everyone won't get paid this month. His savings is down to $100. He's thought about bankruptcy, since he's finding fewer and fewer options to get out of this situation.

1. How would you handle Austin's situation?

2. What other options does Austin have besides bankruptcy?

3. How could Austin have avoided this financial mess?

Yvonne and Student Loan Debt

Yvonne will be graduating in December with a degree in elementary education. Thanks to her hard work, she already has a third-grade teaching job lined up after she graduates. It will be the first time in her life that she will make more than minimum wage. Because she wasn't able to make enough money while in college, she took out student loans to help pay for her education. She has $15,000 in student loan debt and $3,000 in credit card debt. Yvonne must start paying back the student loans once she is out of school, and she is already making payments to her credit card debt.

1. What is the first thing Yvonne should pay back after she graduates? Why?

2. Should Yvonne save up money for an emergency fund first or start paying off her debts first? Why?

3. Now that she will make more than minimum wage, create a game plan for Yvonne's money.

CHAPTER 3

Money in Review

Matching

Match each term to its definition below.

a. debt consolidation	e. cash advance
b. cosigning	f. paradigm
c. debt snowball	g. ARM
d. leasing	h. credit

1 _____ The way you view the world

2 _____ Charges 400% and up for their services

3 _____ Money loaned

4 _____ A mortgage that does not have a fixed interest rate

5 _____ Taking responsibility for someone else's loan

6 _____ Combining several debts into one payment

7 _____ Long-term rental agreement

True or False

Determine whether these statements are true or false. Change the false statements to read true.

8 **T / F :** Debt consolidation is wise.

9 **T / F :** Buying used cars is a good way to avoid depreciation.

10 **T / F :** The typical American millionaire drives a brand new car.

11 **T / F :** The elderly are the number-one target of credit card companies.

12 **T / F :** Co-signing a loan is a way to help out a friend or relative.

13 **T / F :** The lottery is a tax on the poor and on people who can't do math.

14 **T / F :** Home equity loans are a good way to consolidate debt.

15 **T / F :** It is never wise to take out an ARM or balloon mortgage.

16 **T / F :** Paying off the balance of your credit card each month is an acceptable use of credit.

17 **T / F :** The best way to teach teenagers about money is to get them a credit card.

18 **T / F :** It is wise to attack your debt by consolidating many payments into one.

19 **T / F :** Carrying cash results in an increase of spending versus paying with credit.

Short Answer

20 Why do people go into debt when they know that they will have to pay more for an item once they add interest?

21 Why are teens a major target of the credit card industry?

22 How do cash advance and car title companies keep people in the cycle of debt?

23 Why is it better to buy a used car instead of a brand new vehicle?

24 How does the debt snowball work?

25 How can lending money cause problems in a relationship?

CHAPTER 3

Notes

CHAPTER 4

College Student Essentials

UNIT 1: MASTERING THE BASICS

As a college student, a world filled with endless opportunities is set before you. While it's exciting, it can also be difficult to navigate. Every undergraduate needs to understand a few basic principles to be successful—choosing a major, applying for financial aid, landing a job, and preparing for transitions after graduation.

Learning Outcomes

Describe the role of money in deciding a career.

- Money is ultimately never enough compensation for doing a job. While a paycheck is important, you also need to factor in your skills, abilities, personality traits, values, dreams and passions.

Explain the four personality types in the DISC personality profile and identify possible majors that fit each.

- **Dominant (D):** driver, task-oriented, bold
- **Influencing (I):** expressive, outgoing, entertaining
- **Stable (S):** amiable, understanding, loyal
- **Compliant (C):** analytical, factual, serious

Demonstrate how to apply for financial aid.

- Fill out the FAFSA form
- Research grants
- Research scholarships
- Research work opportunities (work study and off-campus jobs)
- Avoid student loans

Describe common transitions that occur after college graduation.

- Working 40 hours a week
- Receiving an income
- Moving to a different location
- Buying a home

Apply effective job-search tools.

- Cover letters
- Résumés
- Interviews

Explain the importance of doing a budget in a marriage relationship.

- Agreement on money is a key factor in a healthy marriage. As a result, the budget committee has two members: the husband and the wife. Both have to be there, both have to participate, and both have to actively engage in the process. Marriage is a partnership.

Summarize the key financial principles to teach children.

- Encourage children to work, "If you work, you get paid; if you do not work, you do not get paid."
- Pay commissions, not allowance
- Teach by example by living debt free, buying insurance, and investing
- Use three envelopes (giving, spending, saving)

Key Terms

Free Application for Federal Student Aid (FAFSA): a form that is completed annually by current and prospective college students to determine their eligibility for financial aid

Grant: a form of federal or state financial aid that does not need to be repaid; usually given to students who demonstrate financial need

Scholarship: a form of financial aid that does not need to be repaid; usually awarded on the basis of academic, athletic or other achievements

Vocation: the work in which an individual is employed; your calling as a career

Work Study: a program that allows students to work part time while continuing their studies

Contact Letter: a letter informing a prospective employer that you are interested in working for their company

Cover Letter: similar to a contact letter but is used to inform the prospective employer of your interest and capabilities as they relate to a specific employment opportunity; always accompanied by a résumé

Résumé: personal and work history used for gaining employment

Reading

UNDERCLASSMEN: the following three sections are tailored to address the needs of freshmen and sophomores.

Choosing a Major: Strengths

To a college underclassman, committing to a major can seem overwhelming at first. The good news is choosing a major is much simpler than it sounds. Simply focus on your strengths. Most people consider the things they're good at as their strengths and the things they're bad at as their weaknesses. But in his book Go Put Your Strengths To Work, author Marcus Buckingham says just because you're good at something doesn't mean it's your strength. In fact, you may be good at a lot of things you'd never want to spend your life doing. The difference between a strength and something you're just good at is passion. Discover what you're passionate about, and you've found your strength. If you can follow these guidelines, you'll choose a major that fits you perfectly. And if you don't, you can always change majors. Your major isn't a life sentence to one field!

Choosing a Major: Personality Types

Why is it that you automatically "click" with some people, while others seem to grate on your last nerve? Why do some people fit right into certain jobs, while others never seem to get the hang of it? A lot of our interactions with people—the good and the bad—connect back to our personality styles. Sometimes, two similar personality styles might butt heads, or totally opposite personality styles might not "get" each other. This can cause tension, conflict and frustration. The DISC personality profile is a great tool in addressing these issues—it explains the differences in how people behave. Keep in mind, the DISC isn't the final word on behaviors; it simply gives you a starting point for understanding how people interact. And once you know that, you'll be more successful understanding your own tendencies, which is key in choosing a major.

Applying for Financial Aid

Going to college doesn't mean you have to go into debt to pay for an education. Yet student loans are becoming more and more the norm instead of the exception. In recent years, graduating college seniors had an average of $22,900 in student loans.[1] Many believe that student loans are just a fact of life. Why settle for that?

With some hard work and a bit of intuition, you can pay for college without going into debt. The average tuition for a public four-year college is $7,605.[2] At first glance that may seem like a lot of money, but there are plenty of ways to foot the bill without taking out a loan. **Apply for Grants and Scholarships.** Once you start looking, there are plenty of grants and scholarships available—and many go unclaimed each year. Do a little research and you'll find grants and scholarships that may allow you to receive financial aid without having to pay it back. **Get a job.** There's no reason why a college student can't pick up a part-time job in the evenings or on the weekends. If you do your homework, you'll find plenty of options to help pay for your college tuition. You don't want to be 22 with a $20,000 pet called Sallie Mae following you everywhere you go!

UPPERCLASSMEN: the following five sections are tailored to address the needs of juniors and seniors.

Transitioning Into Life After Graduation

Imagine yourself as a new college graduate, your diploma still warm off the printer. A whole new way of life will present itself

to you, and you'll be offered countless options. That's why it's important to prepare for this time of transition. If you're like most graduates, you'll likely step into a promising career with a solid income. With this new income, it's a temptation to go on a spending frenzy—leasing a car, buying expensive electronics, getting new furniture, and the list goes on and on. Don't be that person or you'll wreck your future with debt. This is also a transitional period when it comes to housing. You may move to another city or back in with your parents. A mistake many graduates make is buying a home too quickly. You should purchase a house when you have an emergency fund, you are out of debt, you have a down payment, and you pay no more than a quarter of your take-home pay on your 15-year fixed rate mortgage. Graduating into the real world brings responsibilities that can be a blessing or a curse, depending on how you handle your new freedom.

Landing a Job

It's an age-old dilemma. You work hard to get your degree so you can land your dream job, but because you've been in school, you don't have much work experience. And the jobs you want require experience. It's frustrating, maybe a little frightening. But it's certainly not the end of the story. Your degree isn't a guarantee that you'll land the perfect job right out of school. But it does give you the opportunity to move up into that position once you've gotten some solid job experience. So, instead of focusing on your dream job right now, get intense about finding your first job. Your first job will get you into the field want to be in—a simple, foot-in-the-door type position that probably won't pay much. Be realistic and expect that even an entry-level job like this will take a lot of work to get. But once you're in, make it a point to learn all you can and prove to the company that you're a smart, hardworking, passionate team member—just the kind of person they want to hire.

Working Part Time

Working part time during school may not seem like the ideal situation, but it might be a reality in order to graduate debt free. Try to think outside the box when it comes to finding a part-time job as a college student. Think about babysitting or cleaning homes. Or maybe mowing lawns or pressure washing driveways is more your speed. Get creative. At this point in your life, you don't need to limit yourself to a job in your career field (though that would be ideal)—simply try to find a position that works with your class schedule. After you graduate, you may want to consider working part time if you're having difficulty finding a job in your career. If you earn a steady income through part-time work, you aren't as desperate to find a vocational job, which frees you up to wait for the best possible position. It's the perfect temporary solution.

Entering Marriage

Agreement on money is a key factor in a healthy marriage. Every marriage has a Nerd, Free Spirit, Spender and Saver. Mix all this together, and it's really no surprise that money fights so often end in divorce. But there's a better way. I call it the Budget Committee Meeting. In a marriage, the committee has two members: the husband and the wife. Both have to be there, both have to participate, and both have to actively engage the process. Marriage is a partnership. Listen up, nerds. Don't keep the money all to yourself. Don't use your "power" to abuse the Free Spirit. Free Spirits, don't just nod your head and say, "Yeah, that looks great, honey." You have a vote in the Budget Committee Meetings, too. Give feedback, criticism and encouragement. Work on the budget together!

Teaching Children About Money

Every parent needs to understand something: *Someone* is going to teach your kids about money. It will either be you, or it will a shady car dealer, a credit card pusher on their first day of college, a get-rich-quick infomercial pitchman, or just some clown who's after their money. If you want to protect your kids, you need to send them out into the world with some knowledge. First, start paying them a commission for chores they do around the house. Typically, one dollar per completed chore is sufficient with a list of five or six chores each week. Next, don't give them an allowance. After all, what are you making an allowance for? And don't miss out on the teachable moments that come when you give them a commission instead of an allowance. Lastly, encourage them to work. A little hard work isn't going to kill them. Letting a kid sit in front of a TV all day playing video games and eating junk food could be considered child abuse! The lessons you teach them as they earn money and learn to spend, save and give will lay an influential foundation for their lives.[3]

1. "Number of the Week: Class of 2011, Most Indebted Ever." http://blogs.wsj.com/economics/2011/05/07/number-of-the-week-class-of-2011-most-indebted-ever/, May 7, 2011
2. "Trends in College Pricing 2010." http://trends.collegeboard.org/downloads/college_pricing/highlights.pdf, 2010
3. Excerpts were taken from various articles on www.daveramsey.com

CHAPTER 4

Video: Sections 1–8

SECTION 1

Change Happens

The average job is now only __________[1] years in length.

This means that the average worker could have as many as __________[2] different jobs in his or her working lifetime.

Small business is changing the way we think about work. __________[3] of the companies in America have fewer than 100 employees.

Discover Your Strengths and Weaknesses

How can you know __________[4] you ought to be and __________[5] you ought to be doing if you don't know __________[6] you are?

Speaker and author Marcus Buckingham has identified some common myths that often rob people of having fulfillment and enjoyment in their careers.

MYTH: As you grow, you __________[7].

TRUTH: You do not __________[8] your personality.

MYTH: You will learn and grow the most in the areas in which you are __________[9].

TRUTH: You grow in your __________[10]. You will grow the most in the areas that you already know and love the most.

$

The average American lists **6–8 jobs** on his or her résumé by age 25.

ECONOMIC POLICY INSTITUTE

Nine out of 10 college students expect to find a job in their field.

USA TODAY

"Money won't make you happy... but everybody wants to find out for themselves."

ZIG ZIGLAR

American Author and Motivational Speaker

+

In American culture, too many people spend a lifetime chasing wealth in a career they hate. Or they work an excessive number of hours every week. "Do not wear yourself out trying to get rich. Be wise enough to know when to quit." (Proverbs 23:4-5, NLT)

Do something you love and that is fun for you! If you make a lot of money, great! But if you don't, at least you will have spent a lifetime doing something that was rewarding. Money should never become your primary motivation.

Just Because You're Good at Something Doesn't Make It a Strength

According to Marcus Buckingham, author of *Go Put Your Strengths To Work*, "most people think your strengths are what you're good at, and your weaknesses are what you're bad at." He explains that this isn't a good way to measure your strengths and skills.

There may be a lot of things that you're good at, but hate doing. Just because you're good at something doesn't make it a strength. You also must have a passion for what you're doing—that's what qualifies it as a strength.

"A better definition of a strength," said Buckingham, "is an activity that makes you feel strong. And a weakness is an activity that makes you feel weak. Even if you're good at it, if it drains you, that's a weakness."

He recommends writing down activities that drain you or energize you during a regular week. This will prohibit others from confirming or denying your strengths and weaknesses. Instead, you're determining what they are without letting other people's opinions influence you.

Once you have determined your strengths, you need to refine and sharpen your skills. "You grow the most, learn the most, develop the most in the areas where you already have some natural advantage," said Buckingham.

According to Buckingham, there are four clear signs of a strength:

- **Success:** This is effectiveness in the activity you are doing.
- **Instincts:** Find those things that you instinctively look forward to and capitalize on them.
- **Growth:** You're growing when you can concentrate on an activity, and time just flies by.
- **Needs:** Some activities might make you tired, but they fulfill you.

Now that you know your strengths, it's time to put them into action. From your list that you kept throughout the week, write down three strength statements. Buckingham said the statements should be "specific enough to conjure up passion within you, but general enough for you to apply every week." He says you can't build a career around your best unless you know your strengths. "It's one of the skills of life."

$

Students who pursue degrees in **science, technology, engineering and mathematics** will earn higher salaries than students who pursue degrees in art, music, history, culinary arts or sociology.

FASTWEB.COM

Identify Your Motivation and Passion

Career coach Dan Miller reminds us that ______________ is ultimately never enough compensation for doing a job.

11

Discussion Questions: Section 1

- What are your reasons for pursuing a particular major? How has this chapter changed or reinforced your view of your career path?
- If your paycheck wasn't a factor, what kind of career excites you? How does it compliment your strengths?

"What I know is that if you do work that you love and work that fulfills you, the rest will come. I truly believe that the reason I've been able to be so financially successful is because my focus has never, ever for one minute been money."

OPRAH WINFREY

American Television Host, Actress and Philanthropist

SECTION 2

Identify Your Motivation and Passion

(Continued)

Find something that blends your skills, ______________ (12), personality traits, ______________ (13), dreams and ______________ (14).

Understand Your Unique Personality

The ______________ (15) profile is a simple test that will yield tremendous insight into how you process decisions and what your natural tendencies may be.

> **DISC Personality Profile:** A behavior profile test that yields insights into how you process decisions and what your natural tendencies may be

- The D (______________ (16)) person is a hard-charging driver that is task-oriented and first looks to ______________ (17).
- The I (______________ (18)) person is people-oriented, fun, outgoing and generally concerned about pleasing people, so they first look to ______________ (19).
- The S (______________ (20)) person is amiable, loyal, does not like conflict, and is concerned about ______________ (21).
- The C (______________ (22)) person is analytical, loves detail, is factual, can seem rigid, and loves ______________ (23).

Discussion Questions: Section 2

- Which careers compliment your passions and strengths? On the other hand, which careers hinder you?
- In the DISC personality profile, what trait do you predominantly display? How do you see this affecting your choice of a career?

SECTION 3

There are no fill-in-the-blanks for this section.

See Financial Aid To-Do List *on the following pages.*

$

Over an adult's working life, high school graduates can expect, on average, to earn **$1.2 million**; those with a bachelor's degree, **$2.1 million**; and people with a master's degree, **$2.5 million**.

U.S. CENSUS BUREAU

Researchers at Georgetown University predict that by 2018, **63%** of all American jobs will require at least some college education.

CNN MONEY

> ***"The mindset today is you have to know who you are and how you function in the market. That's the only security you have."***
>
> **DAVE RAMSEY**
> Financial Expert

+

The **DISC** is a popular system originating in the 1920s by an American psychologist named William Moulton Marston.

DISC Personality Profile

LOOKING AT YOUR NATURAL TENDENCIES

Understanding your own strengths and weaknesses should be a top priority. Remember, people who only work for money are miserable, because there is no fulfillment or meaning in their career. You must find something that blends your skills, abilities, personality traits, values, dreams and passions.

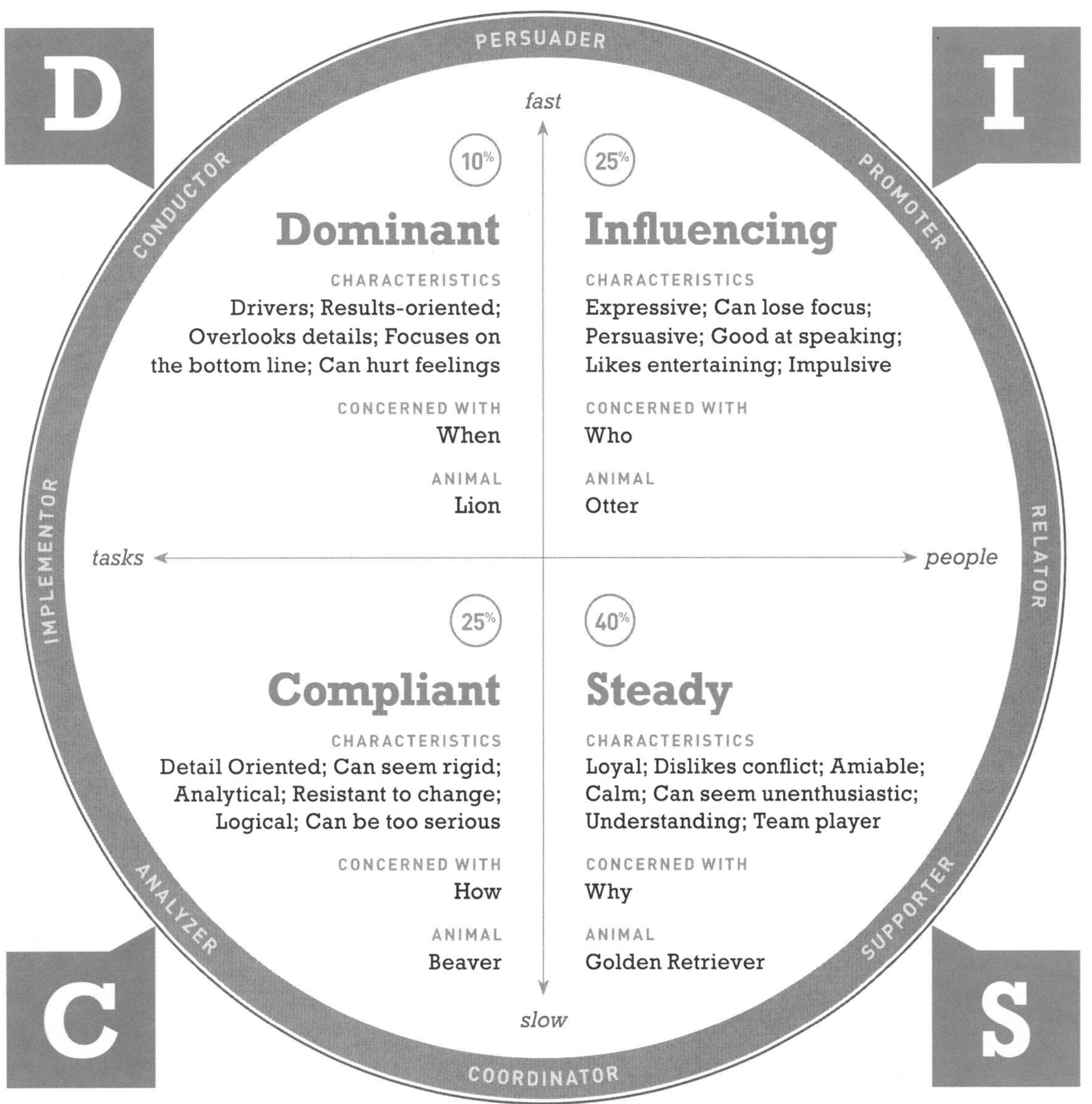

Financial Aid To-Do List

CHECK EACH ITEM OFF THE LIST AS IT'S COMPLETED

COMPLETED ☐

Fill Out the FAFSA Form

- The FAFSA (Free Application for Federal Student Aid) is the first step to receiving any kind of financial aid. Whether you are interested in scholarships, grants, loans, or other financial aids, you'll need to turn it in.
- The FAFSA form needs to be completed each year you are in college. The sooner you turn in the form (by January or February), the more likely you are to get financial help.
- You'll need your family's tax information as you complete the FAFSA. Keep in mind, if you turn it in online, the process moves faster.

COMPLETED ☐

Research Grants

- Consider scholarships and grants "free money," meaning you don't need to pay them back.
- Federal and state governments offer grants that are usually need-based. The FAFSA will determine which grants you qualify for. Examples include the Federal Pell Grant and state-specific grants.

COMPLETED ☐

Research Scholarships

- You should never pay to apply for scholarships. And do not give out your social security number when you apply.

There are several places to search for scholarships:

- University scholarships (examples include academic, athletic, volunteer based, club based, leadership based, ethnic, religious, school of study, fellowship/work based, etc.)
- Community scholarships (like your local Rotary Club and similar community organizations)
- Local business scholarships (like your future employer or your parent's employer)
- Free websites (like fastweb.com, collegeboard.com, finaid.org, and ed.gov)
- Private donors (like relatives or individuals offering unique scholarships)

COMPLETED ☐

Research Work Opportunities

- Research shows that students who work an average of 15–20 hours a week have the highest grade point averages of any type of student in college.
- Students who work often develop good time-management skills and planning skills.
- Research suggests that working over 20 hours a week may affect your grades.

Work-Study

- You can work on campus to pay your tuition bill.
- Usually the school provides hourly positions that pay minimum wage; the good news is you can often study as you work. Check with the financial aid office to see what jobs are offered.

Work Off Campus

- You can also work off campus, which usually pays more than work study. The options are limitless.

COMPLETED ☐

Set Up an Emergency Fund

- Set up a savings account that is set aside just for emergencies.
- As you work in the summer and save money for your school bill, set aside a separate amount in an emergency fund. If something bad happens during school, you have some funds to fix the problem so you don't have to drop out of school.

Avoid Student Loans

- Remember, you have two goals: Stay in school and stay out of debt.
- Avoid student loans! The average repayment period for a student loan is 10 years, if you make the minimum payment each month. You will pay more interest if you go beyond 10 years.

When To Visit the Financial Aid Office

- If your financial situation has changed, a parent has been laid off, or a medical situation has come up, it's important to visit the financial aid office. Your financial aid can be reevaluated and possibly increased.
- You can talk to a financial aid officer as soon as an emergency arises. They will offer you advice, encouragement or help.
- Don't wait to the last minute to go to the financial aid office; see them immediately when a problem arises.

Andrea: $112,623 in Debt

My name is Andrea and I currently have $112,623 in debt. The short version of my story is simply that I used student loans for my entire education, which is how I earned a bachelor's degree in Early Childhood Education. I'm currently a preschool teacher's assistant and I only make $24,000 a year. As a result, I have a second job and work about 80 hours a week, every single week. The majority of "my" student loan debt is a "stupid tax," because I co-signed on a student loan for an ex-boyfriend. I constantly tell my friends to work hard and save to pay cash for everything they buy. A few of them have listened, but I pray that no one else has to endure what I'm going through because they co-signed with an ex-boyfriend. This debt has ruined relationships, and there are many days that I can't quite picture the end.

$

During the last 20 years, tuition has increased at a faster rate than any other major product or service—four times faster than the overall inflation. After adjusting for financial aid, the amount families pay for college has skyrocketed **439%** since 1982.

CNN MONEY

Student loan debt is expected to reach **$1 trillion** in the near future.

CBS MONEYWATCH

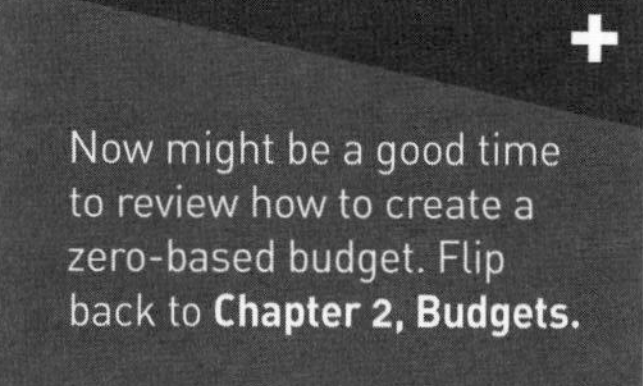

Now might be a good time to review how to create a zero-based budget. Flip back to **Chapter 2, Budgets.**

Discussion Questions: Section 3

- Other than student loans, how do you pay for your tuition? Do you think it's possible to avoid student loans for the rest of your college career? Why or why not?
- If you work, what kind of job do you have? How many hours do you work per week? How have you seen working benefit your life?

SECTION 4

There are no fill-in-the-blanks for this section.

After you graduate from college, you can expect new transitions:

- **Working 40 Hours a Week**

  At your new job, you will be given responsibilities and how you treat those determines your future success in that career. That's why you need to take those responsibilities seriously. Also keep in mind that going from 15 hours in school to 40 hours at work can be difficult. Pace yourself and find a routine/schedule that fits your new way of life. You might have to give up some recreational time in exchange for working time.

› Receiving a Steady Income

Don't be tempted to think a larger income will solve your financial problems. More money simply means more responsibility, so you need to stick to a zero-based budget. Don't go on a spending frenzy because you have more money. Instead, use the extra money to build wealth through investing.

› Moving to a Different City or Moving Back in with Your Parents

Remember, cities all over America have different cost-of-living standards. If you are offered a salary in another city, calculate if you can afford it based on the new cost-of-living situation. Don't take a job because it sounds glamorous or you think it's your only option. Invest time in weighing the costs.

› Buying a Home

Take your time when deciding to purchase a house. You should only buy a home when you have a fully funded emergency fund, you are out of debt, you have a down payment, and when you pay no more than a quarter of your take-home pay on a 15-year fixed-rate mortgage. When you have met all of those requirements, then you are ready for the 10-step process:

1. **Hire an agent.**
2. **Get pre-qualified.**
3. **Meet with your agent.**
4. **Drive by and look at potential homes and neighborhoods.**

$

Another transition to consider is returning to school for a graduate degree. A Master's degree is worth up to **$2.5 million** over a lifetime. Unfortunately, those classes will be more expensive than your undergraduate ones, so make sure you avoid student loans.

US CENSUS BUREAU

Getting Your Degree on Plan B

PROOF THAT YOU CAN GRADUATE FROM COLLEGE DEBT FREE

We recently asked Dave's Facebook friends to tell us how they got through college without debt. We received more than 1,300 comments—proof that debt-free college education *is* possible.

William worked full time on the second shift for a company that offered tuition reimbursement. "Burning the candle on both ends was the hardest thing I've ever done, but it was worth it when I finished summa cum laude," he said.

Work

When scholarships aren't enough, you can always find money the old-fashioned way—work!

"I went to College of the Ozarks near Branson, Missouri," Sandi said. "Every student works their way through on on-campus jobs and graduates debt free. Their logo is 'Hard Work U.'"

Chad ended up with nearly a full-ride scholarship based on his excellent ACT score, a 32. He took the test 18 times, but it was worth it. "I now run my own company working with high school students on their ACT tests and enjoy telling them how they, too, can make it with no debt," he said.

Scholarships

According to Collegeboard.com, the average financial aid payout for a full-time college student was about $10,000. Average tuition at a four-year public college was just over $7,000 per year for in-state students, so it is possible to get enough scholarships to cover tuition and most of your living expenses—you just have to apply!

Jan, a single mom, put herself through college with scholarships. "I applied for every available penny," she said. "My motto was, 'All they can do is tell me *no*—and maybe they will tell me *yes!*'"

Anthony began working toward a U.S. military academy appointment when he was a freshman in high school. He attended the U.S. Naval Academy, receiving a $250,000 education for free. "I paid the government back by serving as a Surface Warfare Officer for 10 wonderful years," he said.

Military

The military isn't for everyone, but it has helped a lot of Dave's Facebook friends get through college debt free.

The Air Force paid for Kate's husband to attend college while they scrimped to pay for books. He worked part time and was even deployed to Iraq, but he graduated in five years with a 4.0 grade point average. He now has his dream job—U.S. Air Force pilot.

Other Options

- Cut your spending down by following a zero-based budget every month.
- The College Level Examination Program (CLEP tests) give you credit for college courses after you pass a series of short tests. CLEP tests are much cheaper than tuition and you get the class credit instantly. Check with your school about their CLEP policy.

Mitchell: $131,684 in Debt

My name is Mitchell and I've attended state universities throughout my entire education. Fortunately I have actually amassed a reasonable amount of scholarships through my studies. Even so, my loan debt piled up quickly and getting myself through medical school has been pricey. My current loan debt is $131,684. The sad part is I've still got three years to go before I see a residency paycheck and even further to go before I see a practicing clinician paycheck. Not to mention, my student loans will likely hit the $250,000 mark before I'm able to begin paying them down.

My goal is to one day call Dave Ramsey's radio show on a Friday afternoon and be able to scream that victorious, "I'M DEBT FREE!" But until then, I'll keep listening to the radio.

Back to studying!

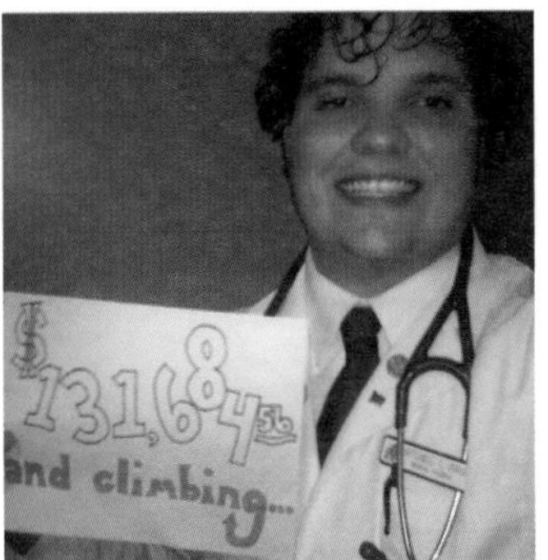

Buying a Home *(Continued)*

5. **Look at the house with an agent.**

6. **Make an offer.**

7. **Meet with a lender.**

8. **Have an inspection.**

9. **Sign the contract.**

10. **Get the keys.**

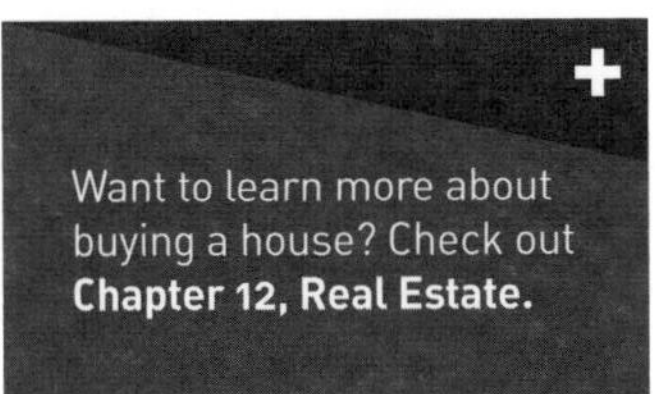

Want to learn more about buying a house? Check out **Chapter 12, Real Estate.**

"Do more than is required. What is the distance between someone who achieves their goals consistently and those who spend their lives and careers merely following? The extra mile."

GARY RYAN BLAIR
Motivational Speaker and Author

Discussion Questions: Section 4

- What do you think will be your easiest transition out of college? The hardest?
- What are the emotions you experience when you think of graduating? How can you start preparing for that transition now?

"The best careers advice to give to the young is 'Find out what you like doing best and get someone to pay you for doing it.'"

KATHERINE WHITEHORN
British Journalist

After College, Then What?

DR Here's the situation: You are a new college graduate, fresh out of school, with high hopes for the future. You've got a great degree—and you've worked extremely hard to get it. But there's a catch. You don't have a lot of job experience—and, of course, every job you want to apply for has some type of minimum experience requirement, right?

So if you are a new graduate in this situation, **what should you do**?

First off, take a deep breath. You're going to find a job. Are you going to hop right into your dream position right out of college? Probably not. But you're going to find a job. **Relax.**

You might have to contact 30 companies. You might have to start out at an entry-level, "gofer" position—getting coffee, running errands, making copies, organizing files. But your primary goal should be to **get your foot in the door.**

Don't just rest on your college degree. You need to clearly communicate to these companies what you have to offer. There are companies out there that are looking for smart and hard-working college grads, and you need to prove that you are just that person.

But, more importantly, you need to remember that money isn't the only factor you need to think about. Career Coach Dan Miller—author of *48 Days to the Work You Love* and *No More Mondays*—says that money is ultimately never enough compensation for doing a job.

Hopefully, you chose your college major because it was something you enjoyed studying. With your first job, find something that blends your **skills, abilities, personality traits, values, dreams and passions.** Don't enroll in law school or work as a salesman if you aren't passionate about working in those fields.

But, remember, you're probably not going to find your dream job right out of college. You might have to suck up your pride. If you have a degree in business management and you want to work in human resources, then you should probably expect to start out at the bottom of an HR department—if you start in the HR department at all. Sometimes it may help you just to get in at a company with a good HR department, taking a job doing something else until an HR position opens.

The average job for the average worker in America is only 2.1 years in length. For workers in their twenties, that timeframe is even shorter. Whether you love or hate your first job out of college, keep in mind that it probably isn't forever. **Continue learning and making yourself a valuable team member, and you'll succeed at whatever you do.**

"Careers, like rockets, don't always take off on time. The trick is to always keep the engine running."

GARY SINISE
American Actor, Film Director and Musician

SECTION 5

Job Hunting

Companies do not start out looking for ______________ (24). They have a specific ______________ (25) and they need someone to meet it.

Develop a strategy:

- Identify your ______________ (26).
- ______________ (27) everything you can about them.

?

"I'm applying for a new job. I like my current job, but the other position would be ideal. Should I tell my boss that I'm applying for the job?"

DAVE'S ANSWER: I think it has a lot to do with your situation at work, and if your integrity comes into play. There's nothing wrong with looking at the menu when you're on a diet, but if you've told your boss or supervisors you're not interested in another job, you need to let them know things have changed.

The big thing here is that you make sure you treat other people the way you would want to be treated. I'm an employer, and I have about 300 people on my team. I don't expect these guys to tell us every time something pops up that might interest them. I do, however, expect my leaders to let me know if they have someone who is so unhappy here that they're looking for other work.

Your relationship with your company and supervisors plays a big part in this, too. I'd speak up if there was something they could do to change my situation from good to ideal. But in a lot of ways, it all goes back to how you would want to be treated if the situation were reversed.

Remember the Golden Rule? Just looking at things from that perspective can answer a whole lot of ethics questions!

Résumés

When it is time to contact the company, think of it like starting a new ______________ (28) with a person.

After you target the companies where you would most like to work, you are going to contact them at least three times.

- Introduction ______________ (29).
- Cover letter and Résumé.
- ______________ (30) follow-up.

Interviews and jobs come from persistent follow-up and ______________ (31).

"Throw a brick through your television! It's time to get excited about your career; get fired up and do some work that matters."

DAVE RAMSEY
Financial Expert

Start Your Job Search Today!

JUST FOLLOW THESE THREE STEPS

After you've determined what your strengths and weaknesses are, identify jobs that compliment your passions and talents. Next, figure out which companies you would like to work for and begin to build a relationship with them. Here are three steps to help you build a relationship with a potential employer:

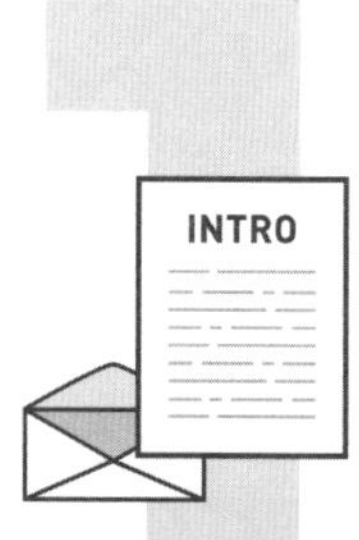

Introduction Letter

Write an introduction letter. This is not a cover letter; this is just a letter introducing yourself and explaining that you intend to apply for a position at the company. Briefly state why you want to work for the company and the top three qualities you bring to the job.

Résumé & Cover Letter

Next, send your résumé and cover letter. Since you've already introduced yourself, they expect this next step. Create a résumé that stands out, but don't go overboard. You don't want it to be an eyesore. And make sure you proof your writing! The last thing you want to do is make a glaring spelling mistake in your cover letter.

Following Up

Follow up the résumé and cover letter with a phone call. In the cover letter, specify that you will call them on a certain date—and then do it. Even if you only get a voicemail, leave a message so the person knows you are serious about getting the job.

Complete these three steps and you'll begin to establish a relationship with the company before you even meet with a human resources representative or your potential supervisor. Remember, persistent follow-up and networking results in interviews and jobs. And never underestimate the power of networking—it is key to finding work you love.

Be Happy at Work

Being content with your job is one of the most important issues you can deal with in your career. No one wants to feel like they're stuck in a job they hate. Here are six tips for making your workplace a happy place:

1. **Embrace your space.** You're at work for at least eight hours a day so make your work space as enjoyable as possible. Display pictures that bring a smile to your face. Bring in a lamp to create a more comfortable atmosphere. Think of things that make you happy and incorporate them into your office space decorating.

2. **Make office buddies.** Befriend people who have the same interests as you. Knowing people who have similar backgrounds or lifestyles will help you feel more at home in the workplace. Plus, you always have someone to hang out with at lunch!

3. **Stay organized.** Don't take on more projects than you can handle. When you can't find something or you feel overwhelmed, this leads to dissatisfaction with your job. Say no when necessary. Create a manageable schedule and organized work area.

4. **Move!** If you sit for long periods of time during the day, make sure you move around. Do some light stretches. Roll your wrists and stretch your hands. Remember to rest your eyes occasionally if you stare at a computer screen all day.

5. **Reward yourself.** Occasionally reward yourself for a job well done. Just like personal stress can interfere with work, the positive sides of life can affect your working mood, too.

6. **Breathe!** Multiple studies have been done that show how deep breathing exercises are great for your overall health. Make a conscious effort to take deep, long breaths throughout the day. Inhaling deeply can boost your energy, make you feel more alert and enhance your overall productivity at work.

Interviews

Present yourself well. You are the ____________________(32), so make it the best one available.

Be on ______________(33), address everyone by __________________(34), offer a firm, confident ______________________(35), and maintain __________(36) contact at all times.

Designate a time to ___________ ______(37) after the interview...and DO IT!

Discussion Questions: Section 5

- If you were an employer looking to hire a recent college graduate, what traits would you look for in interviewees? On the other hand, what traits would hinder them getting the job?
- In the process of finding a job, "luck favors the prepared." What does this mean? How can you use this principle to make yourself stand out from the rest?

+

Remember, **you've got 30 seconds.** They're going to know right then whether or not you can move forward in that organization most of the time.

"It is extremely unlikely that anyone coming out of school with a technical degree will go into one area and stay there. Today's students have to look forward to the excitement of probably having three or four careers."

GORDON MOORE
Co-founder of Intel

The number of Americans working part time for financial reasons is currently **9.1 million.**

BUREAU OF LABOR STATISTICS

Women generally out-earn men in part-time work. Average weekly earnings of female part-time workers were **$229**, compared with **$222** for their male counterparts.

U.S. DEPARTMENT OF LABOR

These part-time jobs are expected to grow over the next 10 years:

- Pharmacist Technician
- Dental Assistant
- Home Healthcare Aide
- Product Demonstrator
- Personal Trainer
- Physical Therapist Aide

HOURLYCAREERS.COM

"We spend the first five to seven years of our marriage trying to attain the same standard of living as our parents. Only it took them 35 years to get there."

LARRY BURKETT
American Author and Radio Personality

Overtime and Extra Jobs

Raising your income ____________ [38] -term means the dreaded part-time job.

How do you get started with an extra job?

- Be willing to ________________ [39] to win.
- Have a detailed ________________ [40] so you can see the finish line. This gives you hope!
- Choose the ___________ [41] or start a ____________________________ [42] business.
- Don't _____________ _______ [43]!

Beware! Do not allow your work to be the source of all your satisfaction and self-________________ [44].

Discussion Questions: Section 6

- What do you hope to earn in your first year of employment? When you consider living on a zero-based budget, can you make ends meet on this salary? If not, what extra jobs do you see yourself getting?
- When you consider your own life, what are the advantages to working extra hours? What are the disadvantages?

?

"What's the best way to ask for a raise at work?"

DAVE'S ANSWER: I think the first 10 sentences that come out of your mouth should be about gratitude. Let your boss know how much you like being there and all the things you appreciate about the business and your job. It's always a good idea to get the point across that you're grateful for what you already have before you go looking for more.

The next step might be to detail the attributes you bring to the company—the traits, habits and accomplishments—that make you valuable to the organization, and why they make you more valuable than your paycheck currently indicates. Then, ask your boss to reconsider your compensation based on these factors. It wouldn't be a bad idea, either, to do a compensation study based on the salaries of people in your line of work, who are employed by comparably-sized organizations in your region. Asking for a raise is one thing, but putting the research into your request that proves what you're asking for is fair and well reasoned never hurts!

Smile a lot and make sure you keep any hints of bitterness or anger out of the conversation, too. You're trying to persuade this person to see things your way.

Just remember, no matter how convincing your argument may be, the answer—for whatever reason—could always be "no." You need to be ready to accept it with the same professionalism and grace that went into your request. If you don't, you just might knock yourself out of a raise or promotion somewhere down the road!

SECTION 7

Marriage and Money

- When you agree on your value system, you will reach a ________ (45) in your marriage that you can experience no other way.

Who does the Financial Decision-Making?

- ________ (46) of you!
- The partner with the natural ________ (47) can prepare the ________ (48), but the decision-making must be done by both of you.

Discussion Questions: Section 7

- What are your weaknesses when it comes to money? How do you think this will affect your marriage? What are ways you and your spouse can work together to overcome your weaknesses?
- What are your expectations for your wedding? Do you think they are realistic? How can you save money in the process?

$

The average income for men in their thirties is **12% lower** than what their dads earned three decades earlier.

ECONOMIC MOBILITY PROJECT

The average income for households under 25 years of age was **$27,047** last year.

U.S. CENSUS BUREAU AND PITNEY BOWES BUSINESS INSIGHT

"Chains do not hold a marriage together. It is threads, hundreds of tiny threads which sew people together through the years."

SIMONE SIGNORET
French Actress

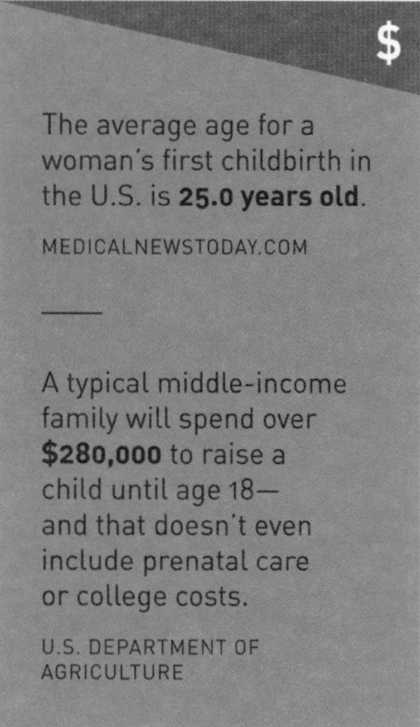

Kids and Money

- Teaching kids how to handle money is not the ______________ 49 responsibility. It is the parents' responsibility.
- Parents should pay ______________ 50, not allowance; we have enough people in our society who expect to be made allowance for.
- Words are ______________ 51.
- If you ____________ 52, you get paid; if you do not ____________ 53, you do not get paid.
- Teach by ______________ 54.

Allowance: Money given to a child, typically on a weekly basis

Commission: Money paid for providing a service

Work Ethic: How motivated, loyal and honest you are in your work

Be Age-Appropriate

- If the children are young, use a clear ______________ 55 to save. Visual reinforcement is powerful.
- Use three envelopes for children ages 5–12:

  ____________ 56, ______________ 57, and ______________ 58.
- Somewhere around 13–15 years old, open a ____________ ______________ 59 for the child and teach him/her how to run it by monthly reviews.

"Isn't it a shame that future generations can't be here to see all the wonderful things we're doing with their money?"

EARL WILSON
American Journalist

\+

If all you give your kids is money and no character, you will be a curse in their lives. You'll change your family tree in a **negative** way.

Discussion Questions: Section 8

- What did your parents teach you about money? What will you do differently when it comes to your kids?
- How can you live by example in the area of finances? How can you live by example in other areas?

Recap & Review

You're Going to Have a Marriage Money Argument

BY JON ACUFF

This is coming. Maybe you've always agreed with your spouse on every other issue in your marriage. Maybe you've had years, even decades of marital bliss usually only reserved for the end of movies on the Lifetime Channel. Maybe your love is so deep and rich that Hallmark has a line of cards inspired by your marriage. Maybe you're so in love you're able to hang wallpaper together, a silent killer of an experience that ends 82% of all marriages. But guess what?

When you start to whip your money into shape, you'll have an argument. And that's okay. More than just okay, that can be the healthy, honest start to a new adventure for you and your spouse. But as you stand on this precipice, on the doorway to a shared experience that just might lead to more unity in your marriage than you thought possible, here are a few things to keep in mind:

1. **Never tell your spouse, "If you would just..."** No good comes of this phrase. I promise. You think it will, but it won't. Those are four words no spouse wants to hear. The problem is, "If you would just" is usually followed by a wildly exaggerated claim. For example, "If you would just stop buying shoes, we'd never have financial problems." Or, "If you would just stop playing golf all the time, we'd have all the money we ever needed." That's not true. There's no one magical step that will completely change all your finances at the drop of a hat. Be realistic (and kind) to your spouse, and never throw them under the bus with, "If you would just..."

2. **Don't pull a "marriage money sneak attack."** You've been reading some Dave Ramsey books for a few weeks. You've been looking at your finances. You've been going over your checking account for hours at a time. And your husband hasn't. So when you say, "We need to talk," he's never going to see it coming. He's going to think you want to talk about where to go to dinner, not how to lay the groundwork for the next 40 years of your financial life. Guys, girls, husbands, wives, never pull a sneak attack. Give them a heads-up on what you'd like to talk about. They might not do their own research, but at least you've put the topic out there before you dissect it in your discussion. While you're thinking ahead, plan it out a few days in advance, get a babysitter, go out to dinner, and start the discussion. This won't be a one-night conversation; this is the start of a lifetime of change.

3. **Sit down for the talk.** If you ever find yourself in an argument and you're physically in motion, the train has jumped the tracks. If you ever decide to have the money conversation while walking through the house and pointing out unused purses in closets or bass boats in garages, slow down. Nothing good comes from a conversation on the move—unless it's about the bear that's chasing you. At that point, run all you want.

4. **The marriage and money talk is a one-on-one conversation. Three's a crowd.** It's not a one-on-one about what your mom and your dad and the girl at work think you should be doing with your money. Keep this a couple thing, not a community thing just yet. You could always talk about your money with a counselor or a trained professional—the right third party can do wonders, but the wrong one can do damage. Keep it one-on-one at first.

5. **Don't throw a "conversation grenade."** I used to specialize in this move. I'd wait until my wife and I were about 15 minutes away from a dinner party, then I would bring up something serious we needed to talk about and drop it in the car like a grenade. After talking about it for a few minutes, we'd get to the party. I'd say, "I'm glad we had this discussion!" and roll out of the car while it was still moving (it's all in how you tuck your shoulder when you first hit the ground). Then later, when my wife wanted to continue the conversation, I'd say, "Oh, I thought we already talked about that." It's such a weasel move, it makes my teeth hurt a little.

Hopefully those tips will help when you and your spouse find yourselves on opposing sides in a money debate. But even more important than those tips is this simple truth:

YOU'RE NOT ALONE.

When you have a money argument, you might feel like you're the only couple who has these kinds of talks. You might feel like if you worked harder or had a better marriage, you'd never get into conversations like these. That's not true. The image of the couple that never disagrees about money is a myth. They've got naturally white teeth and breath that smells like cotton candy, and the only kind of fights they have are "hug fights," where they just hug each other over and over again. It's an idealized, Hollywood version of marriage, where "real life" never gets in the way of the love story.

Talking about money for the first time with your spouse might not be fun, but it doesn't have to be difficult. Here's to honest conversations that help you both get on—and stay on—the same page.

Chapter 4 Key Concepts

- Discover your strengths and weaknesses and identify what motivates you. This will help you decide your career path.
- Do something you love and that blends your talents, skills and abilities. Money doesn't buy happiness.
- Complete the FAFSA form every year and constantly apply for more scholarships.
- Prepare for new opportunities and transitions after you graduate.
- Improve your job-searching skills by having professionals in your field help you with cover letters, résumés and interviewing techniques.
- When you enter marriage, work together on your finances. Unity is key!
- When raising your children, be proactive in teaching them about money.

Video Section Answers

1. 2.1
2. 20
3. 98.3%
4. Where
5. What
6. Who
7. Change
8. Outgrow
9. Weakest
10. Strengths
11. Money
12. Abilities
13. Values
14. Passions
15. DISC
16. Dominant
17. Problems
18. Influencing
19. People
20. Stable
21. Peace
22. Compliant
23. Procedures
24. You
25. Need
26. Target
27. Learn
28. Relationship
29. Letter
30. Phone
31. Networking
32. Product
33. Time
34. Name
35. Handshake
36. Eye
37. Follow up
38. Short
39. Sacrifice
40. Plan
41. Job
42. Home-based
43. Give up
44. Worth
45. Unity
46. Both
47. Gift
48. Budget
49. School's
50. Commissions
51. Powerful
52. Work
53. Work
54. Example
55. Container
56. Giving
57. Spending
58. Saving
59. Checking Account

Case Studies

Tatum and College Courses

Tatum is majoring in marketing and advertising. She has not been very excited about her studies lately and is thinking about switching over to the nursing field. Her income as a nurse will not be as much as what a good advertising firm would pay, not to mention the glamour of working on a big account. Tatum does not want to lose the two years of classes she has already put into college, but she would essentially have to in order to go into nursing.

1. Should Tatum stick with her current major and try out the career first? Why or why not?

2. Or should Tatum switch to the nursing field while she still has two years left of college anyway? Why or why not?

3. What's more important in a life decision, salary or enjoying your job? Justify your answer.

Landon and His Roommate

Landon is having difficulty communicating with his roommate lately. It seems like the two of them disagree on every decision, from what to watch on TV to what temperature to keep the apartment. Landon recently discovered he displays a lot of Dominant (D) traits, while his roommate displays mostly Compliant (C) traits. The two guys like living with each other and neither wants a different roommate.

1. How can Landon change the way he communicates to find solutions with his roommate?

2. How can his roommate change the way he communicates to find solutions with Landon?

3. If Landon was an Influencer (I) and his roommate was Stable (S), how would their situation be different?

Ethan and College Expenses

Ethan is in his third year of college and has run out of savings to pay for school. However, he is determined to finish his degree and graduate. Tuition for his fourth year will amount to $9,000, not including his living expenses. If he keeps his GPA up this semester, he can maintain his academic scholarship for $3,000 and his federal grant for $2,000. This still leaves $4,000 for tuition plus his living expenses, and he only has four months to come up with the money.

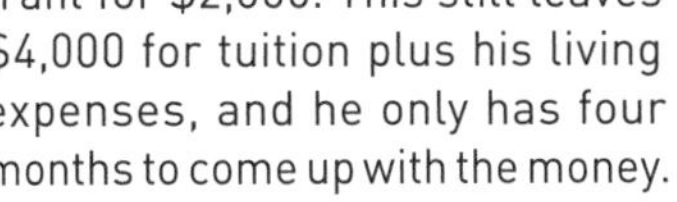

1. If Ethan does not want to use student loans, how can he pay for the rest of school in time?

2. Does it make sense for Ethan to take a year off of school to raise the money?

3. Other than using the financial aid options offered to him, what are some creative ways he can make ends meet?

CHAPTER 4

Money in Review

Short Answer

Underclassmen (Sections 1–3)

1. Would you do something you did not like in order to make more income? Why or why not?
2. What are your strengths and weaknesses?
3. What are the top three majors you are interested in? Of those, which matches your strengths the most?
4. Why is it important to understand different personality styles?
5. What personality trait is the highest for you on the DISC profile? What are the advantages of this trait?
6. What personality trait is the lowest for you on the DISC profile? How does this affect your daily life?
7. How can you go to school and graduate debt free?
8. Do you feel that it is realistic to graduate debt free? Why or why not?
9. What kinds of scholarships do you currently have? What did you have to do to receive those?
10. What information should you never give out when applying for a scholarship?

Short Answer

Upperclassmen (Sections 4–8)

1. What do you think the hardest transition will be after graduation?
2. What do you think the easiest transition will be after graduation?
3. What are three things you should do when targeting possible employment opportunities?
4. Why should an employer hire you over other applicants?
5. Why is it smart to work part time during college?
6. What kind of part-time job would meet your needs the best?
7. Why do money fights cause so many divorces?
8. What are financial discussions you will have with your future spouse?
9. What are some things you can do to teach young children about money?
10. How does getting an allowance differ from earning a commission when it comes to children?

RECAP & REVIEW

CHAPTER 4

Notes

CHAPTER 5

Family, Friends & Philanthropy

UNIT 1: MASTERING THE BASICS

Money and relationships go hand in hand, which means the way you handle your finances affects everyone around you, including your parents, roommates and friends. It has the potential to bless or wreck every relationship you have, so make it a priority to be a giving, generous person.

Learning Outcomes

Describe the general differences that exist between men and women as they relate to money.

- Compare their thoughts about saving for an emergency fund
- Compare their shopping habits
- Compare their reactions to financial problems

Identify the characteristics of a nerd and a free spirit and explain how they approach the budget in different ways.

- The Nerd is organized and likes doing the budget because it results in a sense of control. On the other hand, the Free Spirit prefers less control and enjoys having fun with money.

Integrate healthy communication about money with parents, roommates and friends.

Practice giving time and money to help those in need.

Key Terms

Accountability: the quality or state of being accountable, liable or answerable

Free Spirit: a person who thinks that everything will work out fine; typically hates to deal with numbers

Nerd: a person who is picky about budgeting and numbers

Time Poverty: a situation in which a person is lacking time, which leads to stress

Value System: a person's priorities, beliefs and standards that affect how he or she views the world

Reading

This excerpt, taken from *The Total Money Makeover,* reviews the details of why giving is important. If you constantly hoard your money, you are not experiencing the joy of blessing others by paying it forward. Dave Ramsey explains why giving is the best part of creating a plan for your money. Giving makes you stronger, and hoarding hurts you by making you more selfish and weak. Also, Dave shares the story of a Secret Santa blessing others by giving away over $1.3 million of his own money.

Giving is possibly the most fun you will ever have with money. Every mentally and spiritually healthy person I've met has been turned on by giving as long as it didn't mean his lights got cut off. I can promise you, from meeting with literally thousands of millionaires, the thing the healthy ones share in common is a love of GIVING.

Only the strong can help the weak, and that is true of money too. A toddler is not allowed to carry a newborn; only adults who have the muscular strength to ensure safety should carry babies. If you want to help someone, many times you can't do so without money. The Bible states that pure religion is actually helping the poor, not theorizing over why they are poor (see James 1:27). Margaret Thatcher said, "No one would have remembered the good Samaritan if he hadn't had money." The good innkeeper to help take care of the injured man. Money was involved. Money was at its best that day. Money gives power to good intentions. That's why I'm unashamedly in favor of building wealth.

Let Go

Sadly, I meet people who try to avoid this, mistakenly thinking they will end up with more. Eric Butterworth tells of an interesting system used to capture monkeys in the jungle. The captors use heavy glass bottles with long necks. Into each bottle they deposit some sweet-smelling nuts. The aroma of the nuts

"I can promise you from meeting with literally thousands of millionaires that the thing the healthy ones share in common is a love of GIVING."

attracts a monkey to the bottle. When the monkey puts its hand into the bottle to get the nuts, the neck of the bottle is too small for its fist to come back out. The monkey can't take his hand out of the bottle without dropping the nuts, which he is unwill-

ing to do. The bottles are too heavy to carry away, so the monkey becomes trapped by nothing more than greed. We may smile at these foolish monkeys, but how many times has our freedom been taken away by nothing more than our greed?

Most of us have given something at some time or another, but I have seen some really fun things happen when good people become wealthy. I have one friend who buys seventy-five brand-new bikes for an inner-city ministry every year. He gets these bikes at Christmas and, in conjunction with a missionary group that knows the families in the area, gives them out one at a time to kids in a subsidized housing project. The project is drug-infested and crime riddled, but for one day a year, those young people see someone who wants nothing in return.

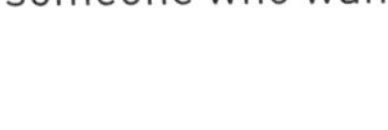

Secret Santa

We have all seen these powerful examples of giving. *USA Today* has followed a guy who calls himself Secret Santa at Christmas for several years. Secret Santa walks the streets around Christmastime and gives away $100 bills. Nothing required, nothing expected, and he remains anonymous. Sometimes he gives to people in need, and other times he just gives. Every year he gives away around $25,000 in $100 bills. He started this tradition years ago in his hometown of Kansas City and has moved out across America. He gave in New York after 9/11 and in the Virginia/Washington, D.C. area after the sniper attacks. He just walks around and hands people $100 bills. He gets some fabulous reactions and hears some wonderful stories.

In late winter of 1971, he worked as a salesman, and when his company went broke, Santa found himself broke, too. He slept in his car for eight days and hadn't eaten for two days when he went to the Dixie Diner. He ordered and ate a big breakfast. He waited for the crowd to clear, then acted as if he had lost his wallet. The diner's owner, Tom Horn, who was also the cook, came over near the stool where Santa had been sitting and picked up a $20 bill and said, "Son you must have dropped this." Santa realized later that Tom had planted that twenty to let him out of a sticky situation with his dignity intact. As he drove way, Santa said, "Thank You, Lord, for that man, and I promise if I ever have the money, I will do the same."

In 1999 Santa, now a very successful businessman, looked up Tom Horn, now eighty-five years old, in the home of Tupelo, Mississippi. Santa recounted the story of the hungry young man of 1971 while standing on Tom's porch in a Santa hat. He asked Tom what he thought that $20 would be worth by that time and Tom laughingly said, "Probably $10,000." Santa then handed Tom $10,000 cash in an envelope. Of course, Tom tried to hand it back, but finally Santa won out, so Tom deposited the money in the bank. He said he might need it to take care of his wife, who has Alzheimer's.

"Secret Santa walks the streets around Christmastime and gives away $100 bills. Nothing required, nothing expected, and he remains anonymous."

Horn says of Secret Santa, "He doesn't want any thanks or praise for what he does. He does it out of the goodness of his heart." After giving to dozens of people this last Christmas, Santa said, "Isn't it fun to lift people up and see the smiles on their faces?" I think I know why this Santa gives. He gives because it is the most fun he can possibly have with money, and you will never know until you try.[1]

---

1. *The Total Money Makeover*, pp. 212–216

CHAPTER 5

Video: Sections: 1–5

SECTION 1

Men, Women and Money *(Over-Generalizing)*

The flow of money in a family represents the ____________ ____________[1] under which that family operates.

Emergency-Fund Savings

Men: "It's boring and not ____________[2] enough."

Women: "It's the most ____________[3] key to our financial plan."

Shopping

Men get good deals by ____________[4]. They want to win.

Women get good deals by ____________[5]. They enjoy the process.

Financial Problems

Men lose ________ - ____________[6] because money usually represents a ____________ ____________[7] to men.

Women face ____________[8] or even ____________[9] because, with them, money usually represents ____________[10].

Marriage And Money

The number-one cause of divorce in America is ____________ ____________[11].

$

Men take more risks. About **3 in 10** men expect to invest in a new product, compared to just **20%** of women.

AXA EQUITABLE STUDY

Women currently report **higher levels of stress** than men regarding money, the economy, job stability and the cost of housing.

AMERICAN PSYCHOLOGICAL ASSOCIATION

"This would be a much better world if more married couples were as deeply in love as they are in debt."

EARL WILSON
American Journalist

+

Now might be a good time to review the reasons for having an emergency fund. Take a look back at **Chapter 1, Savings.**

+

Information not otherwise sourced in this section is based on Dave Ramsey's 20 years of experience counseling families.

AJ: $51,000 in Debt

As a very ignorant and unknowing college student I got into luxury-SUV-size student-loan debt. Part of this time I was a single parent and felt entitled to get the loans... I regret it. I remarried almost three years ago, and now I carry this debt into our marriage. I still owe $51,000. It seems like such a huge mountain to climb. About a year ago, we took FPU at our church and now we facilitate the class! I tell everyone about staying out of debt, no matter what it takes! I teach at a community college, and I throw in "free" Dave lessons just because I care so much about the well-being and financial future of my students. Even though I recently had a baby, I went to full time work again just to be able to get us out of debt faster! By the end of the summer, we will only have our mortgage and student loan to pay off. We have paid off thousands more and had a baby in the last year! Praise the Lord for His guidance in our lives!

I hope someone can learn from my mistake.

Sincerely,
AJ

Discussion Questions: Section 1

- Do you agree with how Dave portrays each gender and how they relate to money? Have you seen exceptions to the rule?
- In your own life, how have you seen men and women handle money differently? How have you seen them handle money similarly?

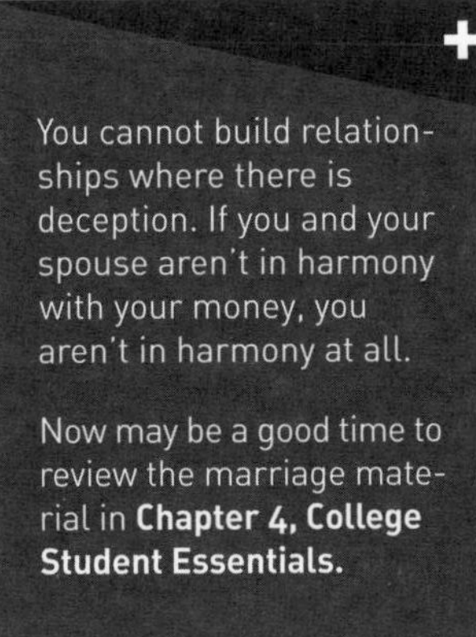

SECTION 2

Who does the Financial Decision Making?

The ________________ likes doing the budget because it gives them control, and they feel like they are taking care of loved ones.
12

The ________________ ________________ feels controlled, not cared for, and can appear irresponsible to the nerd.
13

"A number of times throughout my college career, I have spent entirely too much on just doing fun things with my friends."

CONCERNED COLLEGE STUDENT

Discussion Questions: Section 2

- Are you a nerd or a free spirit? What are the signs in your life?
- How do you communicate with the opposite personality? How can you apply this information to relationships outside of marriage?

$

Americans gave more than $**307 billion** last year to charities.

AMERICAN ASSOCIATION OF FUNDRAISING COUNSEL

83% of philanthropic dollars are contributed by individuals. Corporations and foundations donated the other **17%**.

AMERICAN ASSOCIATION OF FUNDRAISING COUNSEL

"When you try to discuss money with your parents, you may experience 'Powdered-butt syndrome.' Once someone has powdered your butt, they don't want your opinion on money or sex."

DAVE RAMSEY
Financial Expert

"One of the greatest things so far about this class is that it is not just showing me traits about myself—it is helping me relate to others."

COLLEGE STUDENT

SECTION 3

Singles and Money

_____________ _____________ (14) and fatigue can lead to poor money management.

Beware of _____________ (15) buying, which can be brought on by _____________ (16) or even by the "I owe it to _____________ (17)" syndrome.

A written plan gives the single person _____________ (18), self-accountability and _____________ (19).

Prevention

Develop an _____________ (20) relationship.

This is someone with whom to discuss major _____________ (21).

This is someone with whom to discuss your _____________ (22).

Accountability friends must love you enough to be brutally honest and promise to do so for your own good.

Discussion Questions: Section 3

- How well do you and your parents communicate when it comes to money? How can you improve your relationship in this way?
- Have you ever had a money conflict with a sibling, friend or roommate? How could it have been avoided? How did it get resolved?

SECTION 4

Giving

Giving moves people to become less _____________ (23).

You will build wealth and gain better relationships the more you _____________ (24).

Getting Engaged Soon?

If you're getting ready to tie the knot, then one thing you definitely want to talk about with your honey is money!

You probably have lots going on, and emotions are running high. But believe us: *now* is the time to get on the same page about money. Money fights and money problems have been the leading cause of divorce for decades—but the good news is that these issues are preventable! **Getting on the same page creates a strong foundation for a healthy, lifetime marriage.** Plus, you're stopping money fights before they start!

A lot of couples find that being unified with their money increases their intimacy overall. Like Dave says, "When you can talk about money, you can talk about anything." Talking about money is easier than you may think—especially if you start *before* you say, "I do."

The process of bringing your money together doesn't have to add stress to a time of pre-wedding bliss. **It can actually be fun!** Here is a quick five-step checklist to get you started building a solid foundation for your life together:

Step 1: Put It All On The Table. Transparency is the key! Lay out exactly what your current individual situations are openly and honestly, including how much debt you still have and what your views of money are. You might want to discuss what your parents taught you about money—and what you do and don't agree with—kindly, of course. Criticism and judgmental attitudes are not welcome from either party.

Step 2: "Marry" Your Accounts. When you get married, combining your money into a joint account is a crucial step. You are becoming *one*. Keeping one area separated can lead to others, and you want to set a precedent from the get-go. Working together from a shared account brings honesty, unity and a sense that "we're in this together!"

Step 3: Start Budgeting Together. Once you are married, it's time to put your combined income and expenses on paper, on purpose, and determine what a typical month is going to look like. It's good to go ahead and practice budgeting together once you get engaged. That way, you can go ahead and make adjustments so things are set up to work smoothly when game time finally comes. After the wedding, **revisit the budget each month** at your budget committee meeting to make adjustments as needed. Get tips for uniting over the budget.

Step 4: Make A Plan. Once everything is on the table, determine what Baby Step you are on—as a couple! If you were on Baby Step 4, but your bride-to-be is on Baby Step 2, then guess what? You're on Baby Step 2 now. But that's all right! You love this person with all of your heart, so taking "their" debt as "our" debt is a small price to pay in the grand scheme of things. **Set priorities together and make a plan** for moving through Dave's Seven Baby Steps as a team.

Step 5: Put Your Relationship First. Whatever you do, don't stress! It's just money. Your relationship is so much more important. Getting on the same page with money is extremely helpful, but it's not the ultimate end all, be all. Just keep that in perspective when you come to the table together.

As you begin navigating these things together, **you'll be building a stronger marriage, future and family tree!** Congratulations on your decision to make this a priority from the beginning, and blessings on your marriage!

+

Marriage counselor Gary Smalley identifies **five behavioral differences** concerning men and women in his book, *Making Love Last Forever.*

- Men love to share facts; women love to express feelings.
- Men connect by doing things; women connect by talking.
- Men tend to compete; women tend to cooperate.
- Men tend to be controlling; women tend to remain agreeable.
- Men tend to be independent; women tend to be interdependent.

Discussion Questions: Section 4

- Do you feel like giving is important? If so, why?
- Are you currently giving of your time, money or talents? If so, describe an impactful experience that you have had?

"You give but little when you give of your possessions. It is when you give of yourself that you truly give."

KAHLIL GIBRAN
Lebanese Philosopher

"Money is neither my god nor my devil. It is a form of energy that makes us more of who we already are, whether it's greedy or loving."

DAN MILLMAN
Former World Champion Athlete and Author

Get Started Giving!

Giving is one of the most important and rewarding parts of your financial journey. Once you are completely debt-free, you have that much more money to spend, invest and give. Just remember that money given away produces more joy than it could ever buy.

Whatever you make, set aside 10% to give to those less fortunate than you. If you cannot live off 90% of what you make, what makes you think you can live off 100%?

When you are on the earlier Baby Steps and just getting your budget established, money to give may seem hard to come by. That is why you can find creative ways to give. You can give of your time, your knowledge or your services to help other people.

Ways to Give

There are plenty of opportunities to volunteer at a soup kitchen or charity. You can help a single mom down the street by offering to babysit her children while she goes to night school or takes an evening for herself. You can also cook dinner for someone in your church who has lost a loved one.

A person is so encouraged when he or she sees someone else being kind to them. As you learn new ways to give, you will find that money is just another way to give. The real giving comes from you. Save and give like crazy, but always remember where the real spirit of giving comes from.

Each person you give to produces a new story and a new thrill. It is a feeling that never grows dull. Having fun with money is good, but you will tire of golf and travel, and if you eat enough lobster, it tastes like soap. Investing money is good, but going around the Monopoly board eventually loses its appeal once you've hit your investing goals.

You Will Be Fulfilled

The more you give, the more you are fulfilled and the more you want to give. It's a great cycle to be on. Giving is not a matter of moving money from your wallet to a charity or collection plate; it is a matter of realizing that there are others less fortunate than you and you have a genuine desire to help them. Money is just one way to do that.

By helping someone, you give them encouragement, hope and relief. The more people you help, the more joy you will experience.

$

Can't give money? No problem, just consider other options.

For example, last year corporate stock represented the largest category of noncash donations at $23.7 billion. Clothing donations represented the second largest category of noncash donations at $7.6 billion, followed by land donations at $4 billion.

AMERICAN ASSOCIATION OF FUNDRAISING COUNSEL

SECTION 5

There are no fill-in-the-blanks for this section.

Discussion Questions: Section 5

- When have you been impacted because someone gave their time, money or talents to help you? How did this affect you long term?
- If you could start a program where college students focused on giving, what would that look like for you?

Recap & Review

The Generosity of Future Me

BY JON ACUFF

Morning me used to hate night me. That's a bizarre sentence, but it's true. Night me was such a party animal. He'd stay up late, watching horrible reality television shows and reading books into the wee hours of the morning. And then morning me would get up, ready to take over his shift, only to find that he was completely exhausted.

"Come on, you stayed up all night again? How am I supposed to go to work and take care of the day like an adult? Dang you, Night Jon! You are such a punk!"

Okay, that conversation didn't really happen. Although it feels like it, there are not really two versions of me. The same guy who stays up late is the same guy who gets up in the morning. It would be silly to pretend there are two different people working the same day under the same name, Jon Acuff, but you'd be surprised how many people do that when it comes to money.

Especially in regards to the "G" word.

I'm talking about giving. When you get intense with beating debt, sometimes it's easy to make the mistake of thinking that giving is something that will come later. And when we talk about later, it's fun to imagine how generous future me is going to be.

"Right now, giving doesn't really fit into the plan. But in the future? Down the road? I'm going to be like Bill Gates! I'll probably just rent a hot-air balloon and drop stacks of cash out of it. I'll play Natasha Bedingfield music as I do this, and just get people dancing and really enjoying the full depth of my amazing generosity. Gonna change the world, man, really change the world."

But you know the truth about "future me"? He or she is incredibly slippery. Just when you think the future has finally arrived, something else comes up. Something more important or critical or...well, I can start giving later.

Later is a make-believe land that never comes. Future me is a make-believe person who never really gives.

You want to really get gazelle intense? Want to beat debt and have long-term success with everything Dave Ramsey talks about?

Say good-night to future me. Start giving today. Budget some giving right now. You don't have to go crazy, but planning for your tithe to the church or even for a little extra tip money for a struggling, single-mom waitress won't melt your debt snowball. Giving is important no matter where you are in the Baby Steps; that's why Dave put it at the top of his budget form!

The truth is, future me won't know how to be generous with a lot unless present me learns how to be generous with a little.

So, give a little.

Chapter 5 Key Concepts

- Handle your money with wisdom; it will affect all of your relationships.
- Remember, men and women are different when it comes to money.
- Make sure you understand how you relate to money, whether you are a nerd or free spirit.
- Understand how to incorporate better communication in your relationships with your parents, friends and roommates.
- Be a generous, cheerful giver!

RECAP & REVIEW

Video Section Answers

1. Value System
2. Sophisticated
3. Important
4. Negotiating
5. Hunting
6. Self-Esteem
7. Score Card
8. Fear
9. Terror
10. Security
11. Money Fights
12. Nerd
13. Free Spirit
14. Time Poverty
15. Impulse
16. Stress
17. Myself
18. Empowerment
19. Control
20. Accountability
21. Purchases
22. Budget
23. Selfish
24. Give

CHAPTER 5

Case Studies

Mario and Aaliyah's Future

Mario just graduated from college with a degree in marketing. He landed a sales job with a starting salary of $45,000 per year. He has one student loan of $8,000 and is making double payments on it. He also has a fully funded emergency fund. Mario is about to ask his girlfriend, Aaliyah, to marry him. She has a car payment of $279 every month. She also uses a credit card for purchases, although she does pay the balance in full each month. Aaliyah has a fairly good job, but no savings.

1. If they don't talk about money now, predict their first year of marriage.
2. Do you think it's okay for Aaliyah to use credit cards for all of her purchases as long as she pays the balance in full every month? Why or why not?
3. Should Mario pay off his student loan first before buying a ring and proposing to Aaliyah? Why or why not?
4. How do you think Aaliyah's lack of savings will affect Mario's fully funded emergency fund?

Sherry and Her Parents

Sherry is a junior education major. She is one of the lucky students because her parents pay her credit card balance off every month. In fact, Sherry has a nice car, a cool new cell phone and plenty of spending money in her wallet—all courtesy of her parents. She has never had to worry about money. Plus, she doesn't work because her parents told her they wanted her to concentrate on her education instead of a job. However, things took a drastic turn two weeks ago when Sherry's dad lost his job. Her parents told her she was being cut off next month because they can't afford to support her. She is frustrated with her parents and the situation.

1. How will this turn of events affect Sherry's lifestyle and relationship with her parents?
2. Does Sherry have a right to be upset at her parents? Why or why not?
3. What could Sherry have done differently to avoid this situation?
4. What would you tell Sherry to do about supporting herself?

Reggie and Giving

Reggie is a sophomore and recently did a research paper on poverty in the U.S. Writing the paper made him realize that no matter how difficult life is for him, there are always others suffering more. He feels strongly about doing something to make a difference in the area of domestic poverty. The bad news is that he's not sure what he can do since he has no savings and is only in his second year at college.

1. What are some things Reggie can do to make a difference for those in poverty?
2. How much money does Reggie need in order to help those who are living at the poverty level?
3. What are some ideas for how Reggie can start saving money for himself so he's able to give to those in need when the time comes?

CHAPTER 5

Money in Review

Matching

Match each term to its definition below.

a. Free Spirit	d. value system
b. Nerd	e. accountability partner
c. time poverty	

1 ____ The one who likes to deal with numbers and make a budget

2 ____ The one who goes with the flow

3 ____ The one who assists you in making wise decisions

4 ____ How a person views the world and decides what's important

5 ____ A lack of time, which leads to stress

RECAP & REVIEW

True or False

Determine whether these statements are true or false. Change the false statements to read true.

6 **T / F :** The number-one cause of divorce in the U.S. is money fights.

7 **T / F :** You need to find a shopping partner to discuss major purchases with.

8 **T / F :** Men and women are quite similar in how they relate to money.

9 **T / F :** Free spirits are always the savers and nerds are always the spenders.

10 **T / F :** Personal finance is 80% behavior and only 20% head-knowledge.

Multiple Choice

11 For ______, the emergency fund is the most important key to financial security.

a. women

b. men

c. both

d. Dave Ramsey

12 How do men and women relate differently to shopping?

a. men want to find a good deal by hunting; women want to find a good deal by negotiating.
b. women want to find a good deal by hunting; men want to find a good deal by negotiating.
c. women enjoy the process of looking; men want to win by getting the deal.
d. all of the above
e. both b and c

13 A budget committee meeting should last:

a. 45 minutes
b. as long as it takes
c. 10–20 minutes
d. no more than an hour

14 Problems singles might deal with include:

a. time poverty
b. impulse buying
c. "I owe it to myself" syndrome
d. all of the above

15 Which one is not a rule for a budget committee meeting?

a. free spirits must give input
b. the meetings should last no longer than 20 minutes
c. nerds must not let the free spirits change anything on their budget
d. all of the above are ground rules for a budget meeting

Short Answer

16 Explain the advantages and disadvantages that singles have when it comes to finances.

17 Why is it important to give money, time or talents?

18 What are ways you can improve your communication with your parents, roommates and friends?

19 Are you a free spirit or a nerd? Explain the characteristics you have.

20 Compare how men and women differ when it comes to an emergency fund.

RECAP & REVIEW

CHAPTER 5

Notes

UNIT 2

DEVELOPING YOUR SKILLS

CHAPTERS 6–9

CHAPTER 6

Consumer Awareness

UNIT 2: DEVELOPING YOUR SKILLS

Marketing is powerful! Think about it—every single purchase you've made started with advertising. But be careful, debt is also marketed to you. Some salespeople don't want you to think about the product's total cost; they want you to think in terms of how much down and how much a month. Buyer beware!

Learning Outcomes

List the four major ways companies compete for your money.

- Personal selling
- Financing as a marketing tool
- TV, radio, internet and other media
- Product positioning

Identify financing strategies that encourage college students to go into debt.

- 90 days same as cash
- 0% interest
- Car financing

Summarize and apply the five basic rules for making large purchases.

- Wait overnight before making a purchase
- Consider your buying motives
- Never buy anything you do not understand
- Consider the "opportunity cost"
- Seek wise counsel

Explain the role that opportunity cost plays in purchasing decisions.

- Whenever you make a purchase choice, you must pass up opportunities to do other things with your money (like save it or invest it).

Key Terms

Annual Percentage Rate (APR): cost of borrowing money on an annual basis; takes into account the interest rate and other related fees on a loan

Brand Recognition: consumer awareness that a particular brand exists

Buyer's Remorse: regretting a purchase soon after making it

Caveat Emptor: latin term for "buyer beware"

Financing: to buy an item with credit; paying over time

Impulse Purchase: to buy an item without carefully weighing the consequences

CHAPTER 6

Reading

The following excerpt is from *Dave Ramsey's Complete Guide to Money: The Handbook of Financial Peace University.* In this passage, Dave describes the influence that marketing has on your decisions. He also explains how to have power over your purchases and provides helpful guidelines for making large purchases.

When you turn on the TV, listen to the radio, surf the web, or walk into the mall, you are stepping into battle—a battle for your dollars. Today, companies use every angle imaginable to aggressively compete for your money. Marketing is not an option for businesses who want to keep their doors open. Think about it. Between retail stores and online stores, you have thousands of different places to buy that *thing* you can't live without. Every one of those stores is fighting with all the others to get that thing in front of you in the most attractive, compelling way possible.

$10,000 Per Second

In the great book, *Affluenza*, researchers found that the average consumer is struck with over 3,000 commercial messages a day, each one screaming for our attention.[1] Kids will see about one million commercials before they turn 20, and over their lifetime, all the ads strung together would add up to two entire years of watching television commercials![2]

And this is big business. *Affluenza* reported that the typical 30-second national television commercial costs nearly $300,000 to produce—that's $10,000 *per second*![3] Here's the kicker. You know how much it costs to produce one episode of the average television show? About $300,000, roughly the same cost as a 30-second ad. That comes to $83 per second for the actual TV program, compared to $10,000 per second for the advertisements during the commercial breaks. Is it any wonder why some people think the best thing on TV is commercials?

And these campaigns are working. I saw a study not too long ago that showed the average household in the U.S. has more television sets than people![4] Now I'm not mad at these companies. They aren't doing anything wrong. I run a big company myself and we do a lot of different types of advertising. But you need to be aware of what you're walking into whenever you hit the sofa with the remote in your hand.

Do You Smell Cookies?

Think you're really just window shopping when you're walking around the mall? Think again. Stores are using all sorts of creative ways to slip past your buying defenses. For example, a lot of stores are attacking our wallets through our noses! *USA Today* reported that several companies have started pumping different scents through their stores to evoke certain emotions.[5] The Sony Style store, for example, pumps the subtle fragrance of vanilla and mandarin oranges into the store to make you feel relaxed and get your guard down. Bloomingdales uses a lot of different scents, depending on which department you're in. If you're in the baby section, you may catch the faint whiff of baby powder. If you're in the swimwear area, you'll probably catch the smell of suntan lotion. This is designed to slip past our defenses and take the sales message straight into our brains without us ever even realizing it.

If you were to visit my office, one of the first things you'd notice when you walk in the front door is the smell of fresh-baked cookies at our coffee bar in the lobby. Now, we're not trying to put you into a cookie trance so you'll buy our stuff the moment you walk in, but we have found that it is a fantastic way to put people at ease and enable them to enjoy their visit from the moment they walk through the door. Besides, the cookies are free!

Power Over Purchase

Does all this mean that I don't want you to ever spend any money or to ever get anything nice for yourself? Not at all. I have a beautiful home filled with many wonderful things my family enjoys. I don't want you to live in a cave, collect lint, and only come out on triple-coupon Tuesday! But I do want you to think about this stuff and make sure your spending is done according to plan, and that your purchases line up with your financial condition.

It is easy to overspend. That's what the financing industry is all about! Most shoppers *don't have* the cash in their hands on the day they buy! They're spending money they don't have, and that way of life will always keep you broke. Because we can always spend more than we make, we must develop power over purchase. Here are five guidelines that, if followed every time, will guarantee wise buying decisions:

1. **Wait overnight.** Remember, when you're on the edge of a big purchase, your body starts going haywire. When that happens, step away, go home,

and sleep on it. That gives you time to cool down and get some perspective. Trust me, that thing will still be available tomorrow.

2. **Consider your buying motives.** Why are you making this purchase? Is it something you need or want, or are you buying it to make someone else happy or to please the kids? No amount of stuff will ever give you contentment or fulfillment. If I buy a new ski boat, I do it because I know my family and I want it and will enjoy it, not because I believe *that thing* will make me happy. It won't. Money can buy fun, but it can't buy happiness.

   And even if the item is a "want" and not a "need," it could be a perfectly reasonable purchase. There is absolutely nothing wrong with buying some "wants," as long as they fit within your overall financial plan and you understand your motives.

3. **Don't buy what you don't understand.** This is especially true with financial products like investments and insurance. We'll cover those areas in other chapters. For now, just don't buy any gadgets or gizmos just because they're "cool" or someone said you should get one. Buy what you need and get yourself some wants, but *use what you buy*. You don't need a NASA-caliber computer to surf the web and play solitaire. If you don't understand what it is or how to use it, don't buy it.

4. **Consider the opportunity cost.** Your money is finite—it has limits. If you spend it on one thing, you can't spend it on another. That is, if I have $10,000 in the bank and use that money to buy a car, then that $10,000 is gone. For example, I can't buy a $10,000 car *and* put the same $10,000 into a mutual fund. That's opportunity cost. Before you make a significant purchase, ask yourself what else you could do with that money that might be a better idea. You'll likely think of a dozen things *after* you buy the item, anyway, so you might as well ask yourself the question up front!

5. **Seek wise counsel.** Every single time I have made a financial decision that Sharon disagreed with, it cost me money—*lots* of money. She was right. I don't even argue with her anymore. If she has one of those "feeeeeelings," then that's it. I don't do the deal.

And if you're single, talk to an accountability partner. The point here is to get outside your own head, say these things out loud, and give others permission to tell you if the deal is a bad idea.

I want you to have fun with your purchases, but I don't want you to be a victim of clever marketing and impulse buying. Be aware of how, when and where you're being marketed to.

"For example, I can't buy a $10,000 car and put the same $10,000 into a mutual fund."

Look past the glitz and glamour and really see every product for what it is and what its benefits are for you and your family. When you figure out what things you need and want, make a plan and buy with confidence. Then you'll enjoy your stuff without remorse.[6]

---

1. John De Graaf, David Wann, and Thomas H. Naylor. *Affluenza* (2nd ed.). San Francisco:Berrett-Koehler Publishers, page 165.
2. Ibid, page 154.
3. Ibid, page 155.
4. "More TVs Than People in Average Home," www.breitbart.com, September 21, 2006.
5. "Just Browsing at the Mall? That's What You Think." *USA Today*, www.usatoday.com, September 1, 2006.
6. *Dave Ramsey's Complete Guide to Money*, Chapter 6

CHAPTER 6

Video: Sections 1–4

SECTION 1

Buyer Beware

"Caveat Emptor" means ______________ ____________________. 1

Companies use every angle to aggressively compete for your ______________. 2

Four Major Ways Companies Compete

1. ______________ 3 selling.

2. ______________ 4 as a marketing tool.

90-days-Same-As-Cash: If you pay within 90 days, there are no finance fees. It's as if you paid cash today. But if you pay late, you will be charged interest for the entire 90 days, usually with Rule of 78's prepayment penalty.

Rule of 78: Prepayment penalty in a financing contract; the portion of a 90-days same-as-cash agreement that states that the entire loan amount plus the interest accumulated over the first 90 days becomes due immediately

Discussion Questions: Section 1

- What are examples from your life where "Caveat Emptor" applies?
- What is the most effective marketing advertisement you experienced recently?

SECTION 2

Four Major Ways *(Continued)*

3. ________ 5, ______________ 6, ____________________ 7 and other media.

4. Product ____________________ 8.

$

Word of mouth is a great marketing tool. **83%** of shoppers said they are interested in sharing information about their purchases with people they know, while **74%** are influenced by the opinions of others in their decision to buy the product in the first place.

MANAGE SMARTER MAGAZINE

"I forgot to hang up the Resident tag on my car's mirror, so my car was towed. $125 later, I have lost half of what was in my checking account."

COLLEGE STUDENT

+

Ninety Days is Not the Same as Cash For Three Reasons:

1. You won't get a discount off the price, like paying with cash can.
2. You probably won't pay in 90 days. 88% of these convert to payments which are usually at 24% APR with rule of 78's prepayment penalty.
3. You will be charged interest for the whole 90 days if you pay late. Debt is dangerous. Period.

?

"I've been driving an old, used car for years and I'm ready to buy a new one. I've saved up the money, but every time I go to a car dealer they want me to finance a new car instead of paying cash. What should I do?"

DAVE'S ANSWER: Who cares what the car dealers want? This is your purchase, not theirs! Besides, the only reason they want you to finance is so they'll make a lot more money off the deal.

You're a college student who has been smart enough and industrious enough to scrape up that money over the last few years. You don't need to throw a huge chunk of that into something that's going to go down in value like a rock. **New cars lose 70% of their value in the first four years.** A $28,000 car would be worth around $8,400 after that period of time. That's not what I call a smart investment.

You don't need a brand-new car. Once you've got a million dollars in the bank, then you can go out and buy a new car. For now, you need to stick with good, used, low-mileage vehicles that are about three or four years old.

If I were in your shoes and had your budget, I'd shop around and pay cash for a cool little $10,000 car. You can get a great automobile for that kind of money; plus you'll still have the majority of your savings sitting there!

Discussion Questions: Section 2

- How do television marketers use emotion to compel you to buy their product? If you are increasingly aware of marketing techniques like this, how does it affect your spending?
- What are some product-positioning examples that work well on college students?

SECTION 3

Product Positioning *(Continued)*

- Brand Recognition
- Color
- Shelf Position
- Packaging

$

The average consumer mentions specific brands over **90 times** per week in conversations with friends, family and coworkers.

WORD OF MOUTH MARKETING ASSOCIATION

Consumer reviews are significantly more trusted—**nearly 12 times more**—than descriptions that come from manufacturers.

eMARKETER

"He who buys what he does not need steals from himself."

AUTHOR UNKNOWN

?

"What's wrong with buying big things on 12 months same as cash?"

DAVE'S ANSWER: It's a stupid idea. First off, if I buy the item with cash, I'll get a better deal. Plus, if you play with snakes, you'll get bitten.

If they record your payment wrong and it's late, they'll back-charge you through the entire term of the deal at about 24–38% interest.

You'll spend the next year and a half cleaning up this mess. If you can't save up and pay for the item with cash, you can't afford to buy it!

$

The average college senior graduates with more than **$4,100** in credit card debt.

SALLIE MAE

"My spring break was incredible, but I am not happy with the way I managed my money. I went into spring break with about $600 and came back with nearly nothing."

COLLEGE STUDENT

+

If you get into debt, want to know how much you will be paying in interest over your lifetime? Try the Cost of Interest Calculator at **www.foundationsU.com.**

Significant Purchases

A ______________ ______________ is normally anything
9

over ______________.
10

A significant purchase brings on sweat in your palms and across your upper lip. Your eyes dilate. Your pulse rate changes. Proteins and endorphins are released.

We all have that spoiled, red-faced, grocery store kid living inside of us. His name is ______________.
11

Discussion Questions: Section 3

- What would be a "significant purchase" to you right now? How would you go about buying it?
- Are there purchases you've made that disappointed you? How can you ensure that you will genuinely enjoy your purchases?

What College Students *Don't* Need

College students who don't check their spending can find themselves in a jam quicker than you can say "final exam." What's sad is that most who attend school think there are certain things they just *need* to have. We've all got stuff that we *need*, but when you get down to it, most of those items are *wants*.

Here's how you can tell if something is a need or a want. Imagine finding yourself out on the street. You have no home, friends or family, and you're on your own. At that point, you aren't wondering where you can buy a latte or where the nearest place is that you can get on your laptop. You're thinking about where you can go and be safe, get some food, shelter, basic clothing and all that other stuff.

So, on that note . . . let's address some wants masking themselves as needs.

Credit Card
A recent Sallie Mae study found that the average freshman with a piece of plastic will end the academic year with $2,000 in debt. They are just being weaned off of allowance at this point in their lives, so $2,000 might as well be $200,000. Don't start off your financial life behind the eight ball. *Stay away from credit cards and debt.*

Cable TV
TV can be as much of a time-waster as all-night parties, but the wasted hours sneak up on you. Cable is definitely *a luxury item*, so don't continue believing you *need* to watch it if it's available.

Car
There's nothing wrong with owning a paid-for car and having it at school, if you can afford gas and parking. According to AAA, in a nine-month academic year, a car driven 10,000 miles would rack up about $5,800 in expenses such as gas, maintenance and insurance. Permits and parking will drive that number higher, and if your budget is already tight, you might consider leaving the car at home.

Off-Campus Living
This might be the biggest college expense besides the student loan. *Many times, a loan is taken out just to pay for this more expensive lifestyle.* Talk about stupid! You don't need to live like King Tut while you are getting an education. It won't kill you to live on campus and eat cafeteria food. It's a privilege and a responsibility just to go to college. It's not some boot-camp torture, so you don't need to find relief in eating out every night or having a bedroom with a private balcony.

Be smart about school spending. That way, when college is over, so are its expenses.

"The gap in our economy is between what we have and what we think we ought to have—and that is a moral problem, not an economic one."

PAUL HEYNE
Lecturer in Economics

SECTION 4

What to Do

You can always spend more than you __________ (12). You must develop __________ (13) over __________ (14) by following these steps:

1. Wait __________ (15) before making a purchase.

Have you ever wanted to know what was really important to someone?

Look at their checkbook entries. Are they spending a lot on "stuff" like entertainment, clothes, friends, etc? People spend their money on things most meaningful to their hearts. "For where your treasure is"—the money you spend or save—"there your heart will be also" (Matthew 6:21, NKJV).

2. Consider your buying ________________16. No amount of stuff equals ________________17 or fulfillment.

3. Never buy anything you do not ________________18.

4. Consider the "________________ ________________19" of your money.

5. Seek wise ________________20.

Opportunity Cost: The true cost of something in terms of what you have to give up to get the item; the benefits you would have received by taking the other action

Discussion Questions: Section 4

- When has waiting overnight to make a decision benefited you? How do you predict waiting overnight will help you in the future?
- Do you have an accountability partner in any area of your life? If so, how have they been helpful to you?

$

It takes as little as **2.5 seconds** to make a purchasing decision.

STUDY BY BUYOLOGY INC.

When considering a purchase, **54%** of people say price is the most important factor, **34%** say quality and **12%** say good reviews.

SURVEY BY BUZZPLANT

"There is scarcely anything in the world that some man cannot make a little worse and sell a little more cheaply. The person who buys on price alone is this man's lawful prey."

JOHN RUSKIN
Artist and Author

+

Want to learn how to find great deals on your purchases? You will learn more about that in the Chapter 7, **Bargains.**

Recap & Review

Let's Not Get Distracted by the Bright and Shiny

BY JON ACUFF

The other day, my four-year-old, McRae, shared her thoughts on the pet situation at our house. Like many little girls, she and her sister, L.E., are desperate to own a cat that they can dress up like a princess and go on adventures with. But my wife, Jenny, is allergic. So alas, we will not be buying a cat anytime soon.

Pondering this sad reality, McRae remarked at dinner, "We can get a cat when Mom is dead." And although this is technically, scientifically true, I'm not sure we should tell Mom that when she dies, instead of a funeral, we're going to have a cat party. We'll just make it rain felines.

I've been thinking about cats a lot lately because of some credit card commercials I keep seeing. In the commercials, the announcer doesn't mention the rates or the responsibilities or the payments. Instead, he just goes on and on about how you can customize the design of your credit card with photos of your family. You can put your kid's mug on the design. You can get a rainbow, even a double rainbow on the card if you so desire. The sky is the limit with the fun designs you can use to create your dream credit card.

But if you stop and think about that commercial for a second, you'll realize what they're doing to us. They're trying to distract us with the bright and shiny. They're trying to distract us with the colorful and playful. You know who else falls for that? You know who else gets distracted by the bright and shiny?

Cats.

Cats love lasers.

It's true. You can hypnotize a cat with a tiny laser or a colorful piece of yarn.

So when I talk to people about getting their finances in order and not falling for all the tricks of credit card companies, I'm not telling people they need to be financial experts. I don't want us to all win the Nobel Prize for our theories on economics.

I just want us to be smarter than cats.

Don't get distracted. Don't give in to the shiny. Together, I know that we can be smarter than cats. I believe in you and me.

Chapter 6 Key Concepts

- Be aware—companies aggressively market to you and they are experts at getting your money.
- Consider your buying motives. No amount of stuff will equal contentment.
- Learn the five steps to developing power over purchase.
- Always remember, if you can't pay cash, you can't afford it!

Video Section Answers

1. Buyer Beware
2. Money
3. Personal
4. Financing
5. TV
6. Radio
7. Internet
8. Positioning
9. Significant Purchase
10. $300
11. Immaturity
12. Make
13. Power
14. Purchase
15. Overnight
16. Motives
17. Contentment
18. Understand
19. Opportunity Cost
20. Counsel

Case Studies

Joaquin and The Cost of a New Television

Joaquin recently graduated from college and moved into his first apartment. He visits an electronics store to find a plasma television and is approached by a salesperson who tells him about the current store offer of no interest for one year. Joaquin decides that he should purchase the television and take advantage of this free money while it is available. He puts the entire purchase of $1,164.94 (including tax) on his credit card and takes the plasma television home with him.

1. What should Joaquin's monthly payments be if he intends to pay off the television in full before the year is up?
2. Joaquin misses a payment by two days and now has to pay the interest charges for the entire year. If the APR is 22.9%, how much does he owe for the accrued interest?
3. How would the television purchase impact other areas of Joaquin's life?

Ella and the Designer Jacket

While Ella was driving to campus, she noticed a billboard with a girl wearing the same designer jacket she'd seen in a celebrity magazine she was reading over lunch. When she picked up her mail that day, she had a flyer for 30% off at a store that displayed the same jacket.

1. Explain how marketing influenced her.
2. If Ella bought the jacket, would it be a good purchase at 30% off? Why or why not?
3. What else could Ella do with her money instead?

Matt and Video Games

Matt and his college friends spend a lot of their free time playing video games. His friends often talk about the newest version of their favorite game and how much they love the new features in it. Unfortunately, Matt doesn't have the cash to buy the video game. However, if he doesn't practice playing the game, there's no way he'll be able to keep up with his friends when they play together.

1. Predict the possible actions Matt could take and how those actions would affect him.
2. How would Matt's schedule change if he got a job to earn some spending money?
3. Is there a solution for Matt to enjoy the new game without having to purchase it?

CHAPTER 6

Money in Review

Matching

Match each term to its definition below.

a. buyer beware	e. overnight
b. financing	f. opportunity cost
c. counsel	g. 3,000
d. branding	h. significant purchase

1 _____ Seek wise _____

2 _____ Wait _________ before making a major purchase

3 _____ Borrowing money and paying over time

4 _____ Number of advertisements a person views daily

5 _____ Spend $60 on the latest video game, or give $60 to charity

6 _____ Caveat Emptor

7 _____ An amount of money spent that causes some pain

8 _____ Creates consumer awareness for a trademark or product

True or False

Determine whether these statements are true or false. Change the false statements to read true.

9 **T / F :** Color is a product positioning technique used to get the buyer's attention.

10 **T / F :** Advertising slogans that have been around for a long time no longer work.

11 **T / F :** Answering a question with a question is the sign of a well-trained salesperson.

12 **T / F :** Typically, 90-days-same-as-cash contracts convert to payments with interest up to 24% APR.

13 **T / F :** The opportunity cost of purchasing a new cell phone could be the purchase of a spring break trip.

RECAP & REVIEW

Want or Need

Using the Four Walls as a guide, indicate which is a want and which is a need.

14 **W / N :** Cable television

15 **W / N :** Utilities

16 **W / N :** New cell phone

17 **W / N :** Groceries

18 **W / N :** Housing

19 **W / N :** The latest in fashion

20 **W / N :** Transportation

Short Answer

21 Have you ever purchased something and then felt guilty afterward? Explain.

22 How does advertising affect your buying decisions?

23 Describe the five steps to follow before making a significant purchase.

24 Differentiate between a want and a need.

25 Why do so many people fall for financing as a marketing tool? Describe a financing offer that you have recently seen or heard about.

CHAPTER 6

Notes

CHAPTER

7 Bargains

UNIT 2: DEVELOPING YOUR SKILLS

Even if you're not a spender by nature, finding a great bargain on something you really want will send a rush down your spine. It's just plain fun to find a steal of a deal! However, if you want to find the absolute best bargains, you will need to do three things: learn where to find deals, negotiate and have patience. Now, let the fun and games begin!

Learning Outcomes

Summarize the three keys to getting bargains.

- Learn to negotiate everything
- Have patience
- Know where to find deals

Describe the seven basic rules of negotiating.

- Always tell the absolute truth
- Use the power of cash
- Understand and use "walk-away power"
- Shut up
- Say, "That's not good enough"
- Remember good guy, bad guy
- Employ the "If I" take-away technique

List places to find a great deal.

- Individuals, estate sales, public auctions, couponing, garage sales, repo lot, flea markets, refunding, foreclosures, pawn shops, online auctions, classified ads, consignment sales, conventions

Discuss ways to save money while attending college.

Key Terms

Integrity: having to do with a person's honesty and moral attributes

Markup: the difference between the wholesale price and retail price

Negotiating: to bargain for a lower price

Patience: the ability to wait or delay an action without becoming upset or annoyed

Walk-Away Power: the ability to walk away from a purchase when negotiating

Win-Win Deal: a negotiation where both parties benefit

CHAPTER 7

Reading

This excerpt is from *Dave Ramsey's Complete Guide to Money: The Handbook of Financial Peace University.* In this passage, Dave discusses the power bargaining can have on your buying decisions. You'll learn several effective tactics that will help you negotiate with the upper hand.

I spend a lot of time telling people how to save money, invest money, make their money go farther and give money away, but that's only part of the puzzle. The truth is, sometimes, you've just got to spend some money! I mean, even you savers are really spenders part of the time, right? Otherwise, you wouldn't have clothes on your back or food in the fridge. We're all consumers, even the cheapest, most penny-pinching folks in the bunch!

And here's the truth: I love buying things when I know I'm getting a good deal. It's just fun all the way around. If I can work a deal where everyone wins, where I get what I want and the salesperson gets what he wants, it's one of the best feelings in the world to me. I'm happy; he's happy. I have what I want; he has my money, which is what he wants. We both feel good about it, and neither one of us walks away regretting the deal. When those pieces come together, it's magic—and it's true at home and in business.

So in this chapter, I'm going to teach you my absolute favorite phrase in negotiating: "That's not good enough!" Those four little words have saved me more money than I can count over the years. I've taught this so many times and have gotten so much great feedback on this material that I want to spend some time going through this stuff in more detail.

Ground Rules for Big Bargains

We'll start with a fundamental point: It's okay to want a better deal. It's not immoral to want to save more of your hard-earned money. You're not hurting the other party by asking for a deal as long as you follow some basic principles of negotiating.

First of all, you should feel good about a deal only if you have in no way misrepresented the truth. Don't tell half-truths or complete lies just to save a buck. That's wrong, immoral and, if you do this, you should be ashamed of yourself! We're not looking for ways to con people out of their goods, services or money. The goal here is to create an environment where everybody gets what they want.

Second, you must never set out to harm the other party. Negotiating deals is not, and should not be, focused on inflicting pain or hardship on someone else. If you're using a deal negotiation as a way to "get" somebody, back off. You're coming at this from the wrong spirit and you don't deserve the deal.

Third, you've got to set out to create a true win-win deal. Again, the point is to set up a situation where everyone wins. If you've done a good job talking through all the parts of the deal and following the steps we're about to lay out, everyone should walk away feeling fantastic about doing business together.

The Three Keys to Opening the Door to Big Bargains

None of what I'm about to outline is revolutionary, and it's only the rare person who walks up to me and says, "You know, I've never heard this before!" So the problem obviously is not that we don't know what to do; it's that we're just not doing it. My goal in this chapter is to help you do it! To do that, we're going to look at three keys to unlock the door to huge bargains.

The First Key

The first key to opening the door to big bargains is learning to negotiate everything—yes, everything! Just start with the assumption that you can get that thing at a discount. Assume that the sticker or sales tag says, "Price starting at:" before the actual listed price. It's the starting point. It's not the final price. Get it into your head that everything in every store in every city in the world is negotiable. You just have to ask. You have to make it a way of life.

I am amazed at the number of people who shell out huge amounts of money for things and never even think to ask if they can have a better price. And I'm not just talking about cars and computers here. What about asking your plumber for a discount? Or your landscaper? Or your doctor? MSN Money reported awhile back that fewer than one in five consumers had ever asked for a lower price from their doctor, dentist, hospital or pharmacy.[1] That amazes me—only one in five people asked for a deal! But guess what? Of those that actually bothered to ask, HALF of them got a better price![2]

> **"It's okay to want a better deal. It's not immoral to want to save more of your hard-earned money."**

If you really grasp what a win-win deal looks like, it will become perfectly natural and comfortable to ask for the deal every time. The best picture of a win-win deal that I've ever seen is taken from Roger Fisher and William Ury's outstanding book, *Getting to Yes*:

> *There were once two elderly ladies who had one orange between them which they were negotiating for. After a lengthy discussion these two ladies could not come up with a solution except to split the difference, so they cut the orange in half, each taking one half. One lady proceeded to peel the orange and use the peel for baking a cake, while the other peeled her half and ate the fruit.*[3]

I explain the story this way:

If the two had spent time, through good communication, finding out what the other's needs were for the orange, they both could have had the whole orange, and neither would have been the lesser. The point of the story is that if you bring creativity and communication to your purchases you can make excellent buys and help people in the process.[4]

The bottom line of the win-win deal is that, with a little bit of communication, both parties can walk away with 100% of what they want. It doesn't have to be 50/50. Both parties can have it all.

The Second Key

The first key to unlocking incredible deals is learning to negotiate everything. The second key is to have patience. I'll be honest, this is the hardest part for me. I can do it as a matter of personal discipline, but it's not my nature to be patient. My wife can wait days, weeks, months and even years to get back around to buying something she wants. Not me. Once I decide I want something, I want it right now and I'm tired of messing around.

This lack of patience can get rather extreme. Not too long ago, Apple® released their latest gizmo. It went out of stock pretty quickly, and online orders had shipping dates of 3–4 weeks. This drove a lot of people so crazy that they immediately hit eBay and paid enormous premiums—up to 150% of retail—on the darn things! Why would someone pay 50% more for an item they could have at a much better price just a few weeks later? They had no patience. That's definitely not the way to get good deals.

Now, I've got nothing against Apple; I own some Apple products myself and I'm incredibly impressed at their ability to market their products and create demand in the marketplace.

Take a breath, put this stuff in perspective, and make wise decisions.

The Third Key

The third key to unlocking great deals is pretty basic: You have to know where to find them. Finding great buys is like a treasure hunt. It's a skill that will get better the more you sniff out bargains. But remember, most really, really good deals won't be found underneath a giant banner that says, "SALE!" Retail sales are usually a crock. Don't fall for a "lower" price that's still not a good price.

When it comes to specific places to find great deals, I can give you a few ideas, but remember the trick is to be a little creative. Get to know your local area, farmers' markets, mom-and-pop shops, as well as great places online to find bargains. There really isn't a "one-size-fits-all" spot to find good deals, so you'll have to learn the basics and then apply them to your own location.[5]

Now it's your turn to go out and negotiate. Make some deals happen today!

---

1. *"Haggle with Your Plumber, Doctor, or Chimney Sweep,"* MSN Money, March 16, 2003.
2. Ibid.
3. Roger Fisher and William Ury. *Getting to Yes: How to Negotiate Agreement Without Giving In.* Chicago: Nightingale Conant.
4. Dave Ramsey, *Financial Peace Revisited*, New York: Viking Penguin, 2003, p. 164.
5. *Dave Ramsey's Complete Guide to Money*, Chapter 8

CHAPTER 7

Video: Sections 1–4

> The first key to opening the door to huge bargains is to start with the idea that **EVERYTHING** is negotiable at some price, in some quantity, on some delivery date.

> *"Whoever said money can't buy happiness simply didn't know where to go shopping."*
>
> BO DEREK
> Actress and Model

> *"If you are planning on doing business with someone again, don't be too tough in the negotiations. If you're going to skin a cat, don't keep it as a housecat."*
>
> MARVIN S. LEVIN
> Businessman and Corporate Consultant

SECTION 1

Buying Only Big, Big Bargains

It is proper to get a great deal if you:

1. Have in no way ______________________[1] the truth.
2. Have not set out to ______________[2] the other party.
3. Have created a ________ - __________[3] deal.

The First Key

The first key to opening the door to huge bargains is learning to ________________[4] everything.

Win-win deals really work, so don't be __________________[5] to __________[6] for the deal.

Seven Basic Rules of Negotiating

1. Always tell the absolute ________________[7].

Remember, all of the seven negotiating techniques can also be used against you. Be aware of what's happening, and you won't be hooked.

Discussion Questions: Section 1

- Why don't more people negotiate for deals? How can you start negotiating in your life today?
- Why are honesty and integrity important when negotiating?

Here are some tips to help stretch your hard-earned money.

1. **Keep your eye on the calendar.** If you buy your winter clothes in the summer and your summer clothes in the winter, you can save hundreds. Even if you buy a car or house during the off season, you can save big. That whole supply-and-demand thing really is true!

2. **Get outdated technology.** Be willing to buy last year's models of TVs, DVDs, laptops and digital cameras and you can save tons. Chances are the bells and whistles added to the latest versions aren't worth the extra money!

3. **Comparison shop.** You may always shop at one particular store, but venture out to find big bargains at stores you may have never visited before. Discount stores and second-hand shops are fantastic places to find deals and save big time! You can even hop online to find sites that compare products and stores to help you find the best value.

4. **Make a deal.** Don't be afraid to negotiate for a lower price. If you're shopping with cash, your chances of making a sweet deal are a lot better.

5. **Get to know eBay.** Buying stuff at online auction sites is another way to get nice, slightly used items. Just make sure you buy from reputable sellers with a high positive-feedback ranking.

SECTION 2

Seven Basic Rules of Negotiating *(Continued)*

2. Use the power of ____________________.
   8

   - Cash is ________________.
     9
   - Cash is ________________.
     10
   - Cash has ______________.
     11

3. Understand and use "______________ - ______________ power."
   12

Discussion Questions: Section 2

- Cash is emotional, visual and has immediacy. When have you seen one of these features at work in your life? How else is cash powerful?
- Besides shopping for deals, when have you used walk-away power? How did it benefit you?

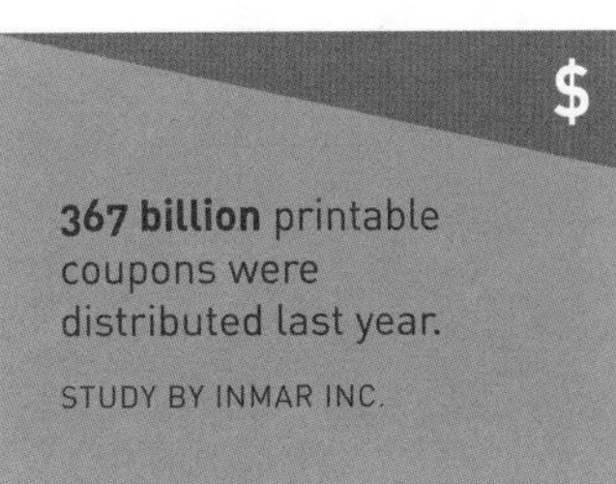

"Let us never negotiate out of fear. But let us never fear to negotiate."

JOHN F. KENNEDY
35th President of the United States

"A bargain ain't a bargain unless it's something you need."

SIDNEY CARROLL
Film and Television Writer

?

"I have used your tips for negotiating and they really work. But how can I get the most money for items I sell? I don't want to get ripped off and I'm not sure how to go about this wisely. Do you have any tips?"

DAVE'S ANSWER: That's a good question and you are right—you don't want to get ripped off when you sell things. First, don't play all your cards face up. The buyer will see that you really need the money. Make it clear that you have walk-away power as a seller. If you can't get the price you want, just walk away from the deal. In the case of antiques or collectible items, get them appraised and sell them slightly below that price. Showing the buyer that you are selling the item for less than the appraisal will make them feel like they are getting a deal. At the same time, you'll know it was a win-win deal because you were armed with information. Try these things and, like everything else, you will get better the more you practice.

$

Where do Americans like to shop? **11.4%** of Americans shop in factory outlet malls, **19.6%** in apparel stores and **21.3%** in major department stores.

AMERICA'S RESEARCH GROUP

"In business, you don't get what you deserve, you get what you negotiate."

CHESTER L. KARRASS
Negotiation Consultant

"Patience is bitter, but its fruit is sweet."

JEAN-JACQUES ROUSSEAU
Philosopher and Writer

Seven Basic Rules of Negotiating *(Continued)*

4. ________ ________.
13

5. "That's not ________ ________."
14

6. ________ guy, ________ guy.
15 16

7. The "If I ________ - ________" technique.
17

If you are patient, willing to negotiate, and educated about what items are on sale during certain seasons, you'll be saving big before you know it!

The Second Key

- The second key to opening the door to huge bargains is that you must have ________.
18

- Don't get ________ to a purchase.
19

The Third Key

- The third key to opening the door to huge bargains is that you must know ____________ (20) to ________________ (21) deals.

Discussion Questions: Section 3

- Of the seven rules of negotiating, which do you use most often? Which would you like to use more often? Why?
- Are you still plagued by impulse purchases? What goes through your heart and mind when you are tempted to spend?

53% of American households get their coupons from the Sunday newspaper. Other ways include the mail, **35%**, and at the stores where people shop, **33%**.

SCARBOROUGH RESEARCH

SECTION 4

The Third Key *(Continued)*

- ________________ (22) something of value, goods or just your ________________ (23).

"Never forget the power of silence (during negotiations), that massively disconcerting pause which goes on and on and may at last induce an opponent to babble and backtrack nervously."

LANCE MORROW
Author and Professor

"Patience is not passive; on the contrary, it is active; it is concentrated strength."

EDWARD G. BULWER-LYTTON
English Politician and Playwright

Places to Find Great Deals

Estate Sale: Type of yard sale with more items, usually the entire contents of a household

Auction: A public sale in which property or items of merchandise are sold to the highest bidder

Foreclosures: Process by which the holder of a mortgage sells the property of a homeowner who has not made interest and/or principal payments on time as stipulated in the mortgage contract

1. ________________ (24)
2. ________________ (25) Sales
3. ____________ ______________ (26)
4. Couponing
5. ______________ __________ (27)
6. Repo Lot
7. __________ ________________ (28)
8. Refunding
9. ____________________ (29)

What do people buy on eBay? On a daily basis, clothing has **20 million** listings, books **12 million** listings, collectibles **11 million** listings, home and garden **7 million** listings and sports memorabilia **6 million** listings.

10 Things You Wish You Knew in College

How many times have you said, "I wish I had known that earlier before I did something stupid"? If you're like the rest of us, probably more times than you care to admit!

However, we can pass along lessons learned to those who follow and hopefully save them some heartache, time and money—especially when it comes to college life.

Dave's Facebook and Twitter fans were quick to offer college advice that they learned the hard way:

1. The "free" T-shirt is not worth the $5,000 credit limit that you will blow through in two months and not pay off for five years.
2. Embrace being poor! It's the only time in your life that no one will look at you funny when you tell them you can't afford it. If you can't buy it with cash, you don't need it.
3. Sallie Mae is like lots of college girls: looks great at first, but she only wants your money!
4. Put a dollar in the bank instead of buying all those snacks from the machines! I'd be rich and skinny today if I had done that.
5. That cheeseburger might be easy to swallow now, but how easy will it be to swallow when you're paying interest on it in five years?
6. Packed lunches do not make you a loser!
7. Find out what your degree really makes. I'm a journalist and it turns out that not every journalist gets to travel the world and make millions.
8. If you need a student loan, apply for more scholarships. If you need a credit card, you can't afford it. If it doesn't benefit your education, you don't need it. Restaurants, cool apartments and nice gadgets do not help you through college.
9. You don't have as much money as your parents, so stop acting like it.
10. A more expensive education does not mean better education.

There are currently more than **30,000** resale, consignment and thrift shops in the United States.

THE ASSOCIATION OF RESALE PROFESSIONALS

Half of online auction participants are men aged 30 to 49, most of whom have college degrees.

THE JOURNAL OF MARKETING THEORY AND PRACTICE

10. ______________________ Shops (30)

11. ______________ ______________________ (31)

12. __________________________ Ads (32)

13. ______________ ____________________________ (33)

14. Conventions

Consignment Shop: Retail store where people sell items and the owner of the shop gets a percentage of the sale

Discussion Questions: Section 4

- How are you saving money right now as a college student? What are three new ways you can save money?
- By the way, how is your envelope system coming along? Are you sticking to your written budget?

Recap & Review

5 Ways to Get Out of a High-Pressure Sales Situation

BY JON ACUFF

I love salespeople. I think they can be some of the most helpful, knowledgeable folks on the planet. I used to be one and would never denigrate them. But there is something you need to know about them:

They are trained to sell you stuff.

Shocking, right? I know, I know, who'd have thought? When you're not in their store or dealership or business, they're training on the best ways to sell you stuff. They're reading books and going to conferences and basically doing everything they can to become the best at getting you to buy stuff.

And when it comes to shopping, we consumers never do the same thing.

Have you ever read a book on how to be a smart consumer? Have you ever gone to a "shopping conference" where you heard shopping experts share tips on making smart purchases? Have you ever received rewards and incentives to get even better at shopping?

Probably not. We don't think about shopping that way. So what happens is that we go into most shopping situations unprepared. The salesperson is like LeBron James. He's trained. He's made a living out of dunking on folks. And we just roll off the couch, straight into the game, and then act surprised when we buy something we really didn't want or can't afford.

Today, I want to level the playing field a little. I want to help give you a fighting chance. I want to train you on some simple ways you can get out of a high-pressure sales situation.

We've all been in those. We're standing with the salesperson on the model floor, looking at something we like, but we're just not sure we love it. And she's going through all her training, dropping jump shots and dunks all over the court. If we could just retreat for a day or two, we might have enough mental space to decide if we really can afford this. But the intensity is cranked up, and we feel stuck. How do you get out of that situation?

Here are five things you can say:

1. "I need to talk to my spouse first." Ahh, the classic "Throw your husband or wife under the bus" move. This is one of the oldest moves in the book, because it works. You're not saying you don't want to buy it; you just want to make sure your significant other is on board, too. If you're not married, then say you want to talk with a parent first. Don't budge on this, and you'll be fine.

2. "This is tough because of the down economy." Even if the economy is up and we're doing well, this is a great angle. Starting in the late 2000s, people started blaming the "down economy" for everything. It started with realistic things, like the struggle to find a job. But before long, folks were crediting the crab grass in their yard and failed dating relationships to the down economy. Tell the salesperson, "I would love to buy this today, but with the whole down economy thing..."

3. "I never pay retail for anything. You'll have to do better than that." Sometimes these are the magic words to unlock a previously unmentioned sale on the item in question. Just tell the salesperson that you've got a family rule, a boundary if you will, that you only buy things that are on sale. (And that should be true, by the way, because everything is on sale if you ask the right way.) If the item is already on sale, tweak it a little and say, "I only buy things that are on deep discount." Chances are, you'll be able to get them to drop the price even further.

4. "Do you have this model in yellow?" Unless you're looking at bananas, chances are the salesperson will not be able to immediately fulfill this yellow request. (And if you are buying bananas through a salesperson, where are you shopping? How many bananas are you going through in a week? So many questions.) Sure, you might not want it in yellow, but that's not what you said. You asked about a color option; there's nothing dishonest about that. And it gives you a chance to put the power back into your hand by taking the conversation from "You need to buy this thing you're looking at right now" to "I might buy something eventually if I really like it."

5. "Sometimes the summer rains remind me of how raindrops sounded on my grandfather's pond when we'd fish for big-mouth bass." That makes no sense at all. But eventually, if you talk enough gibberish, even the most persistent salesperson will bail on you and go talk to someone else.

That last one got away from me a little, didn't it? I'm not even sure what it means. But what I am sure of is that I want you to be prepared. I want you to be able to have a great game with the salesperson. One in which both of you win and you feel good about the whole thing.

Just don't buy the yellow model if they have it. So few things look good in yellow. Except for bananas.

Chapter 7 Key Concepts

- Don't be afraid to ask for the deal.
- Use cash; it has power in negotiations.
- Don't forget walk-away power.
- Be quiet! Silence can make a huge difference in negotiations.
- Remember the key phrase, "THAT'S NOT GOOD ENOUGH!"

Video Section Answers

1. Misrepresented
2. Harm
3. Win-Win
4. Negotiate
5. Afraid
6. Ask
7. Truth
8. Cash
9. Emotional
10. Visual
11. Immediacy
12. Walk-Away
13. Shut Up
14. Good Enough
15. Good
16. Bad
17. Take-Away
18. Patience
19. Married
20. Where
21. Find
22. Trade
23. Services
24. Individuals
25. Estate
26. Public Auctions
27. Garage Sales
28. Flea Markets
29. Foreclosures
30. Pawn
31. Online Auctions
32. Classified
33. Consignment Sales

CHAPTER 7

Case Studies

Jamey and a New Taurus

Jamey is a sophomore in college where she's majoring in economics. Her 1992 Ford Taurus is on its last leg. She's been car shopping and found two possible deals for her situation. The first car she found is in great condition, has low mileage, and is for sale for $9,000. She also found a car for $7,000 which is not in as good of shape and has higher mileage. Jamey only has $7,500 to spend.

1. Which car would you recommend Jamey to buy?
2. Should Jamey negotiate for the higher-priced car? If so, what are three negotiating tips that you would give her?
3. If she decides to buy the less expensive car, could Jamey negotiate for a better deal on it? Why or why not?

Whitney and New Clothes

Whitney works hard to pay as much as she can toward her college tuition and avoids taking out student loans whenever possible. She's noticed that she could use some new clothes before the next semester starts and has saved $300. She prefers to shop at department stores but knows her money won't go very far at stores like that. Whitney is determined not to go over her budget, so she needs to come up with a plan that will help her stick to it.

1. Are there other shopping options that Whitney could take advantage of? If so, what are they?
2. What kind of impact would purchases not made at a department store have on her budget?
3. If you were in Whitney's shoes, what would you do? Why?

Jamal and a Bike

Jamal's roommates bike a lot, and he's becoming interested in the sport after hearing them talk about it so much. He's never done much biking, but it sounds fun and he wants to give it a try. He doesn't want to spend a lot of money on his first bike because he isn't sure how much he will like riding. He is okay with starting with a used bike, because he figures he can always upgrade if he enjoys it. Unfortunately, he went to the bike shop and found their prices to be too expensive.

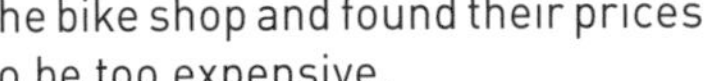

1. How will the high prices affect his enjoyment of biking?
2. Since Jamal doesn't know if he will enjoy riding, what would you advise him to do?
3. Can you think of any ideas of how Jamal could try biking out before he invests money into the equipment?

CHAPTER 7

Money in Review

Matching

Match each term to its definition below.

a. auctions	e. walk-away power
b. estate sale	f. win-win deal
c. integrity	g. patience
d. rebating	

1 ______ The opposite of being married to a purchase

2 ______ Always telling the absolute truth

3 ______ Waiting with hope

4 ______ Both parties benefit

5 ______ Sending in proof of purchase then receiving cash back

6 ______ Type of sale that usually involves the entire contents of a household

True or False

Determine whether these statements are true or false. Change the false statements to read true.

7 **T / F :** Knowing how to deal with a salesperson involves pressure-oriented negotiation.

8 **T / F :** When negotiating, you must use integrity and avoid misrepresenting the truth.

9 **T / F :** You can get great deals if you find a convention that is just setting up.

10 **T / F :** Couponing is when you send in proof of purchase to get cash back.

11 **T / F :** Gathering information on the other person's needs, wants, and fears is only a small part of successful negotiation.

12 **T / F :** You can get a better deal if you're not married to the item.

13 **T / F :** Cash has emotional and visual powers that you can use to your benefit.

14 **T / F :** Thrift and consignment stores only sell used items.

15 **T / F :** You can't negotiate for purchases in our American culture.

Fill in the Blank

Rules of Negotiating:

16 Remember __________ guy, __________ guy.

17 __________ up!

18 Use __________-away power.

19 Say, "That's ______ __________ enough!"

20 Employ the power of __________.

Short Answer

21 What are some reasons people don't negotiate?

22 What are some things that you have recently negotiated (may or may not deal with purchases)?

23 Evaluate the impact that research has on successful bargain shopping. List as many impacts as you can.

24 Explain how walk-away power and silence are powerful tools of negotiation.

25 If you had to place the three keys of successful negotiating in order of importance, which would you put first and why?

CHAPTER 7

Notes

CHAPTER 8

Credit Bureaus

UNIT 2: DEVELOPING YOUR SKILLS

Living on credit is a big part of our culture. We already talked about debt and why you should avoid it, but the fact is, this temptation bombards us every day. We've got to learn how to deal with debt—both in avoiding it, and in cleaning up the mess if we've already stepped in it. At this time in your life, prevention is the best medicine!

Learning Outcomes

Refute the myth of building a credit score.

- A credit score is an "I love debt" score and is not a measure of financial success. The only reason you "need" a credit score is to help you secure a large loan in your future, which defeats the purpose of avoiding debt. Rest assured, everything you "need" a credit score for can be done without having one. Ultimately, the smartest decision is to have a non-existent credit score (a zero credit score).

Describe the value of credit reports.

- A credit report is a detailed history of how you've used debt. Ideally you want to avoid using debt, which results in a non-existent credit report. Even if you don't have a history of using debt, you should still check your credit report annually to make sure your identity hasn't been compromised.

List actions to take when your identity has been compromised.

- Place a fraud-victim alert on your credit report
- Get a police report
- Remember you owe nothing and should pay nothing
- Contact the fraud-victim division of each creditor and furnish documentation
- Be persistent; this will take some time

Summarize laws that protect consumers from illegal collection practices.

- **Fair Credit Reporting Act (FCRA):** Federal law that regulates the collection, distribution and use of consumer information, including consumer credit information
- **Fair Debt Collection Practices Act (FDCPA):** Federal law that prohibits unfair debt-collection practices, such as lying, harassing, misleading and otherwise abusing debtors, by debt collectors working for collection agencies

Communicate effectively with credit bureaus and other agencies about collection issues.

- Cease-and-desist letter
- Pro rata plan
- Lawsuit communication
- Opt-out letter

Key Terms

Bankruptcy: a Legal procedure for dealing with debt problems of individuals and businesses; specifically a legal court case filed under one of the chapters of Title 11 of the United States Code

Credit Bureau: an agency which collects the credit history of consumers so that creditors can make decisions about granting loans

Credit Score: a calculated score that measures an individual's creditworthiness; the two main types of credit scores are the FICO score and the VantageScore

Credit Report: a document showing your credit history, credit inquiries and facts about any accounts you have opened with individual credit lines and on-time or late payment activities

Fraud: a seller's intentional deception of a buyer, which is illegal

CHAPTER 8

Reading

In this excerpt from *Dave Ramsey's Complete Guide to Money,* Dave discusses why having a good credit score doesn't mean you are doing well with money. This passage will help arm you with facts so you won't fall for the myth that the credit score is the end-all-be-all of successful money management.

Before we get started, let me say something to those who don't think they need to read about credit bureaus and debt collectors. If you're reading this book, then you're already miles ahead of the "average" American. Remember, "normal" in North America is broke! If you're taking control of your money, you're totally weird. Maybe you're doing really, really well. Maybe you're out of debt, have a big, fat emergency fund, and will never have to suffer through a bill collector's horrible ranting on the phone. If that's you, then great! Congratulations! But this chapter is still for you.

Here's what we've found. As you take control of your money and get your financial act together, a strange phenomenon starts to happen. All of a sudden, people are going to start coming to you for help. These may be the same people who made fun of you for cutting up your credit cards at first. Over time, they see your life changing and they see you developing a peace about your money, and they realize that you can probably help them.

We see this all the time on our team. It's a joke around our place that if you tell someone you work for Dave Ramsey, you should expect to hear all about their money problems! One guy on our team was having blood drawn for a life-insurance physical, and when the nurse saw "Dave Ramsey" on his paperwork, she started telling him all about her overspending at Christmas—while the needle was still in his arm!

Here's the deal. You've got hurting people all around you. If they see that you're doing well, they will see you as a safe place, someone they can go to for help. So even if you never have to personally deal with a crummy credit card collector, there's a good chance someone you know and love will. And if they come to you for help, you need to have some hope—and information—to give them.

Credit Scores: Forsaking The Almighty FICO

There's a myth running wild out there that sets up a lot of young adults for total failure. I can almost guarantee that you've heard it. In fact, go ahead and finish this sentence: "You need to take out a credit card or car loan to build up your..." If you said, "credit score," you win. If you ever bought into that lie, you lose.

Don't Buy the Lie

Hear me clearly on this: The credit score is NOT a measure of winning financially. It is 100% based on debt. The credit, or FICO, score is simply an "I love debt" rating. No part of the credit score calculation even *hints* at how much wealth you have.

We, as a culture, just take it for granted that a high FICO number means we're doing great! It doesn't. It just shows how much we enjoy being in debt. I'll prove it. Here's a breakdown of how your FICO score is calculated:

35% Debt History

30% Debt Levels

15% Duration of the Debt

10% Type of Debt

10% New Debt

So where does your income, savings account, retirement plan, real estate and mutual fund portfolio factor in? Nowhere. I told you, the score *only* reflects your affinity for debt. It has nothing to do with how much you make or how much you have.

Don't Mind Me. I'm Dead.

I got to thinking about this a while back, and I realized that I have not borrowed money in over 20 years. I wondered what my credit score was, so I went online to pull it. Here's what I got back:

"Our apologies, an error has occurred. We regret that we were unable to fill your score power order request because your credit report does not currently contain enough information to meet the minimum scoring criteria to calculate a FICO score.

In order for a FICO score to be calculated, a report must contain at least one account which has been opened for six months or more, at least one account which has been updated in the past six months, and no indication of being deceased."

"No indication of being deceased!" Translation: In our debt-ridden, credit-addicted culture, you must be DEAD to not have a credit score!

> "Hear me clearly on this: The credit score is NOT a measure of winning financially. It is 100% based on debt."

Not a Measure of Winning

My wife and I have been following these principles for a long time now, so we have some wealth, but we still don't have a FICO score. You could inherit $10 million next week and it will not even change your FICO score by one point. You could go into work tomorrow and get a $1 million-a-year raise and it won't make a bit of difference to your FICO score. What kind of sense does this make? Don't sacrifice your wealth in the name of the almighty FICO. It's a lie, and it can ruin your life.

Credit Bureaus: Untangling The Paper Trail

I want to be clear as we discuss credit bureaus. First, like I said, the FICO score has nothing to do with wealth and success, so building a good credit score should not be a goal. But second, that doesn't mean I want you to intentionally go out of your way to trash your credit score. There's a big difference in having a bad credit history and having no credit history.

I want you to pay your bills, honor your debts, and act with integrity. If you do that, you won't wreck your FICO score all at once. Instead, it will just fade away into nothing as you tick away years and years of not borrowing any money.

Cleaning Up a Mess

Account information stays on your credit report for seven years *from the date of last activity.* That "date of last activity" part is important. This means that you can't just stop paying your credit card bill and wait it out for seven years until it drops off. The collectors or credit card company can do inquiries on the account that can count as "activity," so they have ways of keeping that black mark on your record well beyond seven years. And every time there's activity, that seven-year clock starts over.

This is not a "get out of jail free" card. This system is designed to keep your most recent activity and behavior at the forefront and to allow old mistakes to go away over time. So, missing a few car payments while you were laid off four years ago isn't as important today as it was at the time. The older it gets, the less significant it gets until it eventually just falls off. The only exception to the seven-year rule is a Chapter 7 bankruptcy, which stays on the record for 10 years.

The only information that can be legally removed from your credit bureau report is inaccurate information, so do not fall for credit clean-up scams. You cannot repair a bad credit report unless there are items on the report that are genuinely incorrect. This happens all the time. You've got to stay on top of this. Even if it's someone else's error, it's your responsibility to check the reports regularly and have any inaccuracies removed. Remember this is your electronic reputation. This will impact your ability to do even basic things like get good car insurance. You need to personally check your credit report at least once a year. By law, you are entitled to a free copy of your credit report once a year from each of the three credit reporting agencies, Experian, TransUnion and Equifax. So get a copy, check it closely, and pay attention to this stuff![1]

You need to pay attention to your credit score, but don't fall into a trap of thinking that a good credit score is the way to win with money!

---

1. *Dave Ramsey's Complete Guide to Money*, Chapter 5

CHAPTER 8 Video: Sections 1–5

SECTION 1

Credit Score

One More Myth

MYTH: You need to take out a credit card or car loan to "build up your ____________ ____________."
1

TRUTH: The ____________ score is an "I love ____________" score and is not a measure of winning financially.
2 3

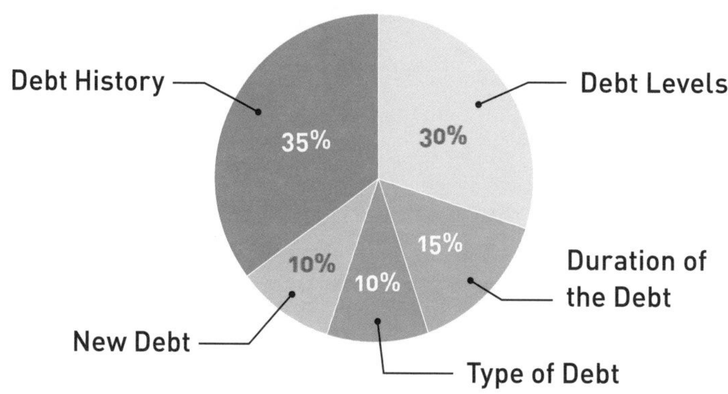

> **Discussion Questions:** Section 1
>
> - What are the disadvantages to building a credit score? What will debt cost you long-term?
> - How can a person succeed financially without using a credit score to get there? How can you implement those things in your life today?

SECTION 2

Credit Bureaus

Account information is removed from your credit report ______ years after the last activity on the account, except for Chapter 7 bankruptcy, which stays on for _______ years.
4 5

Chapter 7 Bankruptcy: Chapter of the Bankruptcy Code providing for liquidation of the debtor's assets in order to repay the creditors; certain assets or aggregate value of assets of the debtor may be exempt based on state law

Beware of credit clean-up scams. The only information that may be legally removed from a credit report is ________________ information.
6

$

The total consumer debt in America is currently **$2.4 trillion**.

FEDERAL RESERVE

"I've never been poor, only broke. Being poor is a frame of mind. Being broke is only a temporary position."

MIKE TODD
American Film Producer

+

There are a lot of companies that measure credit, but two major credit scoring systems are **FICO** and **VantageScore** (which the three credit bureaus jointly created). FICO ranges from 300-850 and VantageScore ranges from 501 to 990. Remember, a credit score measures the risk of your not repaying debt; **it is not a measure of financial success.**

?

"My mom made me an authorized user on her credit card, and now she's having trouble making the payments. Will this affect my credit rating too?"

DAVE'S ANSWER: You are NOT liable and it shouldn't show up on your credit bureau report if you're only an authorized user on the card. There's a huge difference between being authorized to use a credit card and having liability for the card. Even though you're not responsible for her debt, let this be a lesson to you. If you play with fire long enough, you will get burned.

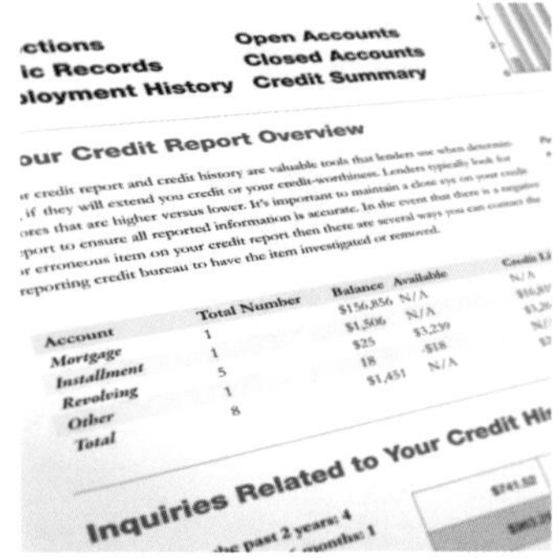

Correcting Credit Report Inaccuracies

Chapter 11 Bankruptcy: Reorganization bankruptcy, usually involving a corporation or partnership; generally includes a plan of reorganization to keep a business alive and pay creditors over time

Chapter 13 Bankruptcy: Chapter of the Bankruptcy Code providing for an individual to repay debts over time, usually three to five years; debtor makes periodic payments to the bankruptcy trustee, who in turn pays the creditors; sometimes includes adjustments to debt balances within the bankruptcy

The National Association of State Public Interest Research Groups (U.S. PIRG) did a survey of 200 adults in 30 states who checked their credit report for accuracy.

________ (7) of those credit reports contained mistakes of some sort and ________ (8) of them contained errors serious enough to result in the denial of credit.

________ (9) of the credit reports contained credit accounts that had been closed by the consumer but incorrectly remained listed as open.

________ (10) listed the same mortgage or loan twice.

You should check your credit report ______________________ (11), which you can do for free.

The three credit bureaus are Experian, TransUnion and Equifax.

$

Of Americans who have credit card debt, the **average balance is $14,750.**

FEDERAL RESERVE

Approximately **10 million** Americans do not use an insured financial institution, such as a bank or credit union.

THE CASE FOR ECONOMIC EDUCATION

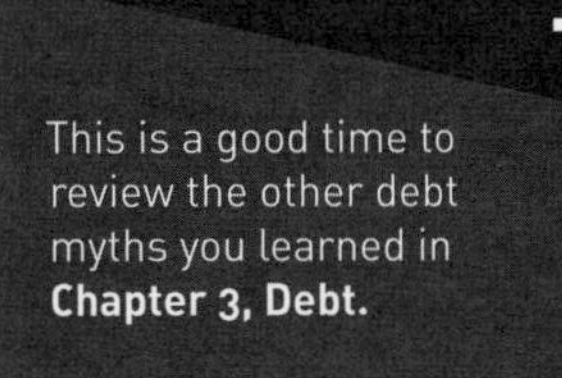

Young people seem to have little to lose from identity theft, which makes them easy targets. College students are particularly vulnerable to identity theft. In fact, people aged 18-25 are the most commonly victimized age group when it comes to this white-collar crime.

A young listener wrote this letter to *The Dave Ramsey Show*:

"My third day of college, I applied for several credit cards on campus. Five years later, I found out my personal information was posted on a web site. I had cars bought in my name and credit accounts across the country. A college student who ran one of the credit card booths was responsible for posting my information. Even though I now have a new Social Security number, I constantly have to monitor my credit reports. I have had to explain all of this to employers who run background checks on me. That free T-shirt wound up costing me $150,000!"

+

Want to know more about identity theft protection? Check out **Chapter 9, Insurance.**

"I was a victim of credit fraud by my mother, and I had no idea what to do. But with the help of this class, I'm not as apprehensive about it."

COLLEGE STUDENT

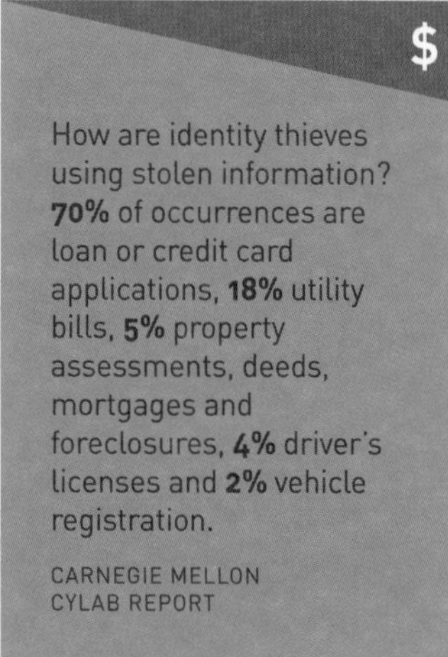

$

How are identity thieves using stolen information? **70%** of occurrences are loan or credit card applications, **18%** utility bills, **5%** property assessments, deeds, mortgages and foreclosures, **4%** driver's licenses and **2%** vehicle registration.

CARNEGIE MELLON CYLAB REPORT

Identity Theft: What to Do

Identity theft is the fastest-growing ____________ ____________ (12) crime in North America today.

1. Place a ____________ ____________ (13) alert on your credit bureau report (stays on 90 days without a police report).

2. Get a ____________ ____________ (14).
   80% of identities are stolen by people you know.

3. Remember, this is ____________ (15). You owe ____________ (16) and should pay ____________ (17).

4. Contact the ____________ ____________ (18) division of each creditor and furnish ____________ (19).

5. Be ____________ (20), this will take some time.
   You now have a new ____________ (21).

How to Protect Yourself from Identity Theft

- Don't give out your personal information, unless you initiated the conversation.
- Shred papers that have your personal information on them, including credit card offers, ATM receipts, bills and FAFSA paperwork.
- Use difficult login passwords with all of your online accounts.
- Install firewall, anti-virus and anti-spyware protection software on your computer.
- Forward your mail to your new address every time you move.
- Opt out of credit card offers in the mail.
- Check your balances online daily.
- Lock your mailbox.
- Be wary if you get an email from a bank or company asking for your personal information by clicking on a link. Close the window and go directly to the website or call them instead.
- Avoid using your pin when charging your debit card. Instead run it as credit. (Rest assured, it is not the same as using a credit card, which is debt.)
- Don't leave your purse or wallet in your dorm or apartment alone.
- Don't make purchases online or enter personal information using a public computer on campus.

An updated version of the 1977 Federal Fair Credit Reporting Act (FFCRA) requires a credit bureau to ______________ (22) all inaccuracies within ________ (23) days of notification of such inaccuracies.

To clean up your credit report of inaccurate information, take the following steps:

Federal Fair Credit Reporting Act: Federal law that regulates the collection, distribution and use of consumer information, including consumer credit information

1. Write a separate letter for each inaccuracy.
2. Staple a copy of your credit report to each letter.
3. Circle the account number

NOTE: You should also request that "inquiries" be removed. All of these letters should be sent ________________________ (24) mail with return receipt requested to prove when they receive the letter.

If the credit bureau does not prove the accuracy of the account within ________ (25) days, request that they remove the ____________________ (26) account from your file.

$

Of all the identity theft victims who call in to *The Dave Ramsey Show*, **approximately half of them know the person who stole their identity**. The thief is often a friend or family member.

460,000 college students' identities are compromised by security breaches per month.

PRIVACYRIGHTS.ORG

"If you think nobody cares if you're alive, try missing a couple of car payments."

EARL WILSON
American Columnist

The Truth About Teens and Credit Cards

MYTH: Make sure your teenager gets a credit card so he or she will learn to be responsible with money.

TRUTH: Getting a credit card for your teenager is an excellent way to teach him or her to be financially irresponsible. That's why teens are now the number-one target of credit card companies.

Over 80% of graduating college seniors have credit card debt before they even have a job! The credit card marketers have done such a thorough job that a credit card is seen as a rite of passage into adulthood. American teens view themselves as adults if they have a **credit card, a cell phone and a driver's license**. Sadly, none of these "accomplishments" are in any way associated with real adulthood.

Vince called my radio show with a problem that has become a trend. Vince signed up for multiple cards during his sophomore year at college to get the **free T-shirt**. He wasn't going to use the cards unless there was an emergency, but there was an "emergency" every week, and soon he was $15,000 in debt. He couldn't make the payments, so he quit school to get a job. The problem was, without his degree, his earnings were minimal. Worse than that, he also had $27,000 in student loans. You aren't required to pay student loans while you are in school, but when you leave school by graduating or quitting, the payments begin in six months.

Vince was one scared 21-year-old with $42,000 in debt but making only $15,000 per year. What's scary is that Vince is "normal." The American Bankruptcy Institute reveals that 19% of the people who filed for bankruptcy last year were college students. **That means one in five bankruptcy filings** were by very young people who started their lives as financial failures. Do you still think it is wise to give a teen a card? I hope not.

$

Think a larger salary will solve your financial problems? Think again!

The average NFL player makes $900,000 a year and a surprising number (some estimate up to 80%) file bankruptcy in the years immediately following their retirement. Recently, former Pittsburgh Steeler lineman Dermontti Dawson joined New York Jets backup QB Mark Brunell in bankruptcy court. Others include Marlin Briscoe, Raghib 'Rocket' Ismail, Johnny Unitas, Deuce McAllister, Mark Brunellm, Travis Henry, Dermontti Dawson, Lawrence Taylor and Arthur Marshall.

CNBC.COM

You will have to be assertive after the 30-day period.

Lodge any ____________________ with the Federal Trade Commission
27
and your state's Consumer Affairs Division.

Discussion Questions: Section 2

- Why do you think there are so many errors on credit reports? Why are those errors so difficult to remove?
- Of the ways to protect yourself against identity theft, which are the three most effective? Other than the ones listed, what are more ways you can protect yourself from identity theft?

SECTION 3

Collection Practices

The best way to pay debt is with a ____________________ (28).

A collector's job is not to help your overall situation. His only job is to get your ____________________ (29).

Collectors are trained ____________________ (30) and ____________________ (31).

They are typically high ____________________ (32) positions with low-pay.

They are taught in their training to evoke strong ____________________ (33).

The way to counteract this technique is to ALWAYS pay ____________________ (34) first, and then you set the order of payment.

Always set your priorities by the Four Walls:

Necessities: Something that is necessary; a requirement or need for something

Disposable Income: Amount of money left over after all necessities and expenses are paid

1. Food
2. Shelter
3. Clothing
4. Transportation

Discussion Questions: Section 3

- In what way is emotion a collector's best weapon? Which emotional tactic would work on you?
- Have you or any of your family members been contacted by a collector or creditor? What tactics were used and did they work?

$

College seniors graduate with an average **credit card debt of more than $4,100.** Close to one-fifth of seniors carried balances greater than **$7,000.**

SALLIE MAE

Be careful when using credit repair companies. Consumer protection officials warn us they often **overpromise, charge high prices, and perform services that you can do yourself.**

CONSUMER FEDERATION OF AMERICA

+

The Federal Trade Commission publishes a brief, semiannual list (March and September) on card pricing by the largest issuers for $5 per copy. It also offers a number of free credit-related publications.

(202) 326-2222

600 Pennsylvania Avenue, NW

Washington, D.C. 20580

www.ftc.gov

$

Nevada has the highest bankruptcy rate of **11 occurrences per 1,000 people.** On the other hand, Alaska has the lowest bankruptcy rate of 1.4 occurrences per 1,000 people.

AMERICAN BANKRUPTCY INSTITUTE

"Creditors have better memories than debtors."

BENJAMIN FRANKLIN
A Founding Father of the United States

"The only man who sticks closer to you in adversity than a friend is a creditor."

AUTHOR UNKNOWN

Federal Fair Debt Collections Practices Act

In 1977, a consumer law was passed by Congress called the Federal Fair Debt Collection Practices Act (FFDCPA) to protect you from unfair collectors. The law technically only applies to collection agencies (not your creditor), but later court cases make most creditors also abide by the FFDCPA.

Federal Fair Debt Collection Practices Act: Federal law that prohibits unfair debt collection practices, such as lying, harassing, misleading and otherwise abusing debtors, by debt collectors working for collection agencies

The Act states that ____________________ (35) is illegal and restricts a collector's calls between the hours of ____________ (36) and ____________ (37) (unless they have your permission).

The Act also allows you to demand that a creditor cease calling you at ____________ (38). You should request this in writing by ____________________ ______________ (39) with return receipt requested.

The Act even allows you to insist that a creditor stop ____________ (40) contact except to notify you of ____________________________ (41) proceedings. This is called a cease-and-desist letter.

Do not use a cease-and-desist letter except in horrible situations, because all _________________________ (42) stop and any hope of a positive resolution is lost.

No collector or creditor may _________________ (43) a bank account or ____________________ (44) wages without proper and lengthy court action, except in the case of delinquent IRS or student loan debt. All such threats are a bluff.

SAMPLE CREDITOR LETTER

(Date) ______________________________

From: ______________________________
____
____

To: ______________________________
____
____

RE: ______________________________

Dear ______________________________,

I am writing to formally request that, in accordance with the 1977 Federal Fair Debt Collection Practices Act, your firm (or agency hired by your firm) no longer contact me at my place of employment, ______________________.

Please take note that this letter was mailed certified mail, return receipt requested, so that I will have proof that you are in receipt of this letter should legal action against you become necessary.

I am willing to pay the debt I owe you, and I will be in touch with you soon to work out arrangements.

Feel free to contact me at my home between _____ AM and _____ PM at the following number: ______________, or by mail at my home address: ____.

Please give this matter your immediate attention.

Sincerely,

(Signature) ______________________________

?

"My boyfriend's credit is in bad shape, and we're thinking about getting married. Will his bad credit rating affect mine?"

DAVE'S ANSWER: Marrying someone with a bad credit rating will not affect your score. In other words, the black marks on his credit rating don't jump across the aisle onto your report as soon as he slips the ring on your finger.

Two things will happen after you're married. First, your credit bureau will begin to reflect the fact that he is your husband. He'll be listed as "spouse" on your report. After this, if they pull your report for any reason, they'll see that half of your "team" has had problems in the past.

His credit score could affect you both the most when you decide to buy a home. If he still has credit issues, purchasing a house could be difficult. But the big issue here is that you seem to have differing views on money management. Make sure you go through premarital counseling together and that the counseling includes a financial component. You could also practice by sitting down together and making a monthly budget. Just keep in mind that this is practice only. Never actually mix your money until your wedding day! If you get married, then money will be a big part of your relationship for the rest of your lives. Money fights and money problems are the leading cause of divorce, so if you agree on your goals now, you'll set a solid foundation for a healthy marriage.

$

Of any age group, 18–34 year olds are more likely to have unsecured debt—**60%** of them do!

MINTEL RESEARCH

"If we don't change, millions of American families are just one medical emergency, or one layoff, away from financial disaster and bankruptcy."

JIM COOPER
Politician

Pro Rata Plan

Your plan should include as much prompt repayment of debt as possible, but YOU must set your priorities of repayment.

Pro Rata Plan: Debt repayment plan by which the borrower repays each lender a fair percentage of the total debt owed when one cannot make the minimum payments on one's debt

DO NOT let a collector use your ______________ ______________ as a paper club.
45

When you are unable to pay the minimum payments, use the ______________ ______________ plan.
46

Discussion Questions for Section 4

- Why would a collector want to contact your family or friends? How do you think they would respond to the collector? How would their conversation make you feel?
- If you were a collector, would you accept a pro rata plan from a delinquent borrower? Why or why not? What other things could they do to gain grace from you?

Pro Rata Debt List

"Pro rata" means the fair share, or the percent of your total debt each creditor represents. This will determine how much you should send them when you cannot make the minimum payments. Even if you cannot pay your creditors what they request, you should pay everyone as much as you can. Send the check for their pro rata share, along with a copy of your budget and this form, every month. Do this even if the creditor says they will not accept it.

Do You Need to Use a Pro Rata Plan?

First, determine your total disposable income by looking over your monthly cash flow plan. Simply write down your income on the line at the top of the form. Then write down the total you spend on necessities (not including consumer debt) each month. Subtract the necessity expense from the income, and you are left with your disposable income. This is the money you have to put toward your debts.

Second, add up your total amount of debt, not including your home, and write that in the blank provided. Below that, write in the total of the minimum monthly payments on all your debts. If the total of your minimum payments is greater than your total disposable income, you need to use the pro rata plan.

For example, Jake and Whitney have a total debt of $2,000, with a combined total minimum payment of $310. However, they only have $200 in disposable income each month, which means they do not have enough money to make the minimum payments. So, they will use the pro rata plan to give each creditor their fair share of the couple's $200.

How to Use This Form

This form has six columns:

1. **ITEM:** the name and type of the account
2. **TOTAL PAYOFF:** the total amount due on the account
3. **TOTAL DEBT:** the combined total of all your debts
4. **PERCENT:** the portion of the total debt load that each account represents. You can calculate this by simply dividing the Total Payoff by the Total Debt for each line.
5. **DISPOSABLE INCOME:** the amount of money you have left after paying necessities
6. **NEW PAYMENT:** the amount you will now send to each creditor. You calculate this by multiplying the numbers in each line's Percent and Disposable Income Columns.

The pro rata plan helps you to meet your obligations to the best of your ability. Of course, your creditors will not like receiving less than their required minimum payments. However, if you keep sending checks, they'll most likely keep cashing them.

Pro Rata Debt List

Income		$3,361
Necessity Expense	–	$3,161
Disposable Income	=	$200

Total Debt:	$2,000
Total Monthly Payments:	$310

ITEM	TOTAL PAYOFF		TOTAL DEBT		PERCENT		DISPOSABLE INCOME		NEW PAYMENT
JC Penney	100	/	2,000	=	5% (.05)	X	200	=	$10
Sears	200	/	2,000	=	10% (.10)	X	200	=	$20
MBNA Visa	200	/	2,000	=	10% (.10)	X	200	=	$20
Citibank Visa	300	/	2,000	=	15% (.15)	X	200	=	$30
Discover	1,200	/	2,000	=	60% (.60)	X	200	=	$120
		/		=		X		=	
		/		=		X		=	
		/		=		X		=	
		/		=		X		=	
		/		=		X		=	
		/		=		X		=	
		/		=		X		=	
		/		=		X		=	
		/		=		X		=	
		/		=		X		=	
		/		=		X		=	
		/		=		X		=	

SECTION 5

Lawsuits

Eventually, if you are making no payments and have cut no deals, you will get sued.

> **Foreclosure:** The process by which the holder of a mortgage sells the property of a homeowner who has not made interest and/or principal payments on time as stipulated in the mortgage contract

Typically, lawsuits for under ____________ (47) are filed in General Sessions Court (or small-claims court), which is a fairly informal proceeding.

> **Bankruptcy:** A legal procedure for dealing with debt problems of individuals and businesses

Before you are sued, you will be served by the local sheriff's department and typically given ________ (48) days notice of the court date.

In court, if the debt is valid, even if you fight, you will ____________ (49). From that date, you will generally have 30 days before the ______________________ (50) becomes final and ________________________ (51) or attachments begin.

> **Garnishment:** A court-ordered attachment that allows a lender to take monies owed directly from a borrower's paycheck; only allowed as part of a court judgment

AT ANY TIME during the process, you may settle with the creditor or their attorney in writing. If you are not able to reach an agreement, you can file with the court a "____________ ____________ (52) motion," called a "pauper's oath" in some states.

Discussion Questions for Section 5

- Does it ever make sense to file for bankruptcy? How can you avoid filing, even in the worst of situations?
- If you filed for bankruptcy because you were irresponsible with debt, how would that experience affect your life long-term? Would you return to your old habits after you filed?

$

One in five (22%) 18–34 year olds **would consider bankruptcy** if their situation became serious enough. This is twice the amount as the generation before.

MINTEL RESEARCH

"Credit is much like being drunk. The buzz happens immediately and gives you a lift... The hangover comes the day after."

JOYCE BROTHERS
American Columnist

"No man's credit is as good as his money."

E.W. HOWE
American Novelist

Free Credit Reports

The FACT Act amendments to the Fair Credit Reporting Act require the three credit bureaus to provide consumers, upon request, one free personal credit report in any 12-month period. You may contact the Central Source online at www.annualcreditreport.com or by calling toll free (877) FACT ACT.

The three credit bureaus each give you a free credit report annually, so in reality you can check your report three times a year. It would be smart to check your report every four months, each time from one of the three bureaus.

Experian
(888) 397-3742
www.experian.com

Equifax Credit Bureau
(800) 685-1111
www.equifax.com

TransUnion
(877) 322-8228
www.transunion.com

Be wary of websites other than www.annualcreditreport.com and the three credit bureau websites. There are many false sites that will try to steal your personal information. Also, remember the Act allows you to get a free credit report, NOT a free credit score. Be cautious of sites that offer a free credit score; they will try to sign you up for credit monitoring and charge you monthly fees.

Be Proactive

Decrease unauthorized direct mail marketing (including pre-approved credit card offers) and unwanted telemarketing calls.

Pre-Screening Opt Out
(888) 567-8688
www.optoutprescreen.com

National Do Not Call Registry
(888) 382-1222
www.donotcall.gov

You can write a letter and request to be removed from direct marketing databases for five years. Be sure to include your name, home phone number, address, and your signature. If your address changes, you must make another request.

Recap & Review

You Wouldn't Buy an $1,800 T-shirt

BY JON ACUFF

My mom once bought a vacuum cleaner from a door-to-door salesman. I can't remember if he closed the sale by sucking up a bowling ball or cleaning blood off our carpet or some other feat, but whatever he did, it worked. She went for it. She bought it right there on the spot, much to the chagrin of my father.

Some people don't like door-to-door salesmen. I don't have a problem with them, because I know how hard they actually work and that lots of them are honest, reputable folks. But some people find that method of selling intrusive. It feels a little like they're invading your personal space and convincing you to buy something you really don't want or need. Asking them to leave feels like a mini-confrontation, and that's hard sometimes. But compared to the technique I hate the most, door-to-door salesmen are the kindest people on the planet.

What technique am I so opposed to?

Credit card location marketing.

I invented that term, because I don't know if we as a culture have agreed on one phrase to describe when credit cards go to college campuses, malls, downtown areas and bars to market their wares.

We've been so accustomed to this practice that we don't even notice it, but there are three distinct reasons why this practice should frustrate you:

1. You Should Never Pay Interest on M&M's®.

One Christmas season at the mall, I saw a table offering a free large bag of M&M's if you signed up for a credit card. They were offering a $2 bag of candy as an incentive to pay potentially hundreds, if not thousands of dollars in interest on the purchases you make with that card. Are we Hansel and Gretel, so easily tricked by the promise of "free" candy that we would let the big bad wolf of credit cards into our finances? (Double fairy tale reference? Yahtzee®!)

2. Credit Card Companies Chum the Waters.

When you want to catch a shark, you go to where the sharks feed. You take your boat to seal island and throw your hook in, hoping that in the frenzy of eating, the sharks won't be able to tell the difference between a seal and bait. Credit card companies do the same thing. The reason they go to the mall is that you're already in shopping mode. There's blood in the water; you're already in the mood to spend some money. *Sign up for a credit card I don't need? Sure! The more, the merrier!* Worst of all is credit cards that go on spring break to chase college kids. Convincing beach-crazed college students to sign up for a credit card so they can get a free T-shirt is practically criminal. If any other company preyed on college students that way, we'd be outraged; but it's normal in the world of credit cards, so we don't even notice. Shame on us.

3. The Only Moment They Talk About is Right Now.

The next time you try to buy a used car, I can promise you the dealer will not say, "This car will drive awesome today. It is such a great car for you to drive today. You will love today's performance. Let's not discuss tomorrow, though—I'm not sure it will still be working." That would be ridiculous. We know the car will work right now, but what about later? When it comes to car shopping, we care about the long-term performance of the car. We question the reliability and the maintenance and a million other factors that impact the lifetime of the car. But not when we sign up for a new credit card on location. "Do you want to save 10% on your purchases today?" It's all about the moment. Not tomorrow's purchases, or the long-term interest we'll pay over time. We're told to focus on the purchases that are right in front of us. Carpe diem, seize the credit!

I hope the next time you're approached by a credit card company when you are out and about, you'll remember this list. Whether you're a college student in Cancun or a mom at the mall, the principles are the same.

That glittery thing dangling in front of you is actually a fishing hook, not a free T-shirt or a bag of candy.

Chapter 8 Key Concepts

- Identity theft is on the rise! Be careful with your personal information, including drivers license, Social Security number, account numbers, phone numbers, addresses and passwords.
- Do not fall for the "I have to build up my credit score" myth. A FICO score is an "I love debt" score.
- Check your credit report annually.
- Remember The Federal Fair Debt Collection Practices Act sets up restrictions that creditors must follow.
- Always set your priorities by the Four Walls: food, shelter, clothing and transportation.

RECAP & REVIEW

Video Section Answers

1. Credit Score
2. FICO
3. Debt
4. 7
5. 10
6. Inaccurate
7. 79%
8. 25%
9. 30%
10. 22%
11. Annually
12. White Collar
13. Fraud Victim
14. Police Report
15. Theft
16. Nothing
17. Nothing
18. Fraud Victim
19. Documentation
20. Persistent
21. Hobby
22. Remove
23. 30
24. Certified
25. 30
26. Entire
27. Complaints
28. Plan
29. Money
30. Salespeople
31. Telemarketers
32. Turnover
33. Emotion
34. Necessities
35. Harassment
36. 8 a.m.
37. 9 p.m.
38. Work
39. Certified Mail
40. All
41. Lawsuit
42. Negotiations
43. Take
44. Garnish
45. Credit Report
46. Pro rata
47. $10,000
48. 10
49. Lose
50. Judgment
51. Garnishment
52. Slow Pay

CHAPTER 8

Case Studies

Michelle and a New Car

After Michelle graduated from college, she decided to purchase a car. She was doing well with the payments, and then things got busy and she fell behind. She started making car payments with her credit card, and now she is behind on both her credit card and car payments. A collector has been calling her at work and threatening to garnish her wages if she doesn't find a way to get current. She is terrified and is considering using her rent payment to make the other payments so the collector will stop calling.

1. Formulate a strategy for Michelle to overcome her fear and deal with the collector.
2. Is it smart for Michelle to use her rent money to make other payments? Why or why not?
3. What solutions would you offer Michelle in negotiating with the collector?

Jeremy and the Loan

Jeremy graduated from college two years ago with a degree in communications. He landed a great job making $40,000 a year. He plans to save up enough money so he can purchase a home with 100% down. Last week Jeremy received a call from the bank telling him that he was late making payments on his loan. The problem is, Jeremy doesn't have a loan with that bank, or any other bank, because he is debt-free.

1. What problem does Jeremy most likely have and how would you help him resolve this issue?
2. Predict the consequences if Jeremy ignores this issue.
3. What rights does Jeremy have in protecting himself?
4. Is there a way he could avoid this situation in the future? If so, how?

Lauren and the Apartment

Lauren is 19 and has never owned a credit card. She plans to move off campus next semester because she's tired of living in the dorm. The apartment complex she's inquiring about runs background checks and views the credit reports of all the prospective tenants. She knows her credit score is zero, and she's worried that will keep her from getting into the apartment complex.

1. What can Lauren do to improve her chances of getting a low rate at the apartment complex?
2. Is it a bad thing to have a credit score of zero? Why or why not?
3. Should Lauren open a credit card account so she can start establishing a credit score? Why or why not?
4. Does Lauren have any other living options?

CHAPTER

8

Money in Review

RECAP & REVIEW

Matching

Match each term to its definition below.

a. FICO score	f. Identity theft
b. Collectors	g. Credit bureau
c. Garnishment	h. FFDCPA
d. Pro rata	i. Fraud
e. Four walls	

1 ______ Gives creditors a "fair share"

2 ______ "I love debt" score

3 ______ Using another person's information to obtain goods or services

4 ______ TransUnion

5 ______ Court order allowing a lender to take money directly from the debtor's paycheck

6 ______ Trained salespeople or telemarketers

7 ______ Food, shelter, clothing, transportation

True or False

Determine whether these statements are true or false. Change the false statements to read true.

8 **T / F :** You should always pay the collectors first.

9 **T / F :** The best way to deal with debt is with a plan.

10 **T / F :** The Federal Fair Debt Collection Practices Act allows creditors to call between 7:00 a.m. and 10:00 p.m.

11 **T / F :** If you are a victim of identity theft, you are only responsible for the first $250 of debt.

12 **T / F :** You should check your credit report every year.

Multiple Choice

13 Passed in 1977 to protect you from unfair collectors:

a. FDIC
b. FHA
c. FFDCPA
d. FFCRA

14 Which of the following is one of the Four Walls:

a. cable television
b. rent payment
c. cell phone bill
d. designer jeans

15 It is a good idea to check your credit report:

a. You don't need to if you've never used debt
b. every year
c. every three years
d. every five years

16 Which of the following tactics are collectors likely to use?

a. lying
b. harassment
c. being friendly
d. all of the above

17 Which of the following is not a factor in determining a FICO score?

a. paying cash for all purchases
b. getting a personal loan from the bank
c. using credit cards
d. all of the above

18 Which piece of information, if stolen, is not likely to lead to identity theft?

a. drivers license
b. library card
c. credit card number
d. Social Security number

19 The Pro rata plan includes which of the following elements:

a. repayment of debt as soon as possible
b. using the Four Walls to set priorities
c. giving a percentage of debt to each creditor
d. all of the above

Short Answer

20 What is the best way to deal with collectors who break the law?

21 Explain the steps to take if you find an error on your credit report.

22 List some ways to protect yourself from identity theft.

23 Describe some common tactics used by collectors. Why do they use these?

24 Refute the myth, "I need to build my credit score."

25 How can a person live comfortably without having a credit score?

RECAP & REVIEW

Notes

CHAPTER 9

Insurance

UNIT 2: DEVELOPING YOUR SKILLS

As a college student, you probably aren't excited about spending money on insurance, especially if you're struggling to make ends meet. However, it's incredibly important to be prepared for unexpected disasters. You never know what the future holds and you'll need that insurance when you least expect it!

Learning Outcomes

Explain why insurance is an essential part of a healthy financial plan.

- The purpose of insurance is to transfer risk from you to the insurance company. Without insurance, certain losses can bankrupt you.

Identify and describe the seven basic types of insurance coverage needed.

- Homeowner's or Renter's Insurance
- Auto Insurance
- Health Insurance
- Disability Insurance (when you are established in your career)
- Long-Term Care Insurance (when you are 60 or older)
- Identity Theft Protection
- Life Insurance

Differentiate between term and cash value life insurance.

- Term life insurance is for a specified period, is substantially cheaper, and has no savings plan built into it. Cash value life insurance is normally for life and is more expensive because it funds a savings plan. Term is definitely the wiser choice.

Key Terms

Claim: paperwork filed with an insurance company in order to get them to cover a loss

Coverage: applies to the amount of protection you have through an insurance company in the event of a loss

Deductible: amount you have to pay out of pocket for expenses before the insurance company will begin to cover all or a portion of the remaining costs

Liability: the state or quality of being obligated according to law or equity

Out-of-Pocket Expense: a specific amount of money that you are required to pay

Policy: describes the type of coverage in an insurance agreement

Premiums: amount you pay monthly, quarterly, semiannually or annually to purchase different types of insurance

CHAPTER 9

Reading

The following excerpt is from *Dave Ramsey's Complete Guide to Money.* In this passage, Dave Ramsey talks about the ins and outs of insurance and how the right types of insurance will save you a lot of headaches when accidents happen.

I get to have a lot of fun, but insurance is one area where even I start to yawn a little bit. Insurance isn't all that exciting—unless you fail to get this stuff done and then wind up with an exciting stack of bills after an exciting emergency! I cannot say it often enough, loud enough or long enough: Get this stuff taken care of! If you don't have health insurance, life insurance and a will in place, do not go to bed until it is done! It is *that* important.

There are a lot of traps and gimmicks in the insurance world, so I'm going to walk you through exactly what you need—and a few things you absolutely *don't.*

Insurance Basics

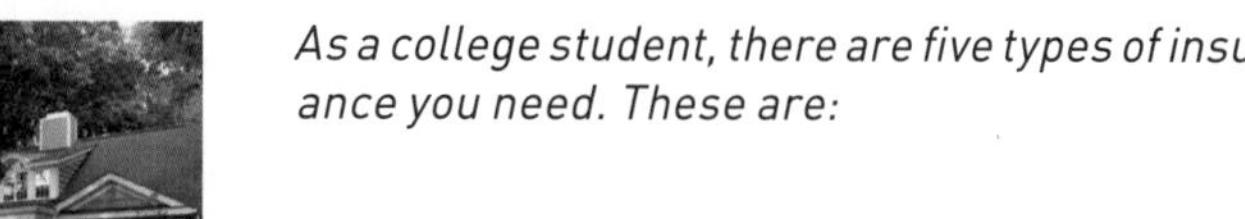

Nobody really *likes* spending money on insurance. It's pretty much the only thing we pay for—and over time spend a lot of money on—and hope we never have to use. But when that time comes, when something major and unexpected happens, we suddenly *love* insurance—as long as we have the right kind.

There are seven key areas of insurance that you need to understand and get—immediately—if you don't have them. They are:

1. **Homeowner's or Renter's:** Save money by raising the deductible. Carry adequate liability. Umbrella policies are a good idea once you have some assets that need an extra layer of protection.

2. **Auto:** Save money by raising the deductible. Carry adequate liability. On older cars, you may consider saving money by dropping your collision coverage (as long as you can afford to buy a replacement car out of pocket).

3. **Health:** Save money by raising the deductible and stop-loss amount. Never accept a maximum payout limit from the insurance company. Check into the Health Savings Account to see if it's a good fit for your family.

4. **Disability:** Sign up for disability insurance once you are established in your career. This replaces your income if a disability prevents you from working. Own-occ coverage provides an income for a specified period, giving you time to learn a new trade if a disability prevents you from continuing your current occupation. Stay away from short-term policies (five years or less).

5. **Long-Term Care:** Buy it the day you turn 60 years old. You may need to have this conversation with your aging parents, especially if you'll be responsible for their elder care.

6. **Identity Theft Protection:** Don't buy a policy that only provides credit report monitoring; you can do that on your own. Only buy those that provide clean-up services. That's the risk you really want to transfer to professionals.

7. **Life Insurance:** Only buy term life insurance. Never mix investments with your insurance. Get 10 times your income, and don't forget the stay-at-home mom. Insurance is not a permanent need, so good term coverage will give you time to become self-insured.

The primary purpose of each one of these is the same: to transfer risk. That's what insurance does. Its sole job is to transfer the risk of financial loss *from* you and *to* the insurance company. Picture it like a big umbrella over your financial life. Without it, you'll be caught out in the rain!

As a college student, there are five types of insurance you need. These are:

Homeowner's/Renter's and Auto Insurance

We can handle these two together, because they're pretty similar. The main job of both is to cover loss or damage to your property (house or car), and to protect you from liability. Homeowner's and auto insurance can get expensive, though. Car insurance, especially, goes way up and down depending on your driving record, how many accidents you've had, how old (or young) you are and several other factors.

Figuring Your Deductible

The best way to keep premiums down is to get a higher-than-normal deductible. A deductible is what you have to pay out of pocket before the insurance company kicks in any money. So if you're flat broke, neck-deep in debt and have two nickels in your savings account, you'd probably opt for a cheap,

$250 or even $100 deductible, right? Big mistake! That's going to cost you a ton of money, maybe 40% or more than a higher deductible would cost!

Health Insurance

I think it's ridiculous that I even have to say this, but the number of uninsured people I talk to every week causes me to say it anyway: You absolutely have to have health insurance! Only 59% of people have health insurance furnished at work.[1] That means the rest of us have to pay all or part of it ourselves. How do we save money on health coverage? The same way we save in other areas of insurance: We raise the deductible and/or your coinsurance amount.

Identity Theft Protection Insurance

The fastest growing white-collar crime in North America today is identity theft. Some studies report that as many as one in three Americans have their identities stolen, and that number grows each year.[2] And if it happens to you, you can expect to spend about 600 hours cleaning up the mess![3] Basically, if someone rips off your identity, getting everything ironed out will be your full-time, 40-hour job for the next 15 weeks. Personally, I don't have time for that, so I better have some quality ID theft protection in place.

When you start looking around at this, you'll find a ton of bad policies and bad information. Do some diligence and check the reviews of the company you're dealing with. One "leading" provider can't stay out of fraud lawsuits long enough to get anything done! Also, a lot of places only offer basic credit-report monitoring. Do not fall for this! That's something you can do yourself. In fact, you should be checking your credit report at least once a year anyway.

Life Insurance

When you're 25, you feel bulletproof, like you have all the time in the world. If you wait until you get sick, you've waited too long. Remember, insurance is all about risk. It's easy and fairly inexpensive to get life insurance when you're young and healthy, but if you wait until after you've been diagnosed with some serious health problem, you're probably out of luck. You'll either be denied coverage or you'll end up paying astronomical premiums on a sub-par policy. So if you don't have life insurance in place, make the call TODAY! You never know what could happen tomorrow.[4]

> **"The primary purpose of each one of these is the same: to transfer risk. That's what insurance does."**

Insurance is a vital part of your financial plan. When accidents happen—and you can be certain they will happen—you must have insurance in place to avoid a potentially disastrous financial hit. Don't make the mistake of ignoring the importance of insurance.

---

1. "Income Stable, Poverty Rate Increases, Percentage of Americans Without Health Insurance Unchanged," U.S. Census Bureau News, August 30, 2005.
2. "Identity Theft: The Aftermath 2006," Identity Theft Resource Center, www.idtheftcenter.org.
3. Ibid.
4. *Dave Ramsey's Complete Guide to Money*, Chapter 7

CHAPTER 9

Video: Sections 1–4

The insurance industry has about **2.3 million** salary jobs. Growing areas of insurance are medical services and financial services, such as securities and mutual funds.

U.S. BUREAU OF LABOR STATISTICS

"It is unwise to hope for the best without preparing for the worst."

ANONYMOUS

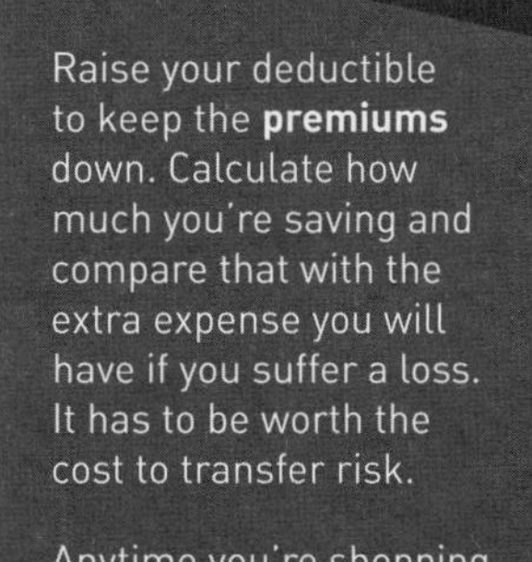

Raise your deductible to keep the **premiums** down. Calculate how much you're saving and compare that with the extra expense you will have if you suffer a loss. It has to be worth the cost to transfer risk.

Anytime you're shopping for insurance, go to an **independent** insurance agent and let them shop among many different plans and companies.

Health, disability, auto and homeowner's insurance catch the big stuff. You handle the little stuff with an emergency fund and solid financial planning.

SECTION 1

Understanding Insurance

Insurance is an essential financial planning tool.

The purpose of insurance is to ________________[1] risk.

Without proper insurance, certain losses can ________________[2] you. Conventional wisdom says that you should transfer risk.

Break-Even Analysis: Method used to evaluate the wisdom of a financial decision by determining the length of time it will take for the cost of the decision to be recouped

Basic Types of Coverage Needed

1. **Homeowner's or Renter's Insurance**
2. **Auto Insurance**
3. **Health Insurance**
4. **Disability Insurance** (when you are established in your career)
5. **Long-Term Care Insurance** (when you are 60 or older)
6. **Identity Theft Protection**
7. **Life Insurance**

?

"My car was recently totaled, but I had full-coverage insurance. The problem is the bank is asking for $3,000 in 30 days because I did not have gap insurance. What is gap insurance?"

DAVE'S ANSWER: Gap insurance covers the difference between what you owe on a car and what the insurance company says it is worth. Your full-coverage policy paid for the current value of the car, but that is less than what you owe the bank. Since you no longer have the car as collateral, the bank is demanding full payment on the loan, or calling their note.

Gap insurance can be pretty expensive, which is another reason not to buy a new car on credit. The minute you drive off the car lot with a new car, it loses value and if you get into an accident, there will be a gap that you are responsible for unless you have gap insurance. All you can do now is pay the bank what you owe and move on, lesson learned.

Types of Insurance

Auto Insurance

Collision: Portion of auto insurance that covers losses due to vehicle damage in an accident

Comprehensive: Pays for damage to your car that is not a result of an accident

If you have a full emergency fund, raise your ____________________.

Carry adequate liability.

Consider dropping your ________________ on older cars.

Discussion Questions: Section 1

- Of the types of insurance college students need, which is the highest priority right now? What about the second highest priority? Finish prioritizing the list and justify your reasons.
- What emergencies should be covered by your emergency fund of three to six months of expenses? On the other hand, what emergencies should be covered by insurance?

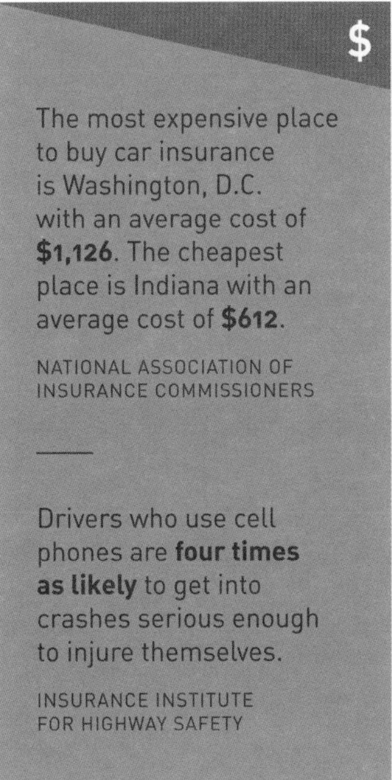

$

The most expensive place to buy car insurance is Washington, D.C. with an average cost of **$1,126**. The cheapest place is Indiana with an average cost of **$612**.

NATIONAL ASSOCIATION OF INSURANCE COMMISSIONERS

Drivers who use cell phones are **four times as likely** to get into crashes serious enough to injure themselves.

INSURANCE INSTITUTE FOR HIGHWAY SAFETY

"I'm glad I understand insurance more, because I honestly had no idea what premiums or deductibles were before this lesson."

STUDENT QUOTES

$

Two-thirds of American renters don't have renter's insurance.

INDEPENDENT INSURANCE AGENTS & BROKERS OF AMERICA

On average, a renter's insurance plan costs roughly **$16 a month**.

ALLSTATE INSURANCE

---

50 million Americans don't have health insurance. This amounts to **16.7%** of the total population.

USA TODAY

People 19 to 24 years old have the highest percentage of uninsured individuals. **30%** of them did not have health insurance last year.

KAISER PERMANENTE INSURANCE

Medical bills and illnesses are the **number one** cause of bankruptcy in the U.S.

HARVARD STUDY

The average cost to insure a family of four is about **$14,000**.

USA TODAY

Homeowner's Insurance

Homeowner's insurance should be "guaranteed ________________ cost."
5

________________ liability policies are a good buy once you have some assets.
6

Umbrella Liability Insurance: High-limit insurance policy that acts as a protective covering over your home and car insurance against liability caused by an accident

Renter's Insurance: Type of insurance that provides coverage for accidents, damages and losses in a rental (apartment or house) or dormitory

Health Insurance

Keys to saving on your health insurance premiums:

Increase your ______________ and/or coinsurance amount.
7

Increase your ______________ - ____________,
8
but never decrease your maximum pay.

See if an ____________, a Health Savings Account, would make sense for your situation.
9

The HSA is a ___________ - ____________________ savings account for medical expenses that works with a high deductible insurance policy.
10

Stop-Loss: Total out-of-pocket expense for health insurance; once reached, the insurance company will pay 100%

Maximum Payment: The amount an insurance company will pay before you are dropped from coverage (with health insurance keep at least a $1 million maximum pay)

Discussion Questions: Section 2

- As a college student, what unexpected accidents could happen to you that would affect your health? Can you afford those medical bills without insurance right now?
- Why is health insurance so expensive? How can you reduce that cost?

Adequate coverage is a must no matter your age.

Think you don't need health insurance? Think again! Of course we're all looking to save money wherever we can. But one area you don't need to skimp on is health insurance. One of the most listed reasons for bankruptcy is unpaid medical bills.

There are hundreds of horror stories about young, single people who choose not to get health insurance because they think they're healthy. Well, you may be healthy at the moment, but you don't know what's going to happen tomorrow! Health problems and accidents seem to happen when you least expect them, always at the worst possible time. Now the single person, who thought he/she was healthy and didn't need insurance, is between a rock and a hard place. So what happens? He/she usually ends up charging the medical bills on a credit card. Within just a few weeks, a once-healthy person is worrying about thousands of dollars of debt.

SECTION 3

Disability Insurance

Disability insurance is designed to replace ________________ lost due to a short-term or permanent disability.
11

Try to buy disability insurance that pays if you cannot perform the job that you were educated or ____________ to do.
12

That is called ______________________, or "own occ," disability. Many times, this is only available for two years.
13

> **Occupational Disability:** Type of insurance that provides an income in case the insured becomes unable to perform the job he/she was educated or trained to do

Beware of ____________ - term policies covering less than ______ years.
14 15

Your coverage should be for _________ of your current income.
16

The ______________ period is the time between the disabling event and when the payments actually begin.
17

A ____________ elimination period will ________________ your premium cost.
18 19

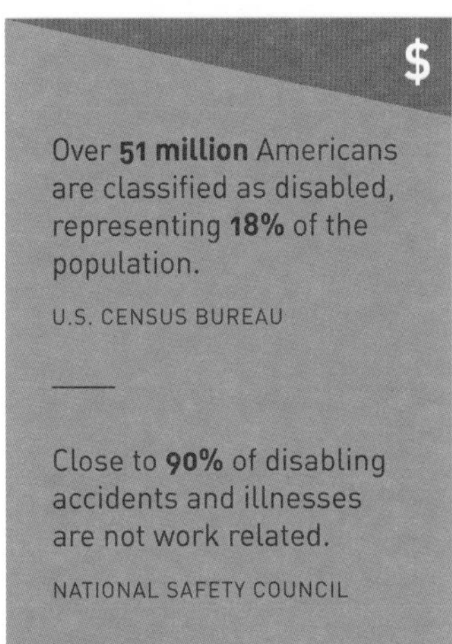

$

Over **51 million** Americans are classified as disabled, representing **18%** of the population.

U.S. CENSUS BUREAU

Close to **90%** of disabling accidents and illnesses are not work related.

NATIONAL SAFETY COUNCIL

Things to Remember About Disability Insurance

Disability insurance is a long-term solution. Your short-term needs should be covered by a full emergency fund of three to six months of expenses.

Buy disability insurance with after-tax dollars. If you become disabled and you bought disability insurance with pre-tax dollars, your disability income will be taxable.

Long-Term Care Insurance

Long-term care insurance is for

__________________ home, assisted living
(20)

facilities or in-home care.

> **Long-Term Care Insurance:** Policy that covers the cost of nursing home or in-home care; recommended for everyone over age 60

____________ of people over the age of 65 will
(21)

require long-term care at some point in their lives.

$

Over **40%** of all seniors will need care in a skilled nursing facility for some portion of their final years.

LONGTERMCARE.GOV

Up to **10 million** Americans are victims of identity theft per year.

JAVELIN STRATEGY AND RESEARCH

Up to **18%** of victims didn't realize their identities were compromised until four years later.

IDENTITY THEFT RESOURCE CENTER

Identity Theft Protection

Don't buy identity theft protection that only provides

credit report ______________________.
(22)

Good protection includes ____________________
(23)

services that assign a ______________________
(24)

to clean up the mess.

> **Restoration Services:** Part of identity theft insurance that assigns a counselor to clean up the mess made when your identity was stolen.

Discussion Questions: Section 3

- Why do you think so few people carry long-term disability coverage? Why is this unwise?
- Do you know anyone whose identity has been compromised? How did it happen? How can you prevent that from happening to you?

Cash Value vs. Term + Roth IRA

CASH VALUE LIFE INSURANCE IS A BAD INVESTMENT. CONSIDER THIS:

For $145 a month, you could have $125,000 in cash value insurance. Or, for that same $145, you could pay $10 a month for $400,000 in 20-year term insurance *and* invest $135 into a Roth IRA. If you start at age 30 your investment will be worth…

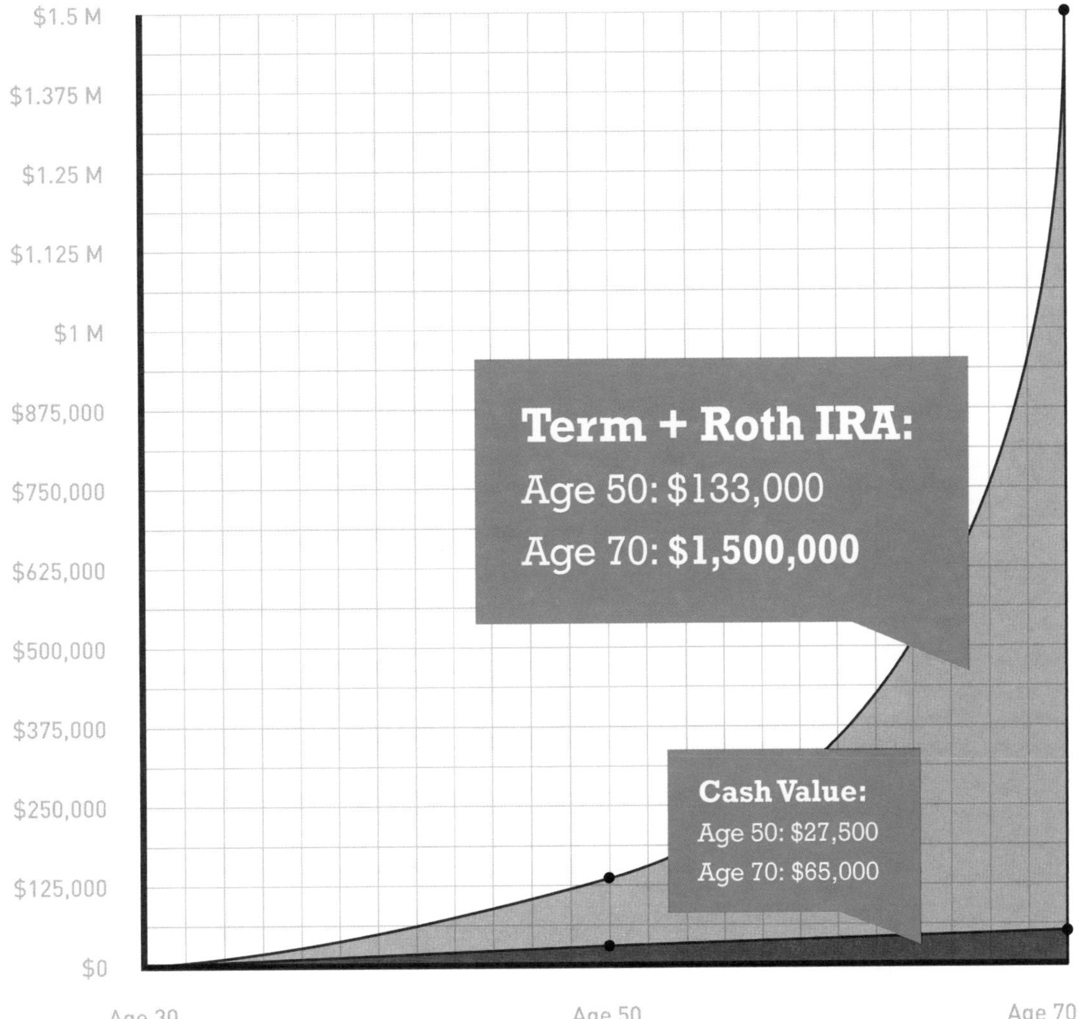

?

"Do young children need life insurance too?"

DAVE'S ANSWER: The people who need life insurance are those with family members depending on them for their livelihood.

Parents should carry about 10 times their annual income in a good, 20-year level term life insurance policy. The only exception for children would be a small rider on the parents' term insurance policy—just enough to take care of a child's funeral expenses—in the event that something awful happens. I did that for years, just a little $15,000 rider, before I decided to self-insure.

$

Almost **one-third** of U.S. households (35 million) don't have any life insurance at all.

LIFE INSURANCE OWNERSHIP STUDY

Half of U.S. households (58 million) readily admit they currently don't have adequate life insurance coverage—the highest level ever.

LIFE INSURANCE OWNERSHIP STUDY

+

Human beings have a 100% mortality rate— we're all going to die someday. If your family depends on your income, it is your responsibility to make sure they'll be taken care of if something were to happen to you.

SECTION 4

Life Insurance

Life insurance is to replace lost income due to ____________.
25

Most people have no ____________ what kind of life insurance they ____________.
26 27

Term Insurance: Life insurance coverage for a specified period of time

Cash Value Insurance: Also known as whole life, universal life, variable life or permanent life insurance; premiums include a death benefit and a plan to build savings within the policy; significantly more expensive than term life insurance

Beneficiary: The recipient of assets passed on from the death of a friend or relative

Two Types of Life Insurance

1. ____________ insurance is for a specified period, is substantially cheaper, and has no savings plan built into it.
28

2. ____________ ____________ insurance is normally for life and is more expensive because it funds a savings plan.
29

The most common insurance myth is that the need for life insurance is a ____________ situation.
30

Twenty years from today, when the children are grown and gone, you are debt-free (including the 15-year mortgage), and you have investments that have grown to a substantial amount, you will have become self- ____________________ (31).

Why Not Life Insurance as an Investment?

1. Returns are historically ______________ (32).

2. When you die with cash value, the insurance company ______________ (33) the cash value.

3. The ______________ (34) deducted from your return are extremely ______________ (35).

Before You Cancel Your Cash Value Policy...

Make sure that you already have a new term policy in place! If, for some reason, you cannot be approved for a new term policy, it is better to hang on to a bad cash value policy than to have nothing at all—until you become self-insured.

> **Self-Insured:** Condition of wealth at which time one no longer needs an outside insurance policy to cover a loss

What to Remember When Purchasing Life Insurance

> **Level Term:** This means you pay the same amount for the entire term of the policy

1. Buy only low-cost level term.

2. Do not forget your spouse.

+

Want to know how to become self-insured? You will learn how to invest to become wealthy in **Chapter 10, Investing**.

"A good rule of thumb is this: you need to have life insurance that pays about 10 TIMES your income, so at a 10% return, your income will be replaced."

DAVE RAMSEY
Financial Expert

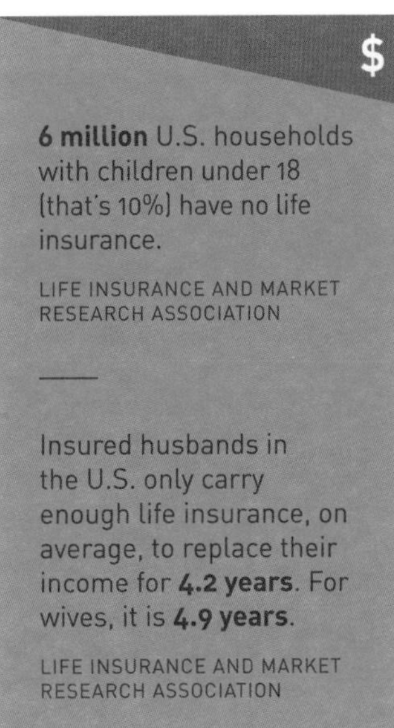

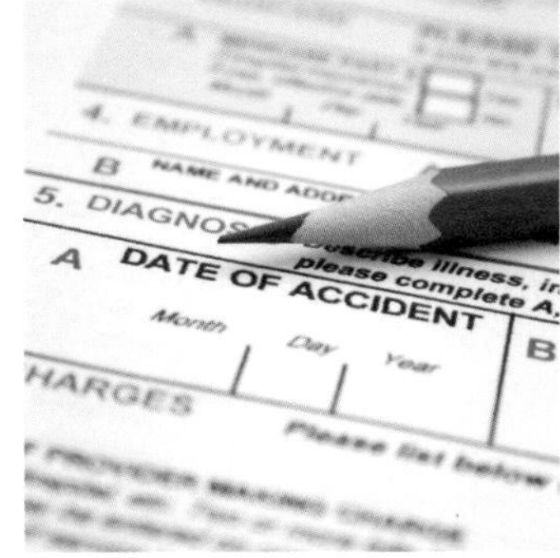

Insurances to Avoid

1. **Credit life/disability:** pays off a borrower's debt if that borrower dies or becomes disabled (your term life insurance already covers this)

2. **Credit card protection:** insures your credit card (you should avoid owning a credit card, period.)

3. **Cancer and hospital indemnity insurance:** insures you against cancer or other medical issues (your health insurance already covers this)

4. **Accidental death:** insures you against unexpected accidents that cause your death (your term life insurance already covers this)

5. **Any insurance with cash value, investments or refunds:** anything that combines insurance with investments is a bad idea

6. **Pre-paid burial policies:** if invested instead, this money would pay for the burial policy many times over

7. **Mortgage life insurance:** pays off your home mortgage if you die unexpectedly or become disabled (your term life insurance, which is 10–15 times cheaper, already covers this)

8. **Any kind of duplicate coverage:** any extra insurance on top of your existing insurance (remember, you only need one policy for each type of insurance); the two companies fight over who pays the bills and nothing gets accomplished

$

Some companies—including insurance companies—will do anything to make a buck. Here are a few bizarre examples of **actual insurance plans** available:

- Alien abduction insurance
- Pet insurance
- Wedding insurance
- Body part insurance

3. Stay away from fancy __________________. (36)

4. Children only need enough for __________________ (37) expenses.

5. You need about _______ (38) times your income. Invested at 10–12%, the annual interest would replace your lost income.

Discussion Questions: Section 4

- Why does cash value insurance look attractive initially? Why is it a terrible choice in the long-run?
- Out of the insurances to avoid, which seems like the worst idea? Justify your reasoning.

Recap & Review

Now that we've covered the seven types of insurance, let's focus on the one we will all use at some point. These simple tips can make a powerful impact over your lifetime of driving.

Distraction from cell phone use while driving (hand held or hands free) extends a driver's reaction as much as having a **blood alcohol concentration of .08%.**

RESEARCH BY UNIVERSITY OF UTAH

The **number one source** of driver inattention is use of a wireless device.

RESEARCH BY VIRGINIA TECH

Top Things to Know About Auto Insurance

BY *MONEY MAGAZINE*

Auto insurance is an important part of owning a vehicle and being a responsible driver. But there are a few things you should know to help you find the right insurer, get the most out of your coverage, and protect your interests when filing a claim.

1. **You're a statistic.** To an insurer, you're not a person—you're a set of risks. An insurer bases its decisions on your "risk factors," including some things that may seem unrelated to driving a car.
2. **Insurers differ.** Prices can vary from company to company. You can save money by comparison shopping.
3. **Don't just look at price.** A low price is no bargain if an insurer takes forever to service your claim. Research the insurer's record for claims service, as well as its financial stability.
4. **Go beyond the basics.** Although most states require only a minimum of liability coverage, you should look for a minimum coverage of $500,000.
5. **Demand discounts.** Insurers provide discounts to reward behavior that reduces risk. However, Americans waste some $300 billion a year because they forget to ask for discounts!
6. **At claims time**, your insurer isn't necessarily your friend. Your idea of fair compensation may not match that of your insurer. Your insurer's job is to restore you financially. Your job is to prove your losses so that you get what you need.
7. **Prepare** before you have to file a claim. Keep your policy updated and reread it before you file a claim, so there are no surprises.

RECAP & REVIEW

Chapter 9 Key Concepts

- Insurance is not an investment. Its only function is to transfer risk.
- You must have auto insurance if you have a car.
- Renter's insurance is essential for renters, including when you live in a dorm at college.
- Health insurance is important, even if you have to pay more than you would like.
- Raising your deductible can save money on your premiums.
- Identity theft is on the rise. Guard your personal information at all times and buy identity theft protection that includes restoration services.

Video Section Answers

1. Transfer
2. Bankrupt
3. Deductible
4. Collision
5. Replacement
6. Umbrella
7. Deductible
8. Stop-Loss
9. HSA
10. Tax-Sheltered
11. Income
12. Trained
13. Occupational
14. Short
15. 5
16. 65%
17. Elimination
18. Longer
19. Lower
20. Nursing
21. 69%
22. Monitoring
23. Restoration
24. Counselor
25. Death
26. Idea
27. Own
28. Term
29. Cash Value
30. Permanent
31. Insured
32. Low
33. Keeps
34. Fees
35. High
36. Options
37. Burial
38. 10

CHAPTER 9

Case Studies

Brianna's Life Insurance Plan

Brianna, a recent college graduate, is single and lives on her own. She has an entry-level job as a reporter at a newspaper and is trying to save up money to purchase a new car. Her brother sold her a $100,000 whole life insurance policy, and she is paying $115 per month in premiums. She started doing some research about life insurance and discovered term insurance. She's considering switching to term insurance, but she's worried about hurting her brother's feelings.

1. Should Brianna stick with the whole life insurance she bought from her brother? Why or why not?
2. Which insurance option is the better option for Brianna?
3. If Brianna does switch to term insurance, help her come up with logical reasons for the switch.

Garret's Car Insurance Options

Garret has an older car worth about $5,000. He thinks he is paying too much for auto insurance and wants to find out how he can save money. He decides to look into raising his deductible from $250 to $1,000. By doing this, he can save $200 per year.

1. If Garret raises the deductible, will it be worth the risk? Defend your answer.
2. What if Garret drops the collision on his car? Would that be a smart idea?
3. Are there other car insurance options that Garret can take advantage of to save money?

John's Healthcare Plan

John is a sophomore in college and used to be on his mother's health insurance plan. His mom recently changed jobs and her benefits package changed. As a result, she can no longer afford to pay for John's health insurance. He is a healthy 20-year-old and a full-time student. He works part time to cover his living expenses, but doesn't have much left over at the end of each month. He's saving up for a car and hates the idea of spending money on health insurance when he hardly ever goes to the doctor.

1. Explain the different health insurance options available for John and assess the risk vs. the reward of each option.
2. Should John go without health insurance and continue saving up for a car? Why or why not?
3. Would a Health Savings Account (HSA) be a good option for John? Why or why not?

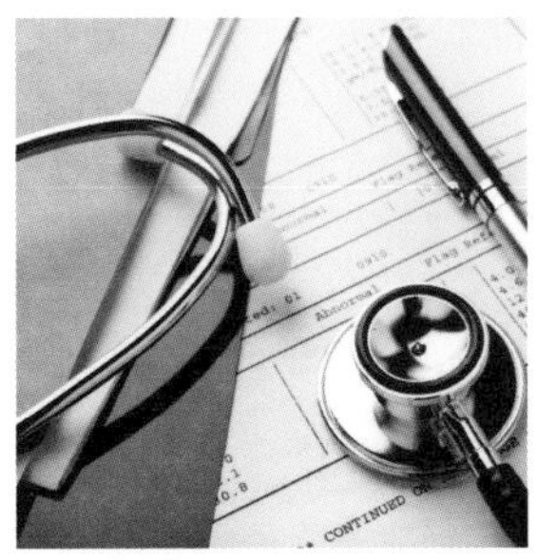

CHAPTER

9 Money in Review

RECAP & REVIEW

Matching

Match each term to its definition below.

a. comprehensive	d. 20
b. collision	e. premium
c. 10	f. out-of-pocket expenses

1 _____ The amount you pay for an insurance policy

2 _____ Costs that insurance doesn't cover; amount you pay

3 _____ The amount of life insurance you should have is ____ times your income

4 _____ Covers damage to a car if there is an accident

5 _____ Covers damage to a car if a tree falls on it

True or False

Determine whether these statements are true or false. Change the false statements to read true.

6 **T / F :** The deductible on any insurance is the portion you have to pay before insurance covers any expenses.

7 **T / F :** If you have an older car, you can consider dropping liability.

8 **T / F :** The purpose of insurance is to transfer risk.

9 **T / F :** Cash value insurance is a good way to invest since it has a savings plan built in.

10 **T / F :** Neither accidental death nor cancer insurance are good insurance policies to carry.

11 **T / F :** Short-term disability is covered by your emergency fund, so only buy long-term disability.

12 **T / F :** The best type of identity theft insurance only provides credit-report monitoring.

Multiple Choice

13 The time between the disabling event and the beginning of payments:

a. deductible
b. out of pocket
c. elimination period
d. stop gap

14 Life insurance policy for a specific period of time:

a. term
b. whole life
c. universal
d. level

15 What can you do to decrease the cost of insurance policies?

a. raise the deductible
b. shop around for rates
c. take advantage of applicable discounts
d. all of the above

Name the Type of Insurance

16 ______________ Covers restoration and monitoring services.

17 ______________ Covers damage to a vehicle

18 ______________ Covers the contents of an apartment

19 ______________ Designed to replace income lost if you cannot perform your job

20 ______________ Covers assisted living, in-home or nursing home care

21 ______________ Designed to replace income lost due to death

Short Answer

22 Explain at least two ways you can save on auto insurance.

23 Why do you need renter's insurance if you don't own valuable items?

24 Explain why life insurance is not a good savings plan.

25 When do you need renter's insurance?

CHAPTER 9

Notes

UNIT 3

CONSIDERING THE FUTURE

CHAPTERS 10–12

CHAPTER

10 Investments

UNIT 3: CONSIDERING THE FUTURE

Becoming wealthy is at the top of everyone's life-goals list, which is why there's always a new "get-rich-quick" scheme. However, it's important to remember that true, reliable wealth building is surprisingly simple—and even a little boring. It's no secret: Investing consistently over time eventually makes you a millionaire.

Learning Outcomes

Explain the KISS rule of investing.

- The "Keep It Simple, Stupid" rule means successful investments are ones that are simple. Avoid complicated investments that are difficult to understand or explain.

Examine the relationship between diversification and risk.

- Diversification, or the spreading around of your investments, causes more stable growth. Many companies work together to increase your investment's value, which in turn lowers risk.

Compare and contrast different types of investments:

- **Money market mutual funds:** A low-risk mutual fund with investments in short-term (usually 90 days or less) maturities; great for your emergency fund
- **Bonds:** Debt tool where an issuer owes you money; a form of I.O.U.
- **Single stocks:** An investment in one particular stock only
- **Mutual funds:** Pool of money managed by an investment company and invested in multiple companies, bonds, etc.
- **Rental real estate:** Buying real estate to rent out as an investment
- **Annuities:** Contract sold by an insurance company, designed to provide payments to the holder at specified intervals, usually after retirement

Key Terms

Diversification: to spread around one's investment dollars among several different classes of financial assets and among the securities of many issuers; results in lowered risk

Investments: account or arrangement in which one would put their money for long-term growth; should not be withdrawn for a suggested minimum of five years

Liquidity: quality of an asset that permits it to be converted quickly into cash without loss of value; availability of money; when there is more liquidity, there is typically less return

Portfolio: a list of your investments

Risk: degree of uncertainty of return on an asset; in business, the likelihood of loss or reduced profit

Risk-Return Ratio: relationship of substantial reward in comparison to the amount of risk taken

Share: piece of ownership in a company or mutual fund

CHAPTER 10

Reading

The following excerpt is from *Dave Ramsey's Complete Guide to Money*. In this section, Dave explains why it's so important to understand investments before you invest. Most of the time, that involves just keeping it simple and picking the right advisor who will explain things to you in terms that make sense.

"Oh, Dave, Investing Is So BORING!"

Every time I teach on investing, I can immediately spot the Nerds and the Free Spirits in the room. The Nerds perk up, pull out their pencils, and start to run the numbers in the margins of their notebooks. The Free Spirits? Well, they go to their happy place. I can see all the Free Spirits in the room start to float out of their bodies. Their eyes glaze over and all of a sudden, they are running through a wheat field or singing in the rain in their minds. They just totally check out.

So here's my suggestion for those of you who find this stuff boring. When I say "investing," picture a vacation home in the French countryside. Or picture a ski trip with your whole family in a beautiful chalet that you've rented for a month. Or picture your spouse being home with you to laugh and play, and to just enjoy life. That's what investing is all about. It's not about the dollars; it's about the kind of life you want to live later on. What you do today will determine that.

"I'm on Baby Step 1! I Can't Even Think About Investing Right Now!"

I know you may just now be getting started with this whole process, and that's okay. Wherever you are in the Baby Steps, I'm on your team. But even if investing is a few years off, you need to learn some basics so you'll know what to do next as you knock out the Baby Steps.

I love to ski. In the snow, on the water, I don't care where. I just like moving fast and having two long planks strapped to my feet. If you've ever been on skis, you know the first thing they tell you is that your whole body will go wherever you're looking. If you're looking straight ahead, you'll go straight ahead. If you look to the right, you'll drift right. If you look down, don't forget to tuck and roll, because you're about to hit the ground. That's true with your money, too. I promise, if you do the things we teach, you're going to get out of debt and save up a full emergency fund faster than you ever thought possible. And when you do, it'll be time to invest for wealth building. So let's get your eyes on that goal, okay?

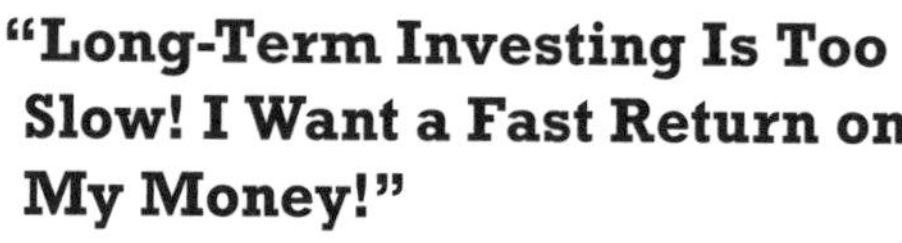

"Long-Term Investing Is Too Slow! I Want a Fast Return on My Money!"

The only people who get rich from get-rich-quick schemes are the people selling them. They play on your emotions, set you up for a quick return, take your money, and then leave you high and dry. And the truth is, risky investments have become a playground for people with gambling problems. Hoping to turn $100 into $1,000 overnight isn't investing; it's gambling. You've heard me say before that the stuff I teach isn't always easy and it isn't a quick fix, but it absolutely works every time.

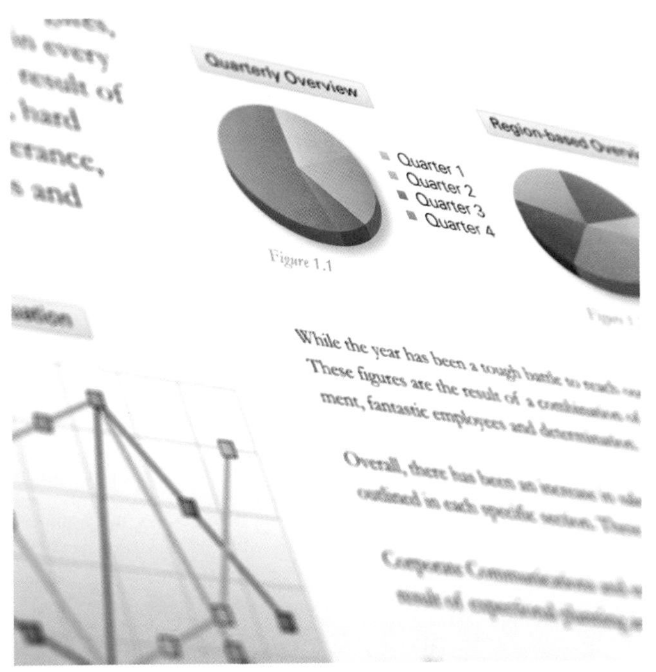

KISS Your Investing

Back when I was just starting to sell houses, one of my biggest problems was that I talked too much. Hard to believe, right? More times than I'd like to remember, I just talked and talked and talked, and ended up talking myself out of a sale. The reason is that I was flooding buyers with information—more information than they wanted or even needed! I went on and on about all these features, contract issues, upgrades, neighborhood stats and everything else I could think of to say. Fortunately, I finally figured out how to shut up, but not before a lot of good people missed out on some good houses, just because I was overcomplicating the whole process.

> **"It's not about the dollars; it's about the kind of life you want to live later on. What you do today will determine that."**

Investing gets like that. Sometimes, "financial people" come in and start talking about all the options and tricks and strategies, and our eyes glaze over. As a result, we either sign whatever they put in front of us and let them make all our financial decisions, or we just decide it's not worth it and walk away. Either way, we lose.

That's why I always recommend the KISS strategy for investing: "Keep It Simple, Stupid." No, this does not mean that you are stupid if you make simple investments! Just the opposite. I'm just saying that people get in trouble when they overcomplicate things. I've met with a lot of really, really rich people over the years—multi-millionaires and even several multi-billionaires—and most of them have a simple, even boring, investment plan. They do the same few, simple things over and over again, over a long period of time. Why? Because it works.

But a lot of people truly believe that investing has to be complicated, or that there's some trick to it—as if there's one big secret to investing, and those people who figure it out get to be rich. But nothing will send you to the poorhouse faster than stupid, long-shot, high-risk investments. It's like that old joke: What's the most common last words for a redneck? "Hey y'all, watch this!" (Don't be offended; I'm a redneck myself!) In investing, I think the most famous last words would be, "Don't worry, I know what I'm doing!"

"Financial People"

Too often, we play these games because "financial people" have sat across the table and talked down to us like we're children. That drives me crazy! A financial advisor is usually an invaluable part of your team, as long as he remembers what his primary job is: to teach you how to make your own decisions. You need someone with the heart of a teacher who will sit down with you and teach you this stuff, so that you can then make your own decisions about how, where and how much to invest. You should never buy any financial product or service if you can't explain to someone else how it works. That level of education is what you're paying your advisor for!

I can only think of two words for financial and insurance people who talk down to you or won't (or can't) teach you how their products work: "YOU'RE FIRED!" Remember, these people work for you. If they aren't doing the job you're paying them for, cut them loose.[1]

Whether you are investing now, or plan to in the future, make sure you understand your investments. If someone asks you to explain your investments, how would you respond? This is your money, and it's your job to understand how you are investing it.

1. *Dave Ramsey's Complete Guide to Money*, Chapter 9

CHAPTER

10 Video: Sections 1–5

SECTION 1

KISS Rule of Investing

Keep it ______________[1], ______________[2]!

Never invest purely for ____________ ____________[3].

Never invest using ______________[4] money.

Diversification

______________[5] means to spread around.

Diversification ______________[6] risk.

Speculative: Purchasing risky investments that present the possibility of large profits, but also post a higher-than-average possibility of loss

Discussion Questions: Section 1

- Why is investing intimidating to many people? At what point is the risk worth it?
- Other than in investing, when does the concept of diversification yield positive results?

SECTION 2

Risk–Return Ratio and Liquidity

With virtually all investments, as the ________[7] goes up, so does the potential return.

When discussing investments, ______________[8] is availability.

Savings Account: Accounts at financial institutions that allow regular deposits and withdrawals; the minimum required deposit, fees charged, and interest rate paid varies among providers

As there is more liquidity, there is typically ______________[9] return.

$

The smartest investment you can make is in yourself. As a college student, you have two goals: **stay in school** and **stay out of debt**.

People with a bachelor's degree or higher have unemployment rates that are about **half the unemployment rate** for people with just a high school diploma.

BUREAU OF LABOR STATISTICS

"Diversification is a protection against ignorance."

WARREN BUFFET
Famous American Investor

+

The Securities Exchange Commission (SEC) is the government agency responsible for regulating the stock market. It was created in 1934 to increase public trust after the 1929 stock market crash and the years of the Great Depression.

The Power of Diversification

WHERE YOU PUT YOUR MONEY MATTERS

What would happen if two people each invested $10,000—one diversifies, the other does not—and left it alone for 25 years? Assume interest is compounded monthly.

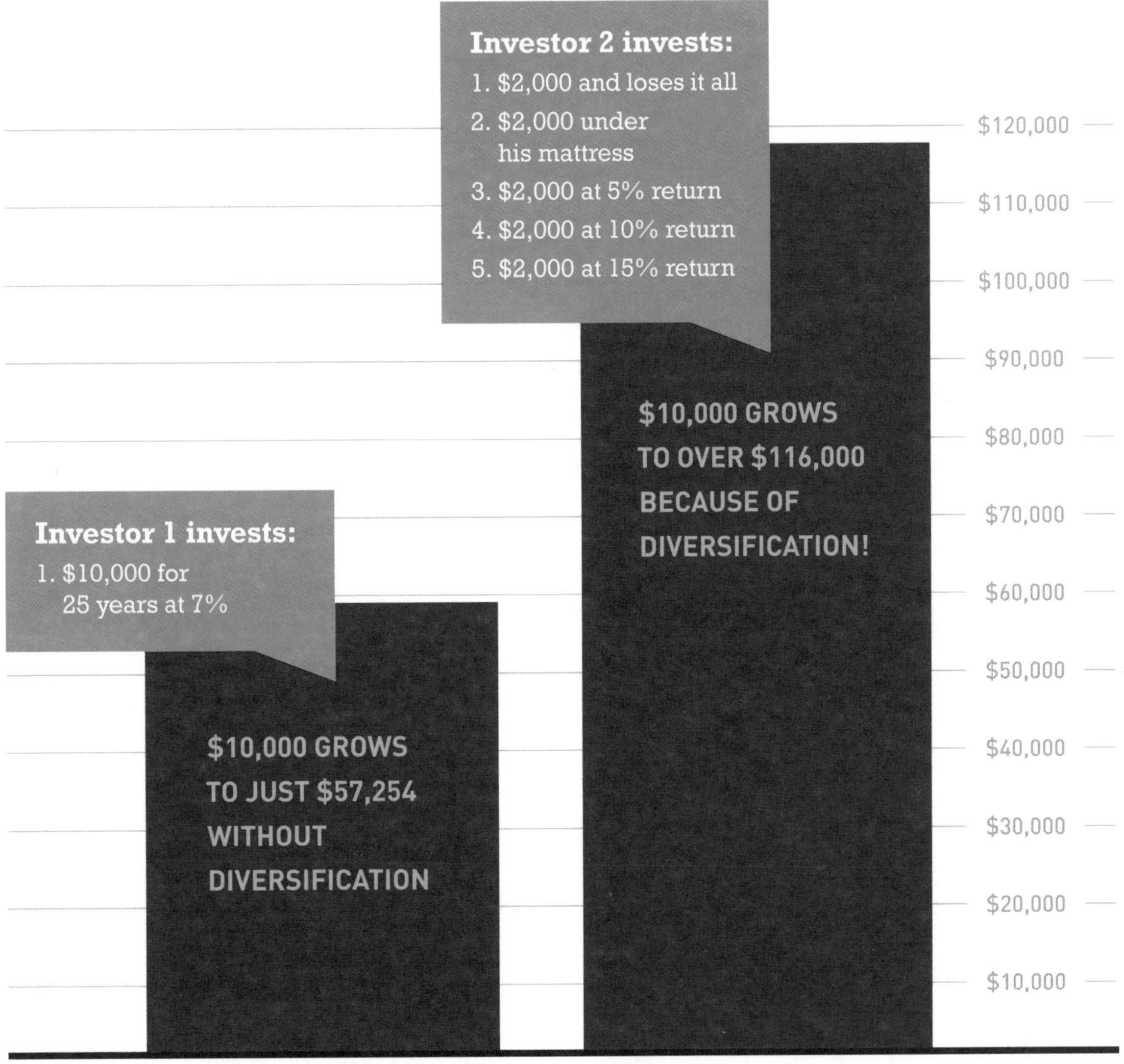

A difference of almost $59,000!

?

"I'm 21 and I'll be receiving an inheritance of about $40,000 soon. I don't know anything about investing and I don't want to lose all this money. I don't have any debt, so what should I do?"

DAVE'S ANSWER: I'm glad you're asking questions. One of the fastest ways to lose money is to put it into something when you don't know how the investment works.

You don't need to change your major to finance to make this happen, but you do have a $40,000 responsibility that you didn't have before. For now, a simple savings account is fine. I'd park $30,000 in there and learn about investing in the meantime. Then use $5,000 to set up an emergency fund, and blow $5,000 on some things just for you. After all, spending and having fun with money is one of the things it's good for!

Here's something to think about once you've educated yourself on investing. If you put that remaining $30,000 in a good mutual fund, by the time you're ready to retire, you'll be looking at millions. Talk about being able to retire with dignity and change your family tree!

"I learned that wealth building doesn't have to begin once I get a job; it can begin NOW."

COLLEGE STUDENT

$

Only **3%** of retirement investors are between the ages of 25 and 29, and they only hold three-tenths of 1% of the assets. Their average balance is $8,663.

THE IRA INVESTOR PROFILE

When it comes to their finances, twentysomethings are hardly carefree.

- **60%** feel they face more financial pressure than past generations.
- **30%** worry frequently about their debts.
- **55%** don't have investments in an IRA or a 401(k) account.

MONEY MAGAZINE

Types of Investments

1. Money Markets

A C.D. is a ____________ ____

____________, typically at a bank.
10

Certificate of Deposit (C.D.): Usually at a bank; savings account with a slightly higher interest rate because of a longer savings commitment (i.e. six months, one year, etc.)

Money market mutual funds are ________ (11) risk money market accounts with check-writing privileges. These are great for

____________ ____________.
12

Money Market Mutual Fund: Mutual fund that seeks to maintain stable share price and to earn current income by investing in interest-bearing instruments with short-term (usually 90 days or less) maturities

2. Single Stocks

Single stock investing carries an extremely

________ degree of risk.
13

Single Stocks: An investment in one particular stock only

Discussion Questions: Section 2

- On a scale of 1 to 10, how comfortable are you with risk? How does this affect your success with investing long-term?
- Why is it important to understand your investment decisions while you work with an investing advisor?

SECTION 3

Types of Investments *(Single Stocks continued)*

Dividend: Distribution of a portion of a company's earnings, decided by the board of directors, to a class of its shareholders; generally distributed in the form of cash or stock

When you buy stock, you are buying a small piece of ______________ 14 in the company.

Your return comes as the company increases in ______________ 15 or pays you, its owner, some of the profits (______________ 16).

Bond: Debt tool where an issuer, such as a corporation, municipality or government agency, owes you money; a form of I.O.U.; the issuer makes regular interest payments on the bond and promises to pay back or redeem the face value of the bond at a specified point in the future (the maturity date)

3. Bonds

A bond is a ______________ 17 instrument by which the company owes ________ 18 money.

Your return is the fluctuation in price and the ______________ 19 rate paid. Few individuals do well with ________ ________ 20 purchases.

Mutual Fund: Pool of money managed by an investment company and invested in multiple companies, bonds, etc; offers investors a variety of goals depending on the fund and its investment charter; often used to generate income on a regular basis or to preserve an investor's money; sometimes used to invest in companies that are growing at a rapid pace

4. Mutual Funds

Investors pool their ______________ 21 to invest.

Portfolio managers manage the pool or ______________ 22.

Your ______________ 23 comes as the ______________ 24 of the fund is increased.

Discussion Questions: Section 3

- Why are single stocks so dangerous? Can you think of current examples that have the potential to destroy countless portfolios based on single stocks?
- Why is it important to be debt-free (except the mortgage) before you begin your long-term investing? Is there a rare situation when it makes sense to invest before getting out of debt?

$

More than half of investors aged 18–34 (51%) and 35–44 (56%) say they will increase the amount they invest over the next five years.

SURVEY BY 24/7 WALL ST./HARRIS

—

There are currently over 10,000 mutual funds in America. If you add all the similar funds together, they are valued in the trillions of dollars.

INVESTOPEDIA

+

Do you remember the power of compound interest from **Chapter 1, Savings?** It's the most effective way to become a millionaire.

Here's how a hypothetical $1,000 investment would have done if invested the day before these events occurred at the stock market average return (if left alone until 2007):

- Great Depression (1/1/1934) $2,528,717
- Pearl Harbor bombed (12/7/1941) $1,790,695
- John F. Kennedy assassination (11/22/1963) $82,504
- Nixon resignation (8/9/1974) $50,104

?

"I'm 19 years old and working during college. I live at home with my parents and my car is completely paid for. How should I start saving for a house and retirement? What do I need to do?"

DAVE'S ANSWER: Your first goal should be to pay for next semester in cash. Then save 3–6 months of your income (since you don't really have any expenses). This will be your full emergency fund. Then you should save for anything you plan on doing in the next few years, like getting married or buying a home.

On top of that, you should invest in a Roth IRA. The contribution limit is currently $5,000 per year, which comes out to about $416 per month. You can do less than that, but not more. If you start that now, you will be extremely wealthy when you retire. Check www.FoundationsU.com periodically to see updated contributions limits.

$

Since the taping of this curriculum, there has been a change in the stock market's trends. The most recent statistic is: Throughout the stock market's history, **97%** of five-year periods made money and **100%** of 15-year periods made money.

IBBOTSON RESEARCH

62% of those who make financial investments rarely change their strategy.

SURVEY BY 24/7 WALL ST./HARRIS

"If you don't feel comfortable owning something 10 years, don't own it for 10 minutes."

WARREN BUFFETT
Famous American Investor

SECTION 4

Types of Investments *(Mutual Funds continued)*

Mutual funds are good ______________-term investments.
25

Mutual funds that are properly diversified will have investment dollars spread equally among four different classes of financial assets.

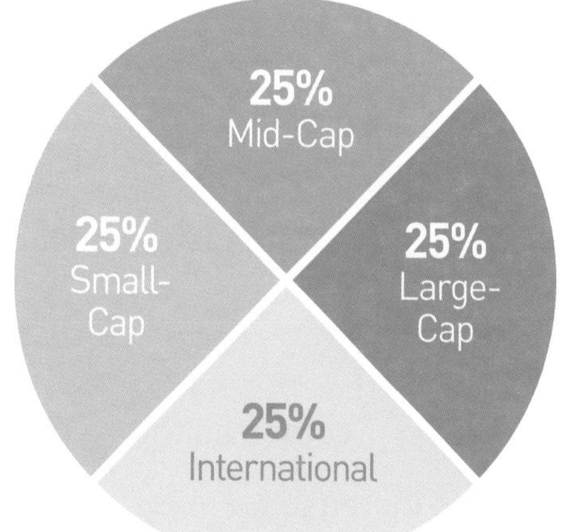

Aggressive Growth Stock Mutual Fund: Fund that seeks to provide maximum long-term capital growth from stocks of primarily smaller companies; the most volatile fund; also referred to as a "small-cap" fund

Growth Stock Mutual Fund: Fund that buys stock in medium-sized companies that have experienced some growth and are still expanding; also called a "mid-cap" fund

Growth and Income Stock Mutual Fund: Fund comprised of large, well-established companies; also called a "large-cap" fund

International Stock Mutual Fund: Fund that contains international or overseas companies

Discussion Questions: Section 4

- What excites you about investing? When will you be ready to invest?
- If you could create the perfect mutual fund, what companies would you put in it?

A Millionaire's Best Friend

THE POWER OF COMPOUND INTEREST

DR As you approach adulthood and start to think about your future, are you really ready to be financially responsible for yourself? If you answered no, you're not alone. A recent study by the Jumpstart Coalition found that **over 75% of young adults believe they are not ready to make smart financial decisions for themselves**. Whether you have never stepped foot in a bank or you are actively saving and investing for your future, all it takes is a little effort and a lot of patience to become confident in your financial decisions.

One awesome thing that you can take advantage of is **compound interest**. It may sound like an intimidating term, but it really isn't once you know what it means. Here's a little secret: compound interest is a millionaire's best friend. It's really free money. Seriously. But don't take our word for it.

Let's take another look at the story of Ben and Arthur from Chapter 1. Remember that Ben invested $16,000 over eight years, and Arthur invested $78,000 over 39 years. Believe it or not, Ben came out ahead...*$700,000 ahead!* How did he do it? **Starting early is the key.** He put in less money but started eight years earlier. That's compound interest for you! **It turns $16,000 into almost $2.3 million!** Since Ben invested earlier, the interest kicked in sooner.

AGE	BEN INVESTS:		ARTHUR INVESTS:	
19	2,000	2,240	0	0
20	2,000	4,749	0	0
21	2,000	7,558	0	0
22	2,000	10,706	0	0
23	2,000	14,230	0	0
24	2,000	18,178	0	0
25	2,000	22,599	0	0
26	2,000	27,551	0	0
27	0	30,857	2,000	2,240
28	0	34,560	2,000	4,749
29	0	38,708	2,000	7,558
30	0	43,352	2,000	10,706
31	0	48,554	2,000	14,230
32	0	54,381	2,000	18,178
33	0	60,907	2,000	22,599
34	0	68,216	2,000	27,551
35	0	76,802	2,000	33,097
36	0	85,570	2,000	39,309
37	0	95,383	2,000	46,266
38	0	107,339	2,000	54,058
39	0	120,220	2,000	62,785
40	0	134,646	2,000	72,559
41	0	150,804	2,000	83,506
42	0	168,900	2,000	95,767
43	0	189,168	2,000	109,499
44	0	211,869	2,000	124,879
45	0	237,293	2,000	142,104
46	0	265,768	2,000	161,396
47	0	297,660	2,000	183,004
48	0	333,379	2,000	207,204
49	0	373,385	2,000	234,308
50	0	418,191	2,000	264,665
51	0	468,374	2,000	298,665
52	0	524,579	2,000	336,745
53	0	587,528	2,000	379,394
54	0	658,032	2,000	427,161
55	0	736,995	2,000	480,660
56	0	825,435	2,000	540,579
57	0	924,487	2,000	607,688
58	0	1,035,425	2,000	682,851
59	0	1,159,676	2,000	767,033
60	0	1,298,837	2,000	861,317
61	0	1,454,698	2,000	966,915
62	0	1,629,261	2,000	1,085,185
63	0	1,824,773	2,000	1,217,647
64	0	2,043,746	2,000	1,366,005
65	0	2,288,996	2,000	1,532,166

What You Can Do Now

The trick is to start as soon as possible. A survey by Charles Schwab found that 24% of young adults believe that since they are young, saving money isn't important. Looks like we just blew that theory out of the water! That same survey also discovered that only 22% of young adults say they know how to invest money to make it grow. Why not change that statistic and learn how to become a smart investor with your money? **And remember, waiting just means you make less money in the end. So get moving!**

Types of Investments

5. Real Estate

Real estate is the least ____________ consumer investment.
26

You should have lots of ____________ before using real estate as an ____________.
27 28

6. Annuities

Annuities are ____________ accounts with an ____________ company.
29 30

____________ annuities are at a low interest rate of around 5%, aren't really fixed, and are a ________ investment.
31 32

____________ annuities are mutual funds sheltered by the annuity covering, thereby allowing the mutual fund to grow tax-deferred.
33

Annuity: Contract sold by an insurance company, designed to provide payments to the holder at specified intervals, usually after retirement; the holder is taxed at the time of distribution or withdrawal, making this a tax-deferred arrangement

Horrible Investments

- Gold
- ____________ & Futures
34
- Day ____________
35
- Viaticals

Commodity: A food, metal or fixed physical substance that investors buy or sell, usually via future contracts

Futures: A term to designate all contracts covering the sale of financial instruments or physical commodities for future delivery on a commodity exchange

$

Men take more risks when investing. Almost 3 in 10 men (28%) will invest in a new product, compared to just 20% of women. In addition, 61% of men will shift the asset mix of their investments, compared to 51% of women.

SURVEY BY AXA EQUITABLE LIFE INSURANCE COMPANY

Roughly 2 in 5 American adults (42%) say gold is usually a good investment.

SURVEY BY 24/7 WALL ST./HARRIS

Young adults are 4–10% more likely to research and purchase their financial products online than older investors.

WALL STREET

+

Want to know how to plan for retirement? You will see more about this in **Chapter 11, Retirement and Savings Plans**.

Discussion Questions: Section 5

- Under what circumstances does it make sense to invest in rental real estate? What are advantages and disadvantages to this type of investment when comparing it to other types?
- From the list of horrible investments, which do you feel is the worst? Why?

Can You Really Get a 12% Return on Your Mutual Fund Investments?

When Dave says you can expect to make 12% on your investments, he's using a real number that's based on the historical average annual return of the S&P 500®. The S&P 500® gauges the performance of the stocks of the 500 largest, most stable companies in the Stock Exchange. It is often considered the most accurate measure of the stock market as a whole. The current average annual return from 1926, the year of the S&P's inception, through 2010 is 11.84%. That's a long look back, and most people aren't interested in what happened in the market 80 years ago.

So let's look at some numbers that are closer to home. From 1991–2010, the S&P's average is 10.66%. From 1986–2010, it's 11.28%. In 2009, the market's annual return was 26.46%. In 2010, it was 8%.

So you can see, 12% is not a magic number. But based on the history of the market, it's a reasonable expectation for your long-term investments. It's simply a part of the conversation about investing.

But What About The 'Lost Decade'?

Dave often points out that every 10-year period in the market's history has made money, and that was true until the latest market drop in 2008. From 2000–2009, the market endured a major terrorist attack and a recession. S&P 500® reflected those tough times with an average annual return of 1% and a period of negative returns after that, leading the media to call it the "lost decade."

But that is only part of the picture. In the 10-year period right before that, 1990–1999, the S&P averaged 19% annually. Put the two decades together, and you get a respectable 10% average annual return.

But that's the past, right? You want to know what to expect in the future. In investing, we can only base our expectations on how the market has behaved in the past. And the past shows us that each 10-year period of low returns has been followed by a 10-year period of excellent returns, ranging from 13% to 18%!

If You're Still Unsure...

Will your investments make that much? Maybe. Maybe more. But the idea here is that you invest and invest for the long haul. Don't let your opinion over whether or not you think a 12% return is possible keep you from investing.

In fact, if you'd rather project your mutual funds to grow at 10% or 8%—that's cool with us. Just set a goal and invest whatever you need to in order to meet that goal.

How To Find Your Funds

It's not difficult to find several mutual funds that average or exceed 12% long-term growth, even in today's market. An experienced investing professional can help you find good mutual funds in each of the four categories Dave recommends.

But the value of a professional advisor doesn't end there. The stock market will have its ups and downs, and the downs are scary times for investors. They react by pulling their money out of their investments—that's exactly what millions of investors did as the market plunged in 2008. But that only made their losses permanent. If they'd stuck with their investments like Dave advises, their value would have risen along with the stock market over the next two years.

Chapter 10 Key Concepts

- Start investing now.
- Diversify. Don't put your money in only one place. Spreading out your money lowers your risk.
- NEVER put money into something you don't understand. If you do not understand an investment well enough to teach someone else how it works, don't buy it.
- Building wealth takes time. It's the tortoise, not the hare, who wins the race.

RECAP & REVIEW

Video Section Answers

1. Simple
2. Stupid
3. Tax Savings
4. Borrowed
5. Diversification
6. Lowers
7. Risk
8. Liquidity
9. Less
10. Certificate of Deposit
11. Low
12. Emergency Funds
13. High
14. Ownership
15. Value
16. Dividends
17. Debt
18. You
19. Interest
20. Single Bond
21. Money
22. Fund
23. Return
24. Value
25. Long
26. Liquid
27. Cash
28. Investment
29. Savings
30. Insurance
31. Fixed
32. Bad
33. Variable
34. Commodities
35. Trading

CHAPTER 10

Case Studies

Jackson and Tanner

Jackson is a senior in college. He and his friend, Tanner, are very close and talk openly about things, including money and investments. Tanner is a business major and tells Jackson that he should put all of his savings into a stock of an internet company that is doing well. He claims that it is a sure way to make money. Jackson is hesitant but also confused because he knows very little about investing.

1. Is Tanner giving Jackson sound advice? Why or why not?
2. Is investing even a good thing for Jackson to do at this time?
3. What options does Jackson have? Predict the financial outcome of those options.
4. If you were Jackson, what would you do? Explain your answer.

Lilly's Inheritance

Lilly graduated from college three years ago with a degree in English. She is now a high school English teacher at a private school. She just inherited $25,000 from her grandparents and is very excited about investing the money and watching it grow. However, she has $2,000 worth of credit card debt and $15,000 in student loans.

1. Would it be better for Lilly to invest the money and watch it grow? Why or why not?
2. Should she pay off her credit card debt and student loans before investing her money? Why or why not?
3. What would you tell Lilly to do with the $25,000 inheritance? Explain your answer.
4. Are there other options of what Lilly can do with the inheritance money besides investing it or paying off debt? What are they?

Geoff's Investment Timing

Geoff recently graduated from a state university with a degree in art history. He has no student loans and has saved $7,000 toward retirement while in school. He's heard rumors about the stock market being unstable right now, and he has friends his age who have seen their investment accounts go down in value. Geoff has decided to keep his money in a savings account until mutual fund returns look better; then he will invest the money.

1. Did Geoff make a good decision to keep his money in a savings account until the market goes back up? Why or why not?
2. If he did put his money in the stock market instead of a savings account, should he leave it alone or take it out when the market goes down? Explain your answer.
3. For long-term savings, what is the better option: Keep your money in a savings account or invest it into the stock market? Why?
4. If Geoff came to you for advice about his money situation, what would you tell him?

CHAPTER 10

Money in Review

Matching

Match each term to its definition below.

a. Real estate	f. Risk
b. Risk–return ratio	g. Small-cap
c. 3–5-year track record	h. Large-cap
d. 5–10-year track record	i. Diversification
e. Annuity	j. Share
	k. Portfolio

1 _____ Growth and Income Stock Mutual Funds

2 _____ Always check this record when investing

3 _____ Spread around the risk

4 _____ Piece of ownership in company stock

5 _____ List of your investments

6 _____ Least liquid of all investments

7 _____ Degree of uncertainty of the return on an investments

8 _____ Aggressive Growth Stock Mutual Funds

9 _____ Savings account within an insurance company

10 _____ Risk goes up, return goes up

RECAP & REVIEW

True/False

Determine whether these statements are true or false. Change the false statements to read true.

11 **T / F :** "Liquidity" means to spread around and lower risk.

12 **T / F :** A single stock is the best place to keep your emergency fund.

13 **T / F :** A certificate of deposit is the best place to keep an emergency fund.

14 **T / F :** Diversification lowers your risk with investing.

15 **T / F :** Commodities and futures are extremely speculative and carry a high risk.

Multiple Choice

16 __% of any 15-year period in the stock market has made money.

a. 53
b. 97
c. 75
d. 100

17 Long-term investments properly diversified include the following mutual funds:

a. Growth, growth and income, bond, aggressive growth
b. Growth, balanced, international, bond
c. International, bond, aggressive growth, growth
d. Growth, growth and income, international, aggressive growth

18 What is the KISS rule of investing?

a. Keep It Simple Stocks
b. Keep It Simple, Stupid
c. Keep It Solo Situated
d. Keep It Somewhere Safe

19 Which of the following is not a good investment?

a. gold
b. viaticals
c. futures
d. all of the above

20 Which statement is true about liquidity?

a. the less liquid the investment, the less return
b. the more liquid an investment, the more return
c. the more liquid an investment, the less return
d. both a and b

21 Which one is not a type of annuity:

a. variable
b. stable
c. fixed
d. none of the above

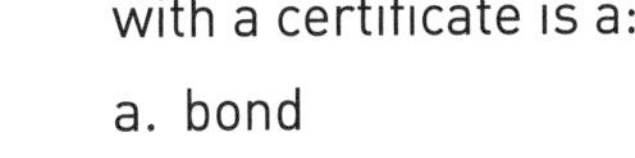

22 A savings account with a certificate is a:

a. bond
b. annuity
c. C.D.
d. viatical

Short Answer

23 Why do you look at the long-term track record with a mutual fund?

24 What are some investments that don't give you a high rate of return?

25 List four types of investments that you should always avoid.

26 How do you go about finding the right person to help you invest?

27 What was the most important fact or idea about investing that you learned in this lesson?

28 Name one thing from this lesson that you could apply to your life right now.

29 Daniel just graduated from college and wants to invest 15% of his income into mutual funds. He earns an annual salary of $32,000 but is $21,000 in debt with his car and student loan. He has $500 in savings. What steps does Daniel need to take?

30 How are single stocks different from mutual funds and which is the better investment?

RECAP & REVIEW

CHAPTER 10

Notes

CHAPTER 11

Retirement and Savings Plans

UNIT 3: CONSIDERING THE FUTURE

In a society that focuses on immediate gratification, saving for retirement seems impossible. The truth is, the fastest way to become wealthy is to choose the slow route—investing small amounts of money over a lifetime. Anyone can retire a millionaire; it simply takes consistency. You can handle that, can't you?

Learning Outcomes

Classify the various retirement account tax treatments.

- **Traditional IRA:** A tax-deferred arrangement in which growth is not taxed until money is withdrawn; contributions to an IRA are often tax-deductible
- **Roth IRA:** An IRA funded with after-tax dollars and grows tax free
- **SEPP:** A pension plan in which both the employee and the employer contribute
- **401(k):** A plan offered by a corporation to its employees and allows individuals to set aside tax-deferred income; in some cases, employers will match their contribution
- **Roth 401(k):** A 401(k) plan that has after-tax contribution benefits
- **403(b):** A plan similar to a 401(k) plan and offered by non-profit organizations
- **457:** A plan established by state and local governments for tax-exempt government agencies; employees are allowed to make salary deferral contributions

Explain how pre-tax and after-tax investments work.

- **Pre-Tax Contributions:** Taken from your gross income before taxes; taxes due upon withdrawal
- **After-Tax Contributions:** Taken from your net income after taxes; no taxes due upon withdrawal

Summarize how to maximize your retirement savings using company matches in combination with other retirement plans.

- First, fund your 401(k) if your company matches the contribution
- Second, fund Roth IRAs
- Third, invest the rest (until you reach 15% of your income) into the 401(k) or other company plans

Compare and contrast the different college-funding options.

- **ESA:** An after-tax college fund that grows tax-free for educational uses; eligibility based on parents' annual income
- **529:** A tax-deferred savings plan that is generally sponsored by a state; these are professionally managed investments
- **UGMA:** Legislation that provides a tax-effective manner of transferring property to minors without the complications of trusts or guardianship restrictions
- **UTMA:** Legislation similar to the UGMA that extends the definition of gifts to include real estate, paintings, royalties and patents

Key Terms

401(k): defined contribution plan offered by a corporation to its employees, which allows employees to set aside tax-deferred income for retirement purposes; in some cases, employers will match their contribution

Direct Transfer: movement of tax-deferred retirement plan money from one qualified plan or custodian to another; results in no immediate tax liabilities or penalties, but requires IRS reporting

Individual Retirement Arrangement (IRA): tax-deferred arrangement for individuals with earned income and their non-income-producing spouses; growth is not taxed until money is withdrawn; contributions to an IRA are often tax-deductible

Rollover: movement of funds from a tax-deferred retirement plan from one qualified plan or custodian to another; incurs no immediate tax liabilities or penalties, but requires IRS reporting

Roth IRA: retirement account funded with after-tax dollars that subsequently grows tax free

Tax-Favored Dollars: money that is working for you, either tax deferred or tax free, within a retirement plan

CHAPTER 11

Reading

The following excerpt is from *The Total Money Makeover.* In this section, Dave Ramsey talks about the power of long-term thinking when it comes to money. The earlier you start, the more financially "in shape" you will become.

I have a friend in his forties who has a bodybuilder physique. He is lean with well-defined muscle groups, but he is not some wild heath nut. He watches what he eats and works out a couple of times a week. I have another friend in his thirties who diets fanatically, runs every day, lifts weights three times a week, but is still forty pounds overweight. The second guy started his health journey a couple of years ago and is losing weight and getting in shape. The first muscleman maintains what he worked hard years ago to get, but he isn't working nearly as hard today.

The Total Money Makeover is the same way. Gazelle intensity is required to get to the wealth steps, but simple maintenance will keep your money muscles maintained. Keep in mind that my muscleman friend never eats three plates of food at a sitting. He is still aware he can lose his fitness, but he can look good and feel good with a lot less effort, assuming he remembers the principles that got him his great body in the first place.

Gazelle intensity has allowed you to get your emergency fund ready. That foundation will allow you to become financially fit by toning your muscles. You have attacked your debt; it is gone. You are now at a crucial time. What do you do with the extra money that you poured into the emergency fund and debt payoffs? This is not the time to give yourself a raise! You have a plan, and you are winning. Keep it up! You are two quarters into a four-quarter game. It is time to begin with the end in mind! It is time to invest.

What Retirement Isn't

Investing for retirement doesn't necessarily mean investing to quit your job. If you hate your career path, change it. You should do something with your life that lights your fire and lets you use your gifts. Retirement in America has come to mean "save enough money so I can quit the job I hate." That is a bad life plan.

When I speak of retirement, I think of security. Security means choices. You can choose to write a book, work or spend time with your grandkids. You need to reach the point where your money works harder than you do. A retirement plan means investing with the goal of security. You already possess the ability to quit your job, and if you don't like your work, you should consider doing that. If not today, develop a five-year game plan for transitioning into what God designed you to do; however, don't wait until your sixty-five to do what you love.

That said, the money part does matter. You want to reach your golden years with financial dignity. That will happen only with a plan. According to a study by Bankrate.com, more than 70

percent of Americans do not believe they will be able to retire with dignity.[1] Not only have we not done anything about retiring with dignity, we have lost hope that it is even possible. Consumer Federation of America found that of people making less than $35,000 per year, 40 percent said that best way for them to have $500,000 at retirement age is to win the Lotto.[2] Wow!

Getting older is going to happen! You must invest now if you want to spend your golden years in dignity. Investing with the long-term goal of security is not a theory to ponder every few years; it is a necessity you must act on now. You must actually fill out the paper-work for your mutual fund. You must actually put money in that thing. According to these statistics, the level of denial the average person has on the subject is alarming.

"Getting older is going to happen! You must invest now if you want to spend your golden years in dignity."

BABY STEP FOUR: Invest 15% of Your Income in Retirement

Those of you concerned about retirement are relieved we have finally gotten to this step. Those who have living in denial are wondering what all the fuss is about. Baby Step Four is time to get really serious about your wealth building. Remember, when you reach this step you don't have any payment but a house payment, and you have three to six months' worth of expenses in savings, which is thousands of dollars. With only one payment, it should be easy to invest heavily. Even with a below-average income, you can ensure your golden years will have dignity. Before this step, you have ceased or have never started investing, and now you have to really pour on the coals.

The tens of thousands of people we have met have helped me develop the 15 percent rule. The rule is simple: Invest 15 percent of before-tax gross income annually toward retirement. Why not more? You need some of your income left to do the next two steps, college saving and paying off your home early. Why not less? Some people want to invest less or none so they can get a child through school or pay off the home super-fast. I don't recommend that because those kids' college degrees won't feed you at retirement. I don't recommend paying off the house first because I have counseled too many seventy-five-year-olds with a paid-for house and no money. They end up selling the family home or mortgage it to eat. Bad plan. You need some retirement investing at this stage before saving for college and the mortgage payoff. Plus, by getting started now, the magic of compound interest will work for you.

When calculating your 15 percent, don't include company matches in your plan. Invest 15 percent of your gross income. If your company matches some or part of your contribution, you can consider it gravy. Remember, this is a rule of thumb, so if you cheat down to 12 percent or up to 17 percent, that is not a huge problem, but understand the dangers of straying far from 15 percent. If you underinvest, you will one day be buying that class cookbook, 72 Ways to Prepare Alpo and Love It. If you overinvest, you will keep your home mortgage too long, which will hold back the wealth-building power of your Total Money Makeover.

By the same token, do not use your potential Social Security benefits in your calculations. I don't count on an inept government for my dignity at retirement, and you shouldn't either. Understand, it is your job to take care of you and yours, so invest now to make that happen.

That's what financial success is all about, isn't it? By taking care of your future, you set up your family, both current and future generations, for long-term financial success. That's winning with money! [3]

1. "Bankrate Survey Finds Americans not Prepared for Retirement." June 23, 2008. Bankrate.com
2. "How we are banking on retirement," USA Today Snapshot, May 9, 2000
3. *The Total Money Makeover*, pgs. 151–156.

CHAPTER

11 Video: Sections 1–4

"A good man leaves an inheritance for his children's children."

PROVERBS 13:22, NIV

"The challenge of retirement is how to spend time without spending money."

AUTHOR UNKNOWN

SECTION 1

Baby Step Review

Once the emergency fund is in place, you should begin retirement and college funding, which falls within long-term investing for

__________ __________. 1

Baby Step 1 is __________ (2) in an emergency fund ($500 if your household income is less than $20,000 a year).

Baby Step 2 is pay off debt using the __________ __________. 3

Baby Step 3 is __________ (4) months of expenses in an emergency fund.

Baby Step 4 is investing __________ (5) of your household income into Roth IRAs and pre-tax retirement plans.

Tax-favored means that the investment is in a __________ __________ (6) or has a special tax treatment.

> **Tax-Favored Dollars:** Money that is working for you, either tax deferred or tax free, within a retirement plan

Qualified Plans

- Individual Retirement Arrangement (__________) 7
- Simplified Employee Pension Plan (__________) 8
- 401(k), 403(b), 457

Think winning the lottery will help you become rich? Think again!

Winning the lottery does not guarantee peace of mind when it comes to your financial future. In fact, Bankrate.com claims the opposite can also happen—some lottery winners go broke!

William won $16.2 million from the Pennsylvania Lottery in 1988. His former girlfriend sued him and won a share of his winnings. His brother was arrested for hiring a hit man to kill him, hoping to inherit the winnings. His other siblings harassed him until he invested in a car business and restaurant, both of which failed. He was $1 million in debt just one year later. Ultimately, he declared bankruptcy and now lives on food stamps.

Willie (not the same William above) won $3.1 million from the Michigan Lottery in 1989. He spent his money on a divorce and crack cocaine. Two year later, he was broke and facing murder charges.

Suzanne won $4.2 million from the Virginia Lottery in 1993. She borrowed $197,746, using her lottery winnings as collateral. She stopped making payments on the loan after she collected the rest of her winnings in a lump sum. The company Suzanne borrowed the money from won a judgment against her for $154,147, but has never seen a dime. Today, she has no assets.

Your success with saving and investing doesn't depend solely on the amount of money you make. It has more to do with making saving a priority and being smart with your money.

Individual Retirement Arrangements

When it comes to IRAs, everyone with an ______________ (9) income is eligible.

The maximum annual contribution for income earners is currently ________________ (10).

An IRA is not a type of ________________ (11) at a bank. It is the tax treatment on virtually any type of investment.

$

Of the working Americans that have some retirement savings:

- **27%:** less than $1,000
- **16%:** $1,000 – $9,999
- **11%:** $10,000 – $24,999
- **12%:** $25,000 – $49,999
- **36%:** $50,000 or more

EMPLOYEE BENEFIT RESEARCH

Roth IRA

The Roth IRA is an ___________ (12)-tax IRA that grows tax ___________ (13).

The Roth IRA has more ________________ (14).

Roth 401(k): A retirement plan similar to a 401(k) which has after-tax contribution benefits

The Roth IRA is best if you're in a higher ______________ (15) at retirement.

+

Want to know how to choose successful investments for your retirement plans? Find more detailed information in **Chapter 10, Investments**.

?

"I'm in college and 21 years old. I've got $1,000 in the bank for my emergency fund, plus I'll be debt-free in about six months. Is it too early to begin saving for retirement?"

DAVE'S ANSWER: You could start a retirement fund, but I'd start a "graduation fund" on top of your emergency fund. You're going to experience lots of transition in the years after college with new jobs, new locations and new relationships. All these things are going to require cash, because you don't want to start your new life by going back into debt. Once you have this in place, I'd suggest investing in mutual funds and maybe a Roth IRA. If you do all this at your age, you'll have a great start in life and you can look forward to being a very rich little old lady when you retire!

+

The **Roth 401(k) Plan** went into effect in 2006, giving employees a tax-free growth 401(k) option.

$

43% of American workers have less than $10,000 in savings.

EMPLOYEE BENEFIT RESEARCH

"This class has affected me so much, I will be starting a Roth IRA this summer."

STUDENT QUOTE

"Retirement is like a long vacation in Las Vegas. The goal is to enjoy it to the fullest, but not so fully that you run out of money."

JONATHAN CLEMENTS
Writer

Investing $5,000 pre-tax is different than investing $5,000 after-tax.

It takes more than $5,000 to get home with $5,000 ____________ (16) taxes.

It would take ____________________ (17).

There are no taxes when you cash it out, so it forces you to ________________ (18) more. It has more ____________________ (19).

Flexibility of a Roth IRA:

The Roth IRA offers tax-free and penalty-free withdrawals at any time equal to contributions. After the emergency fund is depleted, you have a fallback.

After five years, you can make tax-free, penalty-free withdrawals of 100% under these conditions:

1. Over 59 and a half years old
2. Because of death or disability
3. First-time home purchase (max $10,000)

Discussion Questions: Section 1

- How much money total do you need to retire comfortably? Assume you will retire at 65 and live another 20 years after that.
- How do you feel when you see elderly people bagging food in grocery stores or making hamburgers in fast-food establishments? Do you fear this outcome when you consider your own saving habits?

SECTION 2

Simplified Employee Pension Plan

A ____________[20]-employed person may deduct up to _______[21] of their net profit on the business by investing in a SEPP.

Simplified Employee Pension Plan (SEPP): Pension plan in which both the employee and the employer contribute to an individual retirement account

- Current Limitations: The maximum deductible amount is 25% of your total income, up to a $49,000 limit.

401(k), 403(b) & 457 Retirement Plans

Most companies have completely done away with traditional

__________________[22] plans.

It has been replaced by self _______________[23] and ______________[24] type plans, like the 401(k).

- The 401(k) is yours, unlike the pension plan which was an asset of the company.
- If you don't put money into a 401(k), there will be nothing in the fund. A pension, however, is funded automatically by your company.

403(b): Retirement plan similar to a 401(k) plan, but one that is offered by non-profit organizations (rather than corporations); employees invest tax-deferred dollars

- The 403(b) is found in non-profit organizations such as churches, hospitals and schools.

$

25% of Americans have no savings at all. No retirement. No investments. Nothing.

CNN MONEY

24% of American workers say that they have postponed their planned retirement age at some point during the past year.

EMPLOYEE BENEFIT RESEARCH

+

The Rule of 72

Here's a quick way to do compound interest calculations in your head. It isn't exact, but it will give you a quick benchmark to see how long it will take to double your money at a given interest rate.

The Rule of 72 says that by dividing the interest rate into 72, you will know approximately how long it will take to double your money.

Example: How long will it take to double your money at 12%?

- 72/12 = 6 years

What interest rate do I need to earn if I want my money to double in 7 years?

- 72/7 = 10 plus (10.28%)

The 457 is ____________ (25) compensation, which means you are deferring or putting off compensation. Usually this is available for government employees.

Do not use a ____________ (26) Investment Contract (GIC) or bond funds to fund your plan.

- This is like a C.D. inside of your 401(k). You will only make about 3–4% and it will not help you win long-term.

You should be funding your plan whether your company ____________ (27) or not.

457 Plan: Non-qualified, deferred compensation plan established by state and local governments for tax-exempt government agencies and tax-exempt employers; eligible employees are allowed to make salary deferral contributions to the 457 plan; earnings grow on a tax-deferred basis and contributions are not taxed until the assets are distributed from the plan

Rollovers

You should always ____________ (28) over retirement plans to an ____________ (29) when you leave the company.

Don't bring the money home. Instead, move it straight into an IRA by a ____________ ____________ (30).

Roll to a Roth Only If:

1. You will have over $700,000 by age 65.
2. You can afford to pay the ____________ (31) separately, not from the IRA.
3. You understand all the ____________ (32) will become due on the rollover amount.

+

Don't rely on Social Security to take care of you during retirement. The money you put into it has already been paid out to the retirees before you. It's an unreliable source of income. There's supposed to be approximately 2.5 trillion dollars in the Social Security trust fund, but the U.S. government has taken all of that money out and has spent it over the last 30 years.

$

Six of 10 non-retirees believe that Social Security won't be able to pay them benefits when they stop working.

USA TODAY

In 1950, each retiree's Social Security benefit was paid for by **16** workers. Today, each retiree's Social Security benefit is paid for by approximately **3.3** workers. By 2025, it is projected that there will be approximately **two** workers for each retiree.

FINANCIAL REPORT OF THE U.S. GOVERNMENT

+

Want to know how much money you will need for retirement? Go to **www.foundationsU.com** and check out the Retirement Calculator.

Three Mistakes to Avoid

WHEN SAVING FOR RETIREMENT

Saving for retirement is easier than you may think. It's more of an exercise in behavior than head knowledge. That means anyone can save for retirement. All it takes is a little determination and discipline. Unfortunately, in our "I-want-it-now culture," discipline seems to be running quite low. You're jeopardizing your future if you have a habit of:

Staying In Debt

Debt does not help you build wealth for retirement, nor does it save you money. Debt is not a tool that can build prosperity. Every day that you're in debt is a day that you sabotage your retirement. If you want to be rich when you retire, then do what rich people do. According to *Forbes* magazine, most rich people agree that the best way to build wealth is to become and stay debt-free.

Forgetting About Taxes

Some people mistakenly assume that their retirement account is all theirs and Uncle Sam can't lay a finger on it. That's not entirely true. Unless you have a Roth IRA or a Roth 401(k), you will pay taxes on the money you withdraw from your account when you retire. Therefore, your retirement account can easily be 25–30% less than you're expecting.

Failing To Plan

Many people assume that if they simply make a monthly deposit into their 401(k) or IRA, they'll be able to retire with dignity. They don't really have a true plan. These people are playing a risky game of roulette with their retirement. Even if you've done the math and know that your family should have $2 million for retirement if you save a certain amount each month, that's still just half a plan. What if one of you isn't around next year?

Reliable retirement planning prepares for all the risks in life. From making sure you've got term life insurance to having long-term care at the appropriate age, you need a plan for it all. That's why using a professional investment planner is such a great idea. Not only do they help pick the best funds for your situation, they also prepare you for all the risks you don't even know exist.

Monthly Retirement Planning

AIM FIRST, THEN RETIRE WITH DIGNITY

Too many people use the ready-fire-aim approach to retirement planning. That's a bad plan. You need to aim first. Your assignment is to determine how much per month you should be saving at 12% interest in order to retire at 65 with the amount you need.

Step 1

If you save at 12% and inflation is at 4%, then you are moving ahead of inflation at a net of 8% per year. If you invest your nest egg at retirement at 12% and want to break even with 4% inflation, you will be living on 8% income.

Step 2

To achieve that nest egg, you will save at 12%, netting 8% after inflation. So, we will target that nest egg using 8%.

Your Age	Years to Save	8% Factor
15	50	.000126
20	45	.000190
25	40	.000286
30	35	.000436
35	30	.000671
40	25	.001051
45	20	.001698
50	15	.002890
55	10	.005466
60	5	.013610

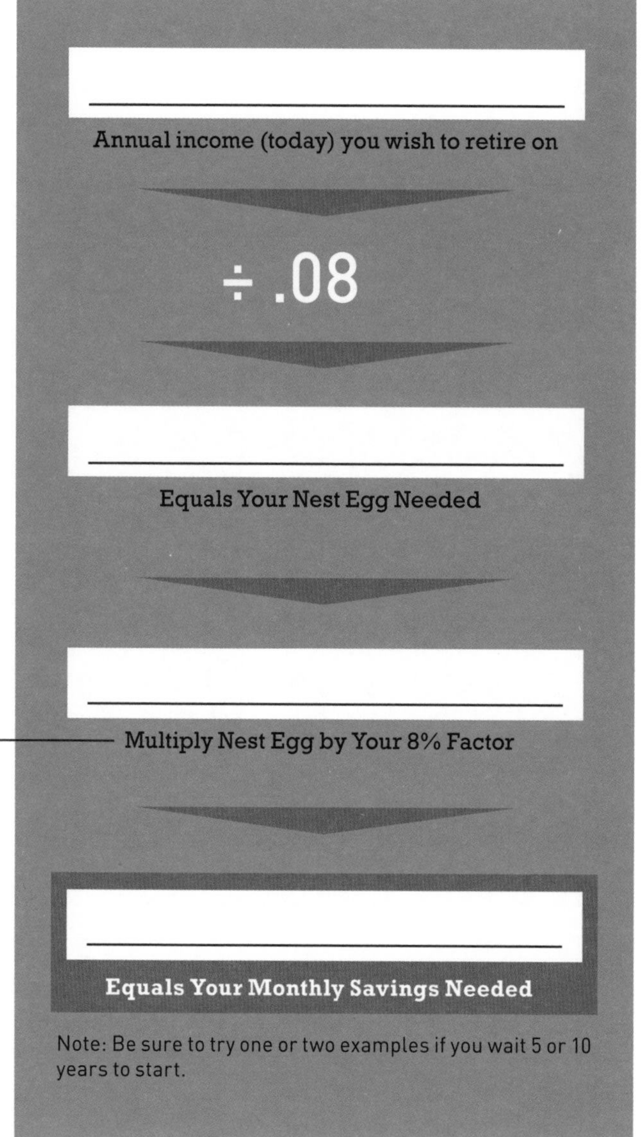

Retirement Loans

Never ______________________ on your retirement plan. NEVER!
33

Discussion Questions: Section 2

- What motivates you to get serious about your retirement plan? What de-motivates you and how can you address this?
- Why are people tempted to borrow money from their retirement? How can they fix their problems without tapping into their retirement?

SECTION 3

Federal Thrift Plan

For federal government workers who have the standard thrift plan, we recommend 60% in the **C** fund, 20% in the **S** fund and 20% in the **I** fund.

Baby Step 4

Baby Step 4: Invest 15% of household income into Roth IRAs and pre-tax retirement.

1. Fund the 401(k) or other employer plan up to the ________________ (if applicable).
   34
2. Above the match, fund _____________ IRAs. If there is no match, start with Roth IRAs.
   35
3. Complete 15% of income by going back to ________________ or other company plans.
   36

Discussion Questions: Section 3

- Should you ever stop adding to your retirement plan? If so, under what conditions? When should you start up again?
- Have you been tempted to think that the government will take care of you during retirement? Why or why not? What would happen if the government was unable to provide for you?

Borrowing Against Your Retirement Plan is a Bad Move.

Even though you pay yourself back some interest, it is nowhere close to what you would have earned if you had left the money in the investment. Plus, if you leave the company or die before it is repaid, you or your heirs will have 60 days to pay it back in full or you will be hit with enormous penalties and interest. Don't do it.

If you do not pay your 401(k) loan off, the tax rate is 30% or 40% for an early withdrawal, and they're going to hit you with 10% in penalties.

Student Without A Loan—In this recent article, Dave Ramsey explains how student loans not only impact individuals, they damage the country's economy as well.

DR Because we have turned a college degree into some kind of "genie-in-a-bottle" formula to help us magically win at life, we go to amazingly stupid extremes to get one. Some people feel they have to get a student loan to cover the cost of tuition. And yes, college tuition is becoming increasingly expensive. But I've found it's the lifestyle choices that students make in college that lead them to borrow excessive amounts of money. When some people go to college, they want to live in an off-campus apartment and eat at restaurants instead of living in the dorms and eating cafeteria food.

Borrowing hurts the economy in multiple ways. More debt means less money invested. If money isn't invested, the economy doesn't grow. More debt also means less money to buy things, which leads to more financing to buy things.

The sad part is that after you've gotten a student loan and paid on it for a couple of years, that's when the reality hits you. That's when you realize that you have obligated yourself to pay thousands of dollars in interest over several years. Instead, you could have kept that money for yourself and invested it, gave it away, or even saved up and bought things with cash.

Well, this is your wake-up call. Don't take out student loans! You can apply for scholarships and grants, work part time or go to a cheaper school. It's not worth it to take out a loan and start life behind the financial eight ball when you graduate.

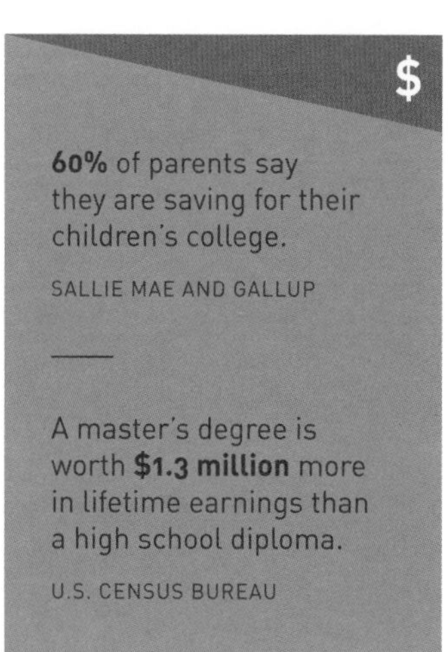

60% of parents say they are saving for their children's college.

SALLIE MAE AND GALLUP

A master's degree is worth **$1.3 million** more in lifetime earnings than a high school diploma.

U.S. CENSUS BUREAU

SECTION 4

Baby Step 5

Baby Step 5: College funding for your kids

First...

Save for college by first using Educational Savings Accounts (ESA), nicknamed the "Education ____________."

Education Savings Account (ESA): After-tax college fund that grows tax free for educational uses; eligibility based on parents' annual income

- You may save $2,000 (after-tax) per year, per child, and it grows tax free! So, if you start when your child is born and save $2,000 a year for 18 years, you would only invest a total of $36,000. However, at 12% growth, your child would have $126,000 for college—TAX FREE!

Above that...

If you want to save more or if you don't meet the income limits for an ESA, use a certain type of __________ plan.
38

> **529 Plan:** College savings plan that allows individuals to save on a tax-deferred basis in order to fund future college and graduate school expenses of a child or beneficiary; generally sponsored by a state, these are professionally managed investments

- Never buy a plan that:

1. _______________ your options.
39

2. Automatically changes your investments based on the __________ of the child.
40

Only then...

> **Custodian:** One who is responsible for an account listed in someone else's name

Move to an _______________ or
41

_______________ plan.
42

> **Uniform Transfers to Minors Act (UTMA):** Law similar to the Uniform Gifts to Minors Act that extends the definition of gifts to include real estate, paintings, royalties and patents

- UTMA/UGMA stands for Uniform

_______________ / Gifts to
43

_______________ Act.
44

- While this is one way to save with reduced taxes, it is __________ as good as the other options.
45

> **Uniform Gifts to Minors Act (UGMA):** Legislation that provides a tax-effective manner of transferring property to minors without the complications of trusts or guardianship restrictions

- The account is __________ in the child's
46

name and a _______________ is
47

named, usually the parent or grandparent.

This person is the manager until the child reaches age 21. At age 21 (age 18 for UGMA), they can do with it as they please.

> $
>
> Women who graduated from college earned about **76%** more than women with only a high school diploma.
>
> *NEW YORK TIMES*
>
> Over the past third of a century, all of the net job growth in America has been generated by positions that require at least some **post-secondary education.**
>
> RESEARCH BY HARVARD UNIVERSITY

> ***"There are ways to get through school, and student loans aren't the way. Last time I checked, W-O-R-K will get them through, too."***
>
> DAVE RAMSEY
> Financial Expert

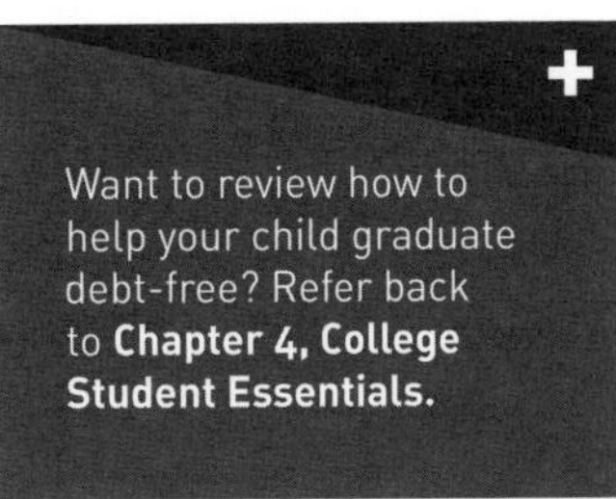

The average amount parents have saved for their children's college is **$28,000.**

SALLIE MAE AND GALLUP

The U.S. economy will create some 47 million job openings over the next 10-year period. Nearly **two-thirds** of these jobs will require that workers have some post-secondary education.

RESEARCH BY HARVARD UNIVERSITY

Avoid Using Certain Plans

1. Never save for college using ________________. (48)

2. Never save for college using ____________ (49) bonds (only earn 5-6%).

3. Never save for college using __________________ (50) tuition.

Discussion Questions: Section 4

- When does it make sense to start saving for your children's college? How much do you think they'll need by then?
- How much do you want to pay for your children's college: all, half or none? Justify your reasons.

Recap & Review

Retire Wealthy Using a Simpler Lifestyle

In this recent article, Dave Ramsey explains how small budget changes make a big impact over a lifetime.

DR Despite being the most affluent generation the world has ever seen, 54% of Americans have saved less than $25,000 for retirement. We're sacrificing our retirement to support our lavish lifestyles—big houses, cars, boats, flat screens, you name it.

Few people can embrace the idea of cutting back their lifestyle and settling for the basics. But, if you're going to "do what rich people do," forget about impressing your neighbors. Instead of seeking satisfaction in what you buy, why not consider gaining satisfaction from a simpler lifestyle?

Proof That Simpler Lifestyles Work

For more than 30 years, Dr. Thomas J. Stanley has studied the habits of wealthy people, revealing his findings in several books, including *Stop Acting Rich* and *The Millionaire Mind.* His groundbreaking research has uncovered the truth about the lifestyles of the wealthiest Americans.

Dr. Stanley posted a letter from "Mrs. C.C." on his blog, thomasjstanley.com. Mrs. C.C. has a net worth of more than $1 million, but she has never made more than $60,000 a year. "I have accumulated most of my net worth by living below my means," she said. "I have everything I want, but I have learned not to want too much."

In another letter, "D. Termined," who, at age 55, has a net worth of $2.4 million, describes his family's lifestyle. "I think I paid $67 for a pair of shoes once, and my watch is a Timex," D. Termined said. "My wife has shopped at thrift stores for many years and uses coupons extensively." There are no granite countertops in his $200,000 house, which was paid off more than 10 years ago. Money saved on the house payments went into savings.

Mrs. T, who is also financially independent, gives 10% of her income to charity, put four kids through college without debt, shops at T.J. Maxx, and drives a Ford Taurus. She told Dr. Stanley, "I am extremely happy with my life."

"Here is yet another case to support my strong contention that satisfaction in life does not come from what you can buy in a store, but rather from the values, beliefs and behaviors that most wealthy people possess," Dr. Stanley concluded.

Finding Balance

While it is important to save and invest for the future, it is also okay to enjoy nice things. Denying yourself the pleasure of new gadgets when you can truly afford them is no healthier than buying gadgets you can't afford.

Some people will be compelled by fear to save more than they need to. Instead of spending money to feel good, they save money to feel good. But the effect is the same—you can never save enough money to feel totally secure if fear is driving you.

★

Chapter 11 Key Concepts

- Save long-term in tax-favored plans—a Roth IRA grows tax-free.
- Contribute to your 401(k), especially when the company offers a match.
- Do not sign up for investment plans that you don't understand.
- NEVER borrow on your retirement plan.
- Avoid student loans. You don't need them to get a college degree.

RECAP & REVIEW

Video Section Answers

1. Wealth Building
2. $1000
3. Debt Snowball
4. 3–6
5. 15%
6. Qualified Plan
7. IRA
8. SEPP
9. Earned
10. $5,000
11. Investment
12. After
13. Free
14. Choices
15. Bracket
16. After
17. $6,000
18. Invest
19. Flexibility
20. Self
21. 15%
22. Pension
23. Funded
24. Matching
25. Deferred
26. Guaranteed
27. Matches
28. Roll
29. IRA
30. Direct Transfer
31. Taxes
32. Taxes
33. Borrow
34. Match
35. Roth
36. 401(k)
37. IRA
38. 529
39. Freezes
40. Age
41. UTMA
42. UGMA
43. Transfer
44. Minors
45. Not
46. Listed
47. Custodian
48. Insurance
49. Savings
50. Pre-paid

CHAPTER 11

Case Studies

Jasmine's 401(k) Strategy

Jasmine, age 29, makes $85,000 at her current job as a Public Relations Director. She's single and completely debt-free. Her company offers a matching program to all employees of 100% up to the first 3%, and 50% of the next 3%. Jasmine is currently funding her 401(k) at 10%.

1. What retirement contribution advice would you give to Jasmine? Explain your answer.
2. How much of her income should Jasmine contribute to retirement?
3. What types of accounts should Jasmine use for her investments?
4. How much should Jasmine contribute to each account and what is the dollar amount of the company match?

Alex and Selena's Future

Alex and Selena are 25 and love to dream about what they will do when they are retired. They want to own a summer home in Florida, travel to Europe, and spend time visiting family around the U.S. To support this dream, they need a retirement income of $100,000 per year throughout their retirement. At their current retirement contribution level, they will have $2 million saved by age 65.

1. Will they have enough money to support their dream by the time they are 65? Support your answer with realistic figures.
2. What should they do to obtain that money so they can live out their dreams?
3. Is their retirement dream realistic? Why or why not?

Krystal's Retirement Goal

Krystal is 47 years old and single. She is a high school principal, making $75,000 a year. She currently owns a 401(k) valued at $85,000. Krystal would like to retire at age 65 with $1.2 million in her retirement nest egg. She plans to contribute $12,000 a year to her retirement fund, growing at 10%.

1. Will Krystal reach her goal? Justify your answer by using the Investment Calculator on Foundations U.
2. If she won't reach her goal, what needs to change in order for her to reach it?
3. Is it really possible to get 10% growth in an investment fund? How?

CHAPTER 11

Money in Review

Matching

Match each term to its definition below.

a. ESA	d. Roth IRA
b. 403(b)	e. SEPP
c. 401(k)	

1 _____ Retirement plan for self-employed people

2 _____ Grows tax-free

3 _____ The typical retirement plan found in most corporations

4 _____ Used for college savings

5 _____ The typical retirement plan found in non-profit groups such as schools and hospitals

True/False

Determine whether these statements are true or false. Change the false statements to read true.

6 **T / F :** Pre-tax contributions are ones the government lets you invest money in before taxes have been taken out of your income.

7 **T / F :** Savings bonds are a good way to save for college.

8 **T / F :** Never borrow money from your retirement plan.

9 **T / F :** When you leave a company, don't move your money from that retirement account.

10 **T / F :** An IRA is a specific type of investment.

Multiple Choice

11 The _____ IRA grows tax-free.

a. Roth
b. traditional
c. original
d. life insurance

12 An Educational Savings Account (ESA) is used for _____.

a. retirement
b. college
c. an emergency fund
d. a new car

13 Which of the following is not a retirement plan?

a. 529
b. 401(k)
c. 403(b)
d. 457

14 Which is not a benefit of the Roth IRA?

a. grows tax-free
b. allows unlimited contributions
c. provides penalty-free withdrawals under certain circumstances
d. offers more choices

15 If your company provides a 100% match up to 6%, how much should you personally contribute to your 401(k) if you earn $35,000 (not including the money the company contributed)?

a. $1,750

b. $2,100

c. $4,600

d. $6,900

16 If you contribute $2,300 to your 401(k) and your company matches up to 3%, how much is in the account (assume you have not gone over the 3% match)?

a. $1,150

b. $2,300

c. $4,600

d. $6,900

17 What should you do with your retirement accounts when you leave a company?

a. cash them out

b. fund deposit

c. fund shift

d. direct transfer

18 Never save for college using:

a. pre-tax dollars

b. pre-paid tuition

c. savings bonds

d. both b and c

19 Baby Step 5 is:

a. 3–6 months of expenses saved

b. college funding

c. 15% of household income into retirement plans

d. the debt snowball

20 If Micayla and Joe are debt-free, how much should they be investing in retirement plans if their combined income is $145,000?

a. $14,500

b. $21,000

c. $21,750

d. $43,500

Short Answer

21 Explain what is meant by tax-favored dollars.

22 What is Baby Step 4? Why does your emergency fund have to be fully funded before you begin this step?

23 Why should you take a 401(k) match (if a company offers one) before you start a Roth IRA?

24 Why worry about retirement when every worker pays into Social Security?

25 Explain how The Rule of 72 works.

Notes

CHAPTER

12 Real Estate

UNIT 3: CONSIDERING THE FUTURE

Whether you're living in a dorm, renting off campus, or considering buying a house, you can benefit from real estate know-how. If you're ready financially, a home is one of the best investments you can make. However, if you jump in too early, it can cause far more damage than good. Take your time and consider all the options.

Learning Outcomes

Describe how to maximize the sale of a home.

- Think like a retailer.
- Make easy fixes and improve the curb appeal.
- Use a real estate agent.
- List it on the internet.

Explain why a home is a great investment.

- It's a forced savings plan.
- It's an inflation hedge.
- It grows virtually tax free.

Determine what to look for when purchasing a home.

- Buy in the bottom price range of the neighborhood.
- Find a good location.
- Purchase one that is attractive from the street and has a good floor plan.
- Have it inspected.

Compare and contrast the various types of home mortgages.

- Fixed-rate mortgage (15-year and 30-year options)
- Adjustable Rate Mortgage (ARM)
- Reverse mortgage
- Accelerated, or biweekly payoff

Identify the pros and cons of renting versus owning a home.

- Renting gives you time to set up an emergency fund, get out of debt, and save money for a home. However, you don't want to lose money on rent payments for an extended period of time. When you are financially prepared, owning a home is a great investment.

Key Terms

Adjustable Rate Mortgage (ARM): Mortgage in which the interest rate changes periodically (i.e. annually); a way for banks to transfer the risk of higher interest rates to the consumer

Equity: The value of a piece of property over and above any mortgage or liabilities related to it

Fixed Rate: An interest rate that does not change over time

Inflation Hedge: An asset rising in value, which helps one to keep up with the rising cost of inflation; real estate can be a great inflation hedge

Multiple Listings Service (MLS): Computer program used by real estate agents to search frequently updated listings of available properties in order to find prospective homes for their clients

Mortgage: Loan secured by the collateral of real estate property, which obligates the borrower to make a predetermined series of payments

Principal: Original amount of money invested, excluding any interest or dividends; also called the face value of a loan

Real Estate Agent: A real estate professional who receives a commission for arranging and facilitating the sale of a property for a buyer or a seller. Also referred to as a real estate broker.

CHAPTER 12

Reading

The following reading excerpt is from *The Total Money Makeover.* Dave Ramsey discusses Baby Step 6—paying off your home mortgage. In this section, he debunks many of the common myths that people believe about mortgages. Although many think he's crazy, Dave explains how it really is possible to entirely pay off your house and not have to worry about monthly mortgage payments ever again. He discusses why you should always get a 15-year fixed-rate loan and how you really can pay cash for a home.

My family has a fabulous dog, a Chinese pug, a dog like Frank in the *Men in Black* movies. Her name is Heaven, and when we talk to her she cocks her little round head sideways in a questioning look as if we have lost our minds. If you heard the way we talk to the dog, you might think we really had lost our minds. We have all seen the cocked-sideways look coming at us when we have said something weird, something against culture. When I say, "Pay off the mortgage," some of you look as if I had told you to build wings and fly to the moon.

Anytime I speak about paying off mortgages, people give me that special look. They think I'm crazy for two reasons. One, most people have lost their hope, and they don't really believe there is any chance for them. Two, most people believe mortgage myths. There are big "reasons" that keep seemingly intelligent people (like me for years) from paying off mortgages, so we will start with those.

MYTH: Take out a thirty-year mortgage and promise yourself to pay it like a fifteen-year, so if something goes wrong you have wiggle room.

TRUTH: Something will go wrong.

One thing I am sure of in my Total Money Makeover, I had to quit telling myself that I had innate discipline and fabulous self-control. That is a lie. I have to put systems and programs in place that make me do smart things. Saying, "Cross my fingers and hope to die I promise, promise, promise I will pay extra on my mortgage because I am the one human on the planet who has that kind of discipline," is kidding yourself. A big part of being strong financially is that you know where you are weak and take action to make sure you don't fall prey to the weakness. And we ALL are weak.

Sick children, bad transmissions, prom dresses, high heat bills and dog vaccinations come up, and you won't make the extra payment. Then we extend the lie by saying, "Oh, I will next month." Grow up!

Short Terms Matter

Purchase Price	$130,000
Down Payment	$20,000
Mortgage Amount	**$110,000**

At 7% Interest Rate		
30-Year Mortgage	$732	$263,520
15-Year Mortgage	$988	$177,840
Difference	**$256**	**$85,680**

Two-hundred-fifty dollars more per month and you will save almost $100,000 and fifteen years of bondage. The really interesting thing I have observed is that fifteen-year mortgages always pay off in fifteen years. Again, part of a Total Money Makeover is putting in place systems that automate smart moves, which is what a fifteen-year mortgage is. Thirty-year mortgages are for people who enjoy slavery so much they want to extend it for fifteen more years and pay thousands of dollars more for the privilege. If you must take out a mortgage, pretend only fifteen-year mortgages exist.

If you have a great interest rate, it is not necessary to refinance to pay a mortgage off in fifteen years or earlier. Simply make payments as if you have a fifteen-year mortgage, and your mortgage will pay off in fifteen years. If you want to pay any mortgage off in twelve years or any number you want, visit my website or get a calculator and calculate the proper payment at your interest rate on your balance for a twelve-year mortgage (or the number you want). Once you have the payment amount, add to your monthly mortgage payment the difference between the new principal and interest payment and your current principal and interest payment, and you will pay off your home in twelve years.

The best time to refinance is when you can save on interest. When refinancing, paying points or origination fees are not in your best interest. Points or origination fees are prepaid interest. When you pay points, you get a lower Annual Percentage Rate (APR) because you have already paid some of the interest up-front. The math shows that you don't save enough on interest rate to pay yourself back for the points. When refinancing, ask for a "par" quote, which means zero points and zero origination fee. The mortgage broker can make a profit by selling the loan; they don't need the origination fee to be profitable.

MYTH: You can't pay cash for a home!

TRUTH: Bet me.

First, let me tell you that mortgage debt is the only kind of debt I don't yell about. I want you to pay off your home as a part of your Total Money Makeover, and, for all the reasons stated in the previous pages, you have to be very careful. When asked about mortgages I tell everyone never to take more than a fifteen-year fixed-rate loan, and never have a payment of over 25 percent of your take-home pay. That is the most you should ever borrow.

I don't borrow money—ever. Luke called me from Cleveland to tell me that some of our listeners and readers are doing what Sharon and I have done, "The 100 Percent Down Plan." Pay cash. Most people don't think that can be done. Luke did it.

"Two hundred fifty dollars more per month and you will save almost $100,000 and fifteen years of bondage."

Luke made really good money. His income at twenty-three years old was $50,000, and he married a young lady making $30,000. His grandfather had preached to him never to borrow money. So Luke and his new bride lived in a very small apartment over a rich lady's garage. They paid only $250 a month for it. They lived on nothing, did nothing that cost money, and they saved. Man, did they save! Making $80,000 in the household they saved $50,000 a year for three years and paid cash for a $150,000 home. They closed on the home on Luke's wife's twenty-sixth birthday. They lived like no one else, and now they are living like no one else. If you make $80,000 per year and don't have any payments, you can become very wealthy very quickly. Keep in mind, though, that Luke's friends and relatives thought he should be committed. They made fun of his cards, his lifestyle and his dream. Only his bride and his grandfather believed in his dream. Who cares what the broke people think?

You may not make $80,000 per year, but you may not need a $150,000 home as your starter either. You may not make $80,000 per year, so your dream might take five years instead of three like Luke's. Ask any eighty-year-old if five years of sacrifice is worth it to change your financial destiny for the rest of your life! Ask any eighty-year-old if five years of sacrifice is worth it to have the satisfaction of knowing you changed your family tree. Paying cash for a home is possible, very possible. What's hard to find is people willing to pay the price in sacrificed lifestyle.

1. *The Total Money Makeover*, pgs. 196–199.

CHAPTER 12

Video: Sections 1–4

SECTION 1

Baby Step Review

BABY STEP 1: $1,000 in an emergency fund ($500 if your household income is less than $20,000 a year)

BABY STEP 2: Pay off all debt except the house utilizing the debt snowball

BABY STEP 3: Three to six months' expenses in savings

BABY STEP 4: Invest 15% of your household income into Roth IRAs and pre-tax retirement plans

BABY STEP 5: College funding for your kids

BABY STEP 6: Pay off your home early

BABY STEP 7: Build wealth and give!

At This Point:

- **You are debt-free except your house.**
- **You have three to six months of expenses in an emergency fund.**
- **You are putting 15% of your before-tax gross income into retirement savings each year.**
- **You are investing for your child's college education.**

$

Residential housing sales account for **15%** of overall economic activity.

NATIONAL ASSOCIATION OF REALTORS

Only **27%** of "for sale by owner" sellers list their homes on the internet.

NATIONAL ASSOCIATION OF REALTORS

"It is through initiatives to further grow homeownership that we empower individuals and families by helping them build wealth and improve their lives."

ELIZABETH DOLE
U.S. Senator

Selling A Home

When selling a home, you should think like a ____________________[1].

The home should be in "near perfect" condition.

The return on investment of fix-up dollars is ____________________[2].

The most important aspect of preparation is attention to the ____________________[3] appeal.

> **Curb Appeal:** The appearance of a home from the street

When selling your home, make sure that it is listed on the ____________________[4].

When selling, statistical research has found that the best real estate agents are worth ____________________[5] than they cost.

The exposure through the ____________________[6] Listing Service is worth it.

When selecting an agent, do not rely on ____________________[7] or ____________________[8].

> **Home Warranty:** An agreement that ensures the structural soundness of a home

These are professionals. You should always ____________________[9] them.

Offering a home ____________________[10] will typically not make a sale. If the buyer asks for a warranty, then consider it with that offer.

Discussion Questions

- Other than the suggestions Dave mentioned, what are additional things you can do to help a house sell?
- How has the internet affected American consumerism? How would you apply online sales techniques to the real estate industry?

$

The median income for real estate agents is **$48,000.**

NATIONAL ASSOCIATION OF REALTORS

"You never get a second chance to make a good first impression."

ZIG ZIGLAR

Famous Businessman and Motivational Speaker

Buying A Home

Homeownership is a great investment for three main reasons:

1. It's a ____________________ savings plan.
   11
2. It's an ____________________ hedge.
   12
3. It grows virtually ____________ ____________.
   13

You can have a gain of $250,000 single or $500,000 married and pay zero tax on the sale of your personal residence if you hold it at least two years.

Title insurance insures you against an ______________ title, which is when your proper ownership is in question. It is a good buy.
14

Always get a land ____________________ if buying more than a standard subdivision lot.
15

Land Survey: A survey that shows where one's property lines begin and end

Real estate agents' access to the ______________ system can make house hunting easier, but be careful. Many agents can only think like retailers, which is not what you want when buying.
16

$

64% of Americans think owning their own home is a safe investment.

NATIONAL HOUSING QUARTERLY SURVEY

Approximately **86%** of the housing units in the United States are currently occupied.

U.S. CENSUS BUREAU

What To Buy

> **Appreciation:** An increase in value

Buy in the ____________________ [17] price range of the neighborhood.

Homes appreciate in good neighborhoods and are priced based on three things: ____________________ [18], ____________________ [19], and ____________________ [20]!

If possible, buy near ____________________ [21] or with a ____________________ [22].

90% of Gen-Yers plan on owning a home.

URBAN LAND INSTITUTE

However, only **19%** of young adults are saving for a home.

STUDY BY VEDA ADVANTAGE & HABBO RESEARCH

22.9% of Americans under 25 own homes in their names.

U.S. CENSUS BUREAU

Discussion Questions

- What does this quote mean? "A man builds a fine house, and now he has a master and a task for life. He is to furnish, watch, show it, and keep it in repair the rest of his days" (Ralph Waldo Emerson, famous American author). Do you feel like this is an exciting task or a daunting one? Why?
- In your opinion, what is the "perfect" house for you? Be as specific as possible.

SECTION 3

Buy bargains by ____________________ [23] bad landscaping, outdated carpet, ugly wallpaper and the Elvis print in the master bedroom.

Always buy a home that is (or can be) attractive from the ____________________ [24] and has a good basic ____________________ ____________________ [25].

> **Home Inspector:** An individual who inspects homes for defects prior to the closing of a home sale to protect the buyer or lender's investment

Have the home inspected mechanically and structurally by a certified ____________________ ____________________ [26].

Appraisals are an "____________________ [27] of value," but it's a better opinion than the current homeowner has. Always order one if in doubt.

?

"I'm a senior in college and I want to buy a house in about five years. How can I save and pay cash when it's time to buy?"

DAVE'S ANSWER: Paying cash is an awesome goal! First and foremost you should stay out of debt. I want you to start building a future on something solid, and that solid ground means being debt-free. Debt is an acid that eats up your income, so stay away from student loan debt and all other kinds of debt. Lots of times people will play around with student loans. They don't take them seriously because they have low payments or really low interest rates. The next thing you know, it's still sitting there 10 years later staring at you like some kind of big, dumb pet!

Next, start looking at neighborhoods you might want to live in and find out how much the homes cost. Then plan backward and figure out when you'll be ready to make that big purchase. If you pile up cash during college and the first few years after graduation, that down payment will be ready and waiting.

+

See how much you will be paying for your mortgage after interest is calculated in! check out the Mortgage Calculator at **www.foundationsU.com**

$

The average sale price of an existing single-family home in America is currently **$220,600**.

NATIONAL ASSOCIATION OF REALTORS

Owner-occupied housing units make up **57.2%** of total housing units.

U.S. CENSUS BUREAU

Just over **17 million** persons younger than 25 own and occupy their homes.

NATIONAL ASSOCIATION OF REALTORS

What Not To Buy

1. ____________ (28) or ____________ ____________ (29)

2. ____________ (30)

Timeshare: Vacation property in which a company sells a small segment of time to a customer; the costs of running the property are shared among all of the owners who bought into the timeshare

Mortgages

First, remember to ____________ (31) debt.

The best mortgage is the ____________ (32) down plan.

But If You Must Take A Mortgage...

Do not buy until you are ready. That means you are out of debt with a fully funded emergency fund.

Discussion Questions

- When does it make sense to rent rather than to buy a home? How can you minimize living costs in a renting situation?
- Do you believe it's possible to get a mortgage with a zero (nonexistent) credit score? Why or why not? Support your answer with reasons.

How Much Will You Save?

30- VS. 15-YEAR MORTGAGE AT 6%

If you take out a $225,000 mortgage, you save more than $143,000 with a 15-year mortgage, paying only $550 more each month!

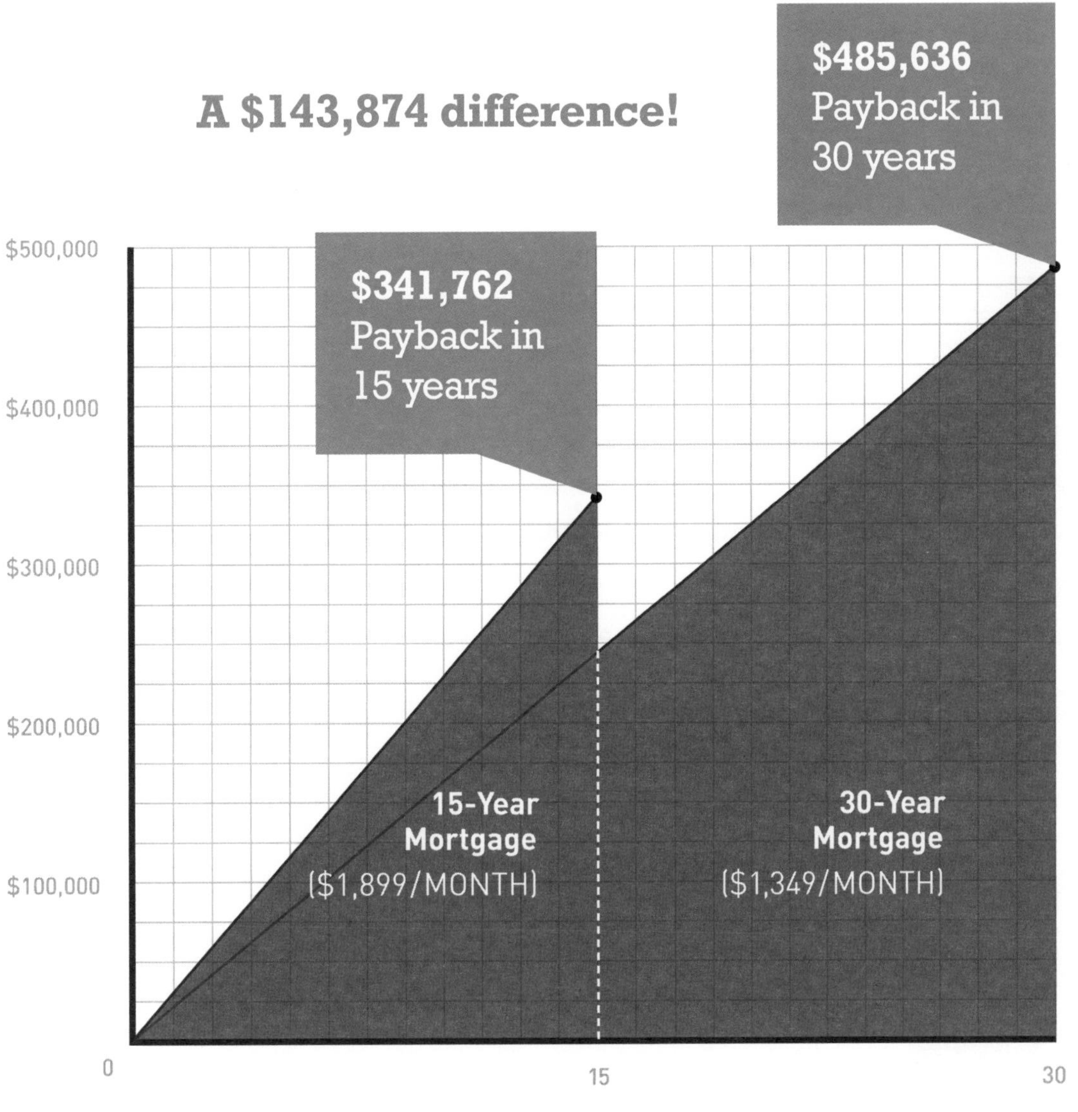

?

"I've saved $10,000 and I'm thinking about using it as a down payment on a $140,000 home right after I graduate next year. Would this be a good idea?"

DAVE'S ANSWER: I wouldn't do it. I love the fact that you're working while you're in school. Saving that much money is fabulous, especially for someone who's young!

I almost did the same kind of thing when I was in college. I was into real estate, and I really wanted to test my wings and buy something. Looking back on it, though, I'm glad I didn't.

It would have been a huge mistake. College can be a bumpy enough ride, even for the most responsible student. If you lost your job you'd be in a real mess, and you wouldn't have a lot of breathing room. Plus, the two years following graduation have the potential to be the most permanently life-changing period you'll ever experience. You could move across the country for a new job, get married, or decide to attend graduate school. In any of these situations, a house would turn into an anchor around your neck.

Renting is a great idea while you're young. Just keep piling up cash until you're ready to settle down.

+

Get a house, but don't let the house get you. Do not buy until you're financially ready, and then that home will be a blessing rather than a curse.

Reasons to rent right after you graduate:

- It's flexible. You can move anytime you want.
- It's cheaper. There are more expenses with owning a house than renting it.
- It frees up your money. You can use your money for other things like your emergency fund or paying off debt.
- It's less maintenance. The property owner is responsible for fixing broken things.

SECTION 4

Get a payment of no more than ____________ (33) of your take-home pay on a ______________ (34) fixed-rate loan, with at least ____________ (35) down.

Have a fully funded emergency fund left over after closing.

Horrible Mortgage Options

1. Adjustable Rate Mortgages (ARMs) were brought on with the advent of ________________ (36) interest rates in the early 1980s.
   - The concept of the ARM is to ____________________ (37) the risk of higher interest rates to the ______________________ (38) and, in return, the lender gives a lower rate up front.
   - Of course, ____________________ - ______________________ (39) loans are a bad idea because you are only paying the interest.
   - You can qualify for more home with ARMs, but the risk of financial stress later is not worth it.

Reverse Mortgage: Used to release the home equity in a property. The homeowner either makes no payments and the interest is added to the lien of the property, or the homeowner receives monthly payments thereby increasing the debt each month.

Accelerated Payment: Biweekly mortgage payments that allow for one additional payment on your mortgage annually

2. ____________________ Mortgages
   40

   - Bad idea because you are putting a paid-for home at risk and the fees are horrible.

3. ____________________, or Biweekly Payoff
   41

   - Allows you to make a half-payment every two weeks, which equals 13 payments a year. The reason it pays off early is because you make one extra payment a year.
   - Do not pay a fee for this option. You can easily do this on your own.

4. ____________ Advantages of a Mortgage
   42

   - Do not fall for the myth that you should keep your mortgage for the tax advantages. The math doesn't work.

Basic Ways To Finance A Home

Conventional Loan: Mortgage obtained through the Federal National Mortgage Association (FNMA), which insures against default; generally includes a down payment of 5–20% or more

Private Mortgage Insurance (PMI): Policy paid by the mortgage borrower that protects the lender against loss resulting from default on a mortgage loan

1. ____________________ are usually through the Federal National Mortgage Association (FNMA) and privately insured against default.
   43

   - Down payments range from 5–20% or more.
   - These loans are available in all forms and formats.
   - PMI is ____________________ Mortgage Insurance.
     44

$

34% of Americans believe mortgages are an acceptable type of debt.

NATIONAL ASSOCIATION OF REALTORS

2.9 million U.S. homes received foreclosure filing last year.

USA TODAY

Reverse mortgage options have the **most fraud** in the mortgage business.

FEDERAL TRADE COMMISSION

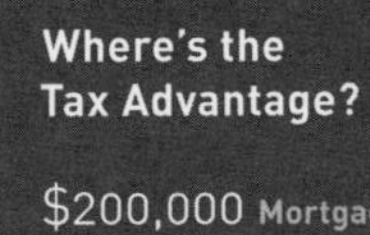

Where's the Tax Advantage?

$200,000 **Mortgage Amount**

5% **Interest Rate**

$10,000 **Annual Interest Paid**

Mortgage interest is tax-deductible, so you would not have to pay taxes on this $10,000. That is why many people tell you to keep the mortgage. But what does this really save you?

$10,000 **Taxable Amount**

25% **Tax Bracket**

$2,500 **Annual Taxes Paid**

So, if you keep your mortgage just for the "tax advantages," all you are really doing is sending $10,000 to the bank instead of sending $2,500 to the IRS. Where's the "advantage" in that? Why would you pay $10,000 when you could pay just $2,500?

$

The government, through Fannie Mae, sister firm Freddie Mac, and the Federal Housing Administration, is now backing almost **nine in 10** new mortgages.

REUTERS.COM

FHA loans now insure over **50%** of all new mortgages.

URBAN LAND INSTITUTE

2. ____________ 45, which is insured by the U.S. Department of Housing and Urban Development (HUD)—the federal government.

- Down payments are as low as __________ 46 and are used on lower-priced homes.
- These loans are currently ______________ 47 expensive than conventional financing and should be avoided.

Federal Housing Administration (FHA) Loan: Type of loan that is issued by the Federal Housing Authority; geared toward providing a mortgage to moderate- and low-income families that would not otherwise be able to afford a mortgage

3. ____________ 48, which is insured by the Veterans Administration (VA).

- Designed to benefit the veteran; the seller pays everything, allowing a true zero-down purchase.
- With a good down payment, the conventional loan is a ________________ 49 deal.

Owner Financing: Type of mortgage in which the existing owner acts as the mortgage holder; payments are made to the owner rather than to a mortgage company or bank

4. ____________________ 50 Financing is when you pay the owner over time, making him/her the mortgage holder.

- This is a ________________ 51 way to finance because you can be creative in the structure of the loan.
- Example: No payments for a year, interest rates that graduate, or a discount for early payoff.

Discussion Questions

- What does it mean to be "house poor"? Do you know anyone in that situation? How did they get into that position? How can they get out of that position?
- Imagine yourself ten years from now—you have a steady job and a growing family to support. How would paying off your home early make you feel? How would it affect your investing potential, your job performance and your relationships?

Recap & Review

Extreme Makeover, Dave Ramsey Style

BY JON ACUFF

Dave Ramsey has ruined me for most reality television shows. Before Dave, I used to be able to watch reality TV without thinking about the financial consequences of the show. I could watch blissfully without questioning the foolish decisions people were making on House Hunters International®. I could laugh along with the hosts of remodeling shows as people went upside down on home renovations. But now? Now? I see price tags and debt.

And it's all Dave's fault. The biggest example of all is *Extreme Makeover: Home Edition.* On that show, ABC builds a brand-new home for a family in need. Custom designed and tricked out to the max, the homes are always amazing. At the end of the show, the family stands behind a bus before they get to see the finished project. Then everyone yells, "Move that bus!" and voila! Their new home is revealed.

Now, though, when I watch it, instead of cheering, "Move that bus!" I think to myself, *Pay those taxes, pay those taxes!* I know deep down, chances are the property taxes on that mansion are going to put a whupping on that family in the future. ("Put a whupping on" is a financial term—sorry for the jargon.)

But maybe it could be different. Maybe we wouldn't have those problems if Dave Ramsey created his own version of *Extreme Makeover: Home Edition.* What would that look like?

Six ways *Extreme Makeover* would be different if Dave Ramsey created it:

1. At the start of each *Extreme Makeover: Home Edition,* the ABC crew shows up at someone's house and sketches their ideas for the house on a big piece of paper. With crayons. And smiley faces. Planning the home takes about 13 seconds of effort. Since Dave is far more realistic than that, and big projects, whether building a house or getting out of debt, are time-intensive, the planning wouldn't happen instantly. In fact, if I had to guess, the house would be built using a series of small actions, or "baby steps," if you will.

2. Instead of those monochromatic T-shirts all the volunteers wear, every volunteer would wear a signature Dave Ramsey blue button-down shirt. Probably something in a periwinkle.

3. Instead of a bus for the reveal, there would be a giant debt snowball that would have to be rolled out of the way. It would be the size of a tank, and the family would have to roll it away together as a final sign of the new life they're starting and the debt they're kissing goodbye.

4. Instead of the wrecking ball, we'd start your demolition off by cutting all your credit cards in half. Instead of yelling at you with a bullhorn to wake up, we'd yell at you to bring out your credit cards.

5. Instead of the participants on the show crying, credit card companies around the country would weep because one more person was escaping from debt. Title pawn places, predatory lenders—there would be a long list of people in bad suits, crying large, sad tears.

6. In order to celebrate how you need "gazelle intensity" to get out of debt, we'd give you a herd of gazelles for your new backyard. We'd also give you a book on how to raise gazelles, so no worries there. It would probably be called *Total Gazelle Makeover.*

I'd watch that show. Especially to see how those gazelles adjust to suburbia. A giant snowball rolling down the street and a herd of gazelles prancing in the backyard? That's a reality television show winner right there.

★

Chapter 12 Key Concepts

- Your rent or house payment should never be more than 25% of your take-home pay.
- Always work with a good real estate agent and make sure to have the home inspected.
- Stay away from Adjustable Rate Mortgages and interest-only loans.
- If you must take out a mortgage, do not do so until you have a fully funded emergency fund, you are debt-free, and you have at least a 10% down payment. (A down payment of 20% is even better because you can avoid paying PMI).

RECAP & REVIEW

Video Section Answers

1. Retailer
2. Enormous
3. Curb
4. Internet
5. More
6. Multiple
7. Friendships
8. Relatives
9. Interview
10. Warranty
11. Forced
12. Inflation
13. Tax Free
14. Unclean
15. Survey
16. MLS
17. Bottom
18. Location
19. Location
20. Location
21. Water
22. View
23. Overlooking
24. Street
25. Floor plan
26. Home Inspector
27. Opinion
28. Trailers
29. Mobile Homes
30. Timeshares
31. Hate
32. 100%
33. 25%
34. 15-year
35. 10%
36. High
37. Transfer
38. Borrower
39. Interest-only
40. Reverse
41. Accelerated
42. Tax
43. Conventional
44. Private
45. FHA
46. 3%
47. More
48. VA
49. Better
50. Owner
51. Great

CHAPTER

12 Case Studies

Jennifer and Chase

Jennifer and Chase have house fever. After searching for four months, they believe they've found the right house. They're debt-free, have good jobs, and have a 20% down payment. However, when they applied for a 15-year fixed-rate mortgage, they were rejected by their bank because they have no credit history.

1. What options do they have? Be sure to explain.
2. If they were your friends, what advice would you give them? Justify your answer.
3. Why are they a safer risk for the bank than someone who has a history of credit?

Terell And Sheree

Newlyweds Terell and Sheree have found a house they want to purchase. However, they'll need some creative financing in order to make it work. They've lined up a 30-year fixed-rate loan but need to have a 10% down payment to get a good interest rate. They need to find another loan for the down payment, and Sheree has asked her dad to co-sign.

1. Predict possible outcomes of Terell and Sheree's position. Explain your predictions.
2. Is it a good idea for Sheree to ask her dad to co-sign on the loan? Why or why not?
3. Is a 30-year fixed-rate loan a good idea for Terell and Sheree? Explain your answer.
4. If you were in Terell and Sheree's situation, what would you have done?

Derrick's Mortgage Options

Derrick is going to graduate from college in three months with a degree in criminal justice. However, his real passion is real estate and he has found his dream home. Derrick has the option of getting a conventional loan or a balloon mortgage. He "knows" he will be making more money when the balloon payments increase in three years. The monthly payment of the conventional loan is $1,000. The monthly payment for the balloon mortgage is $700 for the first three years, and then it jumps to $1,300 after that. At his current job, Derrick makes enough to cover a $1,000 mortgage payment.

1. Is the conventional loan the better option for Derrick? Why or why not?
2. Should Derrick take advantage of the balloon mortgage? Explain your answer.
3. Are there any better options available to Derrick that he hasn't thought about yet? If so, what are they?
4. What would you advise Derrick to do in this situation? Justify your answer.

CHAPTER 12

Money in Review

Matching

Match each term to its definition below.

a. Mortgage	e. Title insurance
b. Equity	f. Home warranty
c. Principal	g. Land survey
d. MLS	h. Appreciation

1 _____ The value of your house over and above the mortgage

2 _____ Listing service real estate agents use

3 _____ Protects you from an unclean title

4 _____ Loan secured by the collateral of a specific real estate property

5 _____ Shows where property lines are

6 _____ The face value of your mortgage, not including interest

7 _____ An increase in value

8 _____ An agreement that ensures the structural soundness of a house

True or False

Determine whether these statements are true or false. Change the false statements to read true.

9 **T / F :** Baby Step 7 is to pay off your house.

10 **T / F :** The best mortgage is an adjustable rate mortgage.

11 **T / F :** Real estate agents are usually worth the price.

12 **T / F :** Friends or relatives always make the best real estate agents.

13 **T / F :** Your rent or mortgage payment should be at least 25% or more of your take-home pay.

Multiple Choice

14 What type of mortgage is an ARM?

a. Advanced Rate Mortgage
b. Adjustable Rate Mortgage
c. Average Rate Mortgage
d. none of the above

15 Which is not a type of mortgage?

a. Reverse
b. Veterans Administration
c. Lease to own
d. Conventional

16 Which is not an investment benefit of homeownership?

a. Lower tax bracket
b. Grows virtually tax free
c. Inflation hedge
d. Forced savings plan

17 How much do you need for a down payment in order to avoid paying PMI?

a. 0%
b. 10%
c. 20%
d. 50%

18 Which is true about owner financing?

a. The buyer makes payments to the owner
b. You can be creative in structuring the terms of the loan
c. You can include a discount for early payoff
d. All of the above

Short Answer

19 Describe two things you can do to increase the chances of selling your home.

20 Why is a good real estate agent worth the money you pay in commission?

21 What are three reasons why home-ownership is a great investment?

22 What conditions need to be in place before you buy a house?

23 Explain why people take out ARM or balloon mortgages.

24 What are the best benefits of paying at least 20% down?

25 Outline the differences between a Conventional, VA and FHA loan.

CHAPTER 12

Notes

STUDENT RESOURCES

Financial Forms

Basic Student Budget

ITEM	MONTHLY TOTAL	ACCOUNT
GIVING	______	______
SAVING		
General Savings	______	______
Emergency Fund	______	______
Next Semester: Tuition, Books, Fees	______	______
HOUSING		
Rent / Rental Insurance	______	______
UTILITIES		
Cell Phone	______	______
Electric	______	______
Cable / Internet	______	______
Water / Trash	______	______
FOOD		
Groceries / Meal Plan	______	______
Eating Out	______	______
TRANSPORTATION		
Car Payment	______	______
Gas / Oil Change / Repairs & Tires	______	______
Registration & Insurance	______	______
Public Transportation	______	______
Trips & Traveling	______	______
PERSONAL		
Clothing / Laundry	______	______
Personal Hygiene / Toiletries	______	______
Entertainment	______	______
Blow Money	______	______
Health / Medical	______	______
OTHER MISC.	______	______
TOTAL MONTHLY NECESSITIES	______	

Major Components of a Healthy Financial Plan

	ACTION NEEDED	ACTION DATE
Written Cash Flow Plan	______________	________
Will and/or Estate Plan	______________	________
Debt Reduction Plan	______________	________
Tax Reduction Plan	______________	________
Emergency Funding	______________	________
Retirement Funding	______________	________
College Funding for Kids	______________	________
Charitable Giving	______________	________
Teach My Children	______________	________
Life Insurance	______________	________
Health Insurance	______________	________
Disability Insurance	______________	________
Auto Insurance	______________	________
Homeowner's Insurance	______________	________

I ______________________________, a responsible adult, do hereby promise to take the above stated actions by the above stated dates to financially secure the well-being of my (our) family and myself (ourselves).

Signed:______________________________ Date:______________

Signed:______________________________ Date:______________

Consumer Equity Sheet

ITEM / DESCRIBE	VALUE	-	DEBT	=	EQUITY
Real Estate ________	________		________		________
Real Estate ________	________		________		________
Car ________	________		________		________
Car ________	________		________		________
Cash On Hand	________		________		________
Checking Account	________		________		________
Checking Account	________		________		________
Savings Account	________		________		________
Money Market Account	________		________		________
Mutual Funds	________		________		________
Retirement Plan 1	________		________		________
Retirement Plan 2	________		________		________
Cash Value (Insurance)	________		________		________
Household Items	________		________		________
Jewelry	________		________		________
Antiques	________		________		________
Boat	________		________		________
Unsecured Debt (Neg)	________		________		________
Credit Card Debt (Neg)	________		________		________
Other ________	________		________		________
Other ________	________		________		________
Other ________	________		________		________
TOTAL	________		________		________

Income Sources

SOURCE	AMOUNT	PERIOD / DESCRIBE
Salary 1		
Salary 2		
Salary 3		
Bonus		
Self-Employment		
Interest Income		
Dividend Income		
Royalty Income		
Rents		
Notes		
Alimony		
Child Support		
AFDC		
Unemployment		
Social Security		
Pension		
Annuity		
Disability Income		
Cash Gifts		
Trust Fund		
Other______________		
Other______________		
Other______________		
TOTAL		

Lump Sum Payment Planning

Payments you make on a non-monthly basis, such as insurance premiums and taxes, can be budget busters if you do not plan for them every month. Therefore, you must annualize the cost and convert these to monthly budget items. That way, you can save the money each month and will not be caught offguard when your bimonthly, quarterly, semi-annual or annual bills come due. Simply divide the annual cost by 12 to determine the monthly amount you should save for each item.

ITEM NEEDED	ANNUAL AMOUNT		MONTHLY AMOUNT
Real Estate Taxes	______________	/ 12 =	______________
Homeowner's Insurance	______________	/ 12 =	______________
Home Repairs	______________	/ 12 =	______________
Replace Furniture	______________	/ 12 =	______________
Medical Bills	______________	/ 12 =	______________
Health Insurance	______________	/ 12 =	______________
Life Insurance	______________	/ 12 =	______________
Disability Insurance	______________	/ 12 =	______________
Car Insurance	______________	/ 12 =	______________
Car Repair/Tags	______________	/ 12 =	______________
Replace Car	______________	/ 12 =	______________
Clothing	______________	/ 12 =	______________
Tuition	______________	/ 12 =	______________
Bank Note	______________	/ 12 =	______________
IRS (Self-Employed)	______________	/ 12 =	______________
Vacation	______________	/ 12 =	______________
Gifts (including Christmas)	______________	/ 12 =	______________
Other __________	______________	/ 12 =	______________

Recommended Percentages

How much of your income should be spent on housing, giving, food, etc.? Through experience and research, we recommend the following percentages. However, you should remember that these are only recommended percentages. If you have an unusually high or low income, then these numbers could change dramatically. For example, if you have a high income, the percentage that is spent on food will be much lower than someone who earns half of that.

If you find that you spend much more in one category than we recommend, however, it may be necessary to adjust your lifestyle in that area in order to enjoy more freedom and flexibility across the board.

ITEM	ACTUAL %	RECOMMENDED %
Charitable Gifts	________	10–15%
Saving	________	5–10%
Housing	________	25–35%
Utilities	________	5–10%
Food	________	5–15%
Transportation	________	10–15%
Clothing	________	2–7%
Medical/Health	________	5–10%
Personal	________	5–10%
Recreation	________	5–10%
Debts	________	5–10%

Monthly Cash Flow Plan

Every single dollar of your income should be allocated to some category on this form. When you're done, your total income minus expenses should equal zero. If it doesn't, then you need to adjust some categories (such as debt reduction, giving or saving) so that it does equal zero. Use some common sense here, too. Do not leave things like clothes, car repairs or home improvements off this list. If you don't plan for these things, then you're only setting yourself up for failure later.

Yes, this budget form is long. It's *really* long. (Pages 282–285.) We do that so that we can list practically every expense imaginable on this form to prevent you from forgetting something. Don't expect to put something on every line item. Just use the ones that are relevant to your specific situation.

Every main category on this form has subcategories. Fill in the monthly expense for each subcategory, and then write down the grand total for that category. Later, as you actually pay the bills and work through the month, use the "Actually Spent" column to record what you really spent in each area. If there is a substantial difference between what you budgeted and what you spent, then you'll need to re-adjust the budget to make up for the difference. If one category continually goes over or comes up short for two or three months, then you need to adjust the budgeted amount accordingly.

Use the "% Of Take-Home Pay" column to record what percentage of your income actually goes to each category. Then, use the "Recommended Percentages" form to see if your percentages are in line with what we recommend.

Notes:

- An asterisk (*) beside an item indicates an area for which you should use the envelope system.
- The emergency fund should get all the savings until you've completed your full emergency fund of three to six months of expenses (Baby Step 3).
- Don't forget to include your annualized items from the "Lump Sum Payment Planning" form, including your Christmas-gift planning.

Monthly Cash Flow Plan *(Continued)*

BUDGETED ITEM	SUB TOTAL	TOTAL	ACTUALLY SPENT	% OF TAKE HOME PAY
CHARITABLE GIFTS		______	______	______
SAVING				
Emergency Fund	______		______	
Retirement Fund	______		______	
College Fund	______	______	______	______
HOUSING				
First Mortgage	______		______	
Second Mortgage	______		______	
Real Estate Taxes	______		______	
Homeowner's Ins.	______		______	
Repairs or Mn. Fee	______		______	
Replace Furniture	______		______	
Other ______	______	______	______	______
UTILITIES				
Electricity	______		______	
Water	______		______	
Gas	______		______	
Phone	______		______	
Trash	______		______	
Cable	______	______	______	______
*FOOD				
*Groceries	______		______	
*Restaurants	______	______	______	______
TRANSPORTATION				
Car Payment	______		______	
Car Payment	______		______	
*Gas and Oil	______		______	
*Repairs and Tires	______		______	
Car Insurance	______		______	
License and Taxes	______		______	
Car Replacement	______	______	______	______
PAGE 1 TOTAL		______	______	

Monthly Cash Flow Plan *(Continued)*

BUDGETED ITEM	SUB TOTAL	TOTAL	ACTUALLY SPENT	% OF TAKE HOME PAY
***CLOTHING**				
*Children	______		______	
*Adults	______		______	
*Cleaning/Laundry	______	______	______	______
MEDICAL/HEALTH				
Disability Insurance	______		______	
Health Insurance	______		______	
Doctor Bills	______		______	
Dentist	______		______	
Optometrist	______		______	
Medications	______	______	______	______
PERSONAL				
Life Insurance	______		______	
Child Care	______		______	
*Baby Sitter	______		______	
*Toiletries	______		______	
*Cosmetics	______		______	
*Hair Care	______		______	
Education/Adult	______		______	
School Tuition	______		______	
School Supplies	______		______	
Child Support	______		______	
Alimony	______		______	
Subscriptions	______		______	
Organization Dues	______		______	
Gifts (incl. Christmas)	______		______	
Miscellaneous	______		______	
*Blow Money	______	______	______	______
PAGE 2 TOTAL		______	______	

Monthly Cash Flow Plan *(Continued)*

BUDGETED ITEM	SUB TOTAL	TOTAL	ACTUALLY SPENT	% OF TAKE HOME PAY
RECREATION				
*Entertainment	______		______	
Vacation	______	______	______	______
DEBTS (Hopefully None)				
Visa 1	______		______	
Visa 2	______		______	
MasterCard 1	______		______	
MasterCard 2	______		______	
American Express	______		______	
Discover Card	______		______	
Gas Card 1	______		______	
Gas Card 2	______		______	
Dept. Store Card 1	______		______	
Dept. Store Card 2	______		______	
Finance Co. 1	______		______	
Finance Co. 2	______		______	
Credit Line	______		______	
Student Loan 1	______		______	
Student Loan 2	______		______	
Other ______	______		______	
Other ______	______		______	
Other ______	______		______	
Other ______	______		______	
Other ______	______	______	______	______
PAGE 3 TOTAL		______	______	
PAGE 2 TOTAL		______	______	
PAGE 1 TOTAL		______	______	
GRAND TOTAL		______	______	
TOTAL HOUSEHOLD INCOME		______ ZERO		

Allocated Spending Plan

Now that you've planned out the entire month on the "Monthly Cash Flow Plan," let's get just a little bit more precise. On this form, you will allocate—or spend—all of your money from each individual pay period.

There are four columns on this form, representing the four weeks in a given month. You will use one column for each week you get paid. If you are married and your spouse earns an income, then you will both use this same form. For weeks in which you both receive a paycheck, simply add those two incomes together and use a single column. Be sure to write the pay date at the top of the column.

Now, go down the list and allocate each expense to a specific payday, using your bills' due dates as a guide. For example, if your phone bill is due on the 22nd and you get paid on the 15th and 30th, then you know that you would probably pay that bill from your income on the 15th. Some things like utility bills will be paid monthly, while other items, such as food and gasoline, could be paid weekly. The point here is to anticipate both your upcoming expenses and your upcoming income and plan accordingly.

Beside each line item, you'll see two blanks separated by a slash (/). Put the expense to the left of the slash and the remaining income from that pay period to the right of the slash. As you work your way down the column, the income remaining should diminish until you reach a perfect zero at the bottom of the list. If you have money left over at the end of the column, go back and adjust an area, such as savings or giving, so that you spend every single dollar.

This level of detail may be uncomfortable to you at first, but the payoff is worth it. By specifically "naming" every dollar before you actually get it in your hands, you will remove an incredible amount of stress and curb your overspending.

Notes:

- If you have an irregular income, such as self-employment or commissions, you should use the "Irregular Income Planning" form instead of the "Allocated Spending Plan."
- If you know that you have an impulse spending problem, then you may want to allocate more money to the "Blow" category. That way, you are at least planning for it and setting up some boundaries for yourself.
- An asterisk (*) beside an item indicates an area for which you should use the envelope system.

Allocated Spending Plan *(Continued)*

PAY PERIOD:	___/___	___/___	___/___	___/___
ITEM:				
INCOME	______	______	______	______
CHARITABLE	___/___	___/___	___/___	___/___
SAVING				
Emergency Fund	___/___	___/___	___/___	___/___
Retirement Fund	___/___	___/___	___/___	___/___
College Fund	___/___	___/___	___/___	___/___
HOUSING				
First Mortgage	___/___	___/___	___/___	___/___
Second Mortgage	___/___	___/___	___/___	___/___
Real Estate Taxes	___/___	___/___	___/___	___/___
Homeowner's Ins.	___/___	___/___	___/___	___/___
Repairs or Mn. Fees	___/___	___/___	___/___	___/___
Replace Furniture	___/___	___/___	___/___	___/___
Other ______	___/___	___/___	___/___	___/___
UTILITIES				
Electricity	___/___	___/___	___/___	___/___
Water	___/___	___/___	___/___	___/___
Gas	___/___	___/___	___/___	___/___
Phone	___/___	___/___	___/___	___/___
Trash	___/___	___/___	___/___	___/___
Cable	___/___	___/___	___/___	___/___
*FOOD				
*Groceries	___/___	___/___	___/___	___/___
*Restaurants	___/___	___/___	___/___	___/___

Allocated Spending Plan *(Continued)*

TRANSPORTATION				
Car Payment	____/____	____/____	____/____	____/____
Car Payment	____/____	____/____	____/____	____/____
*Gas and Oil	____/____	____/____	____/____	____/____
*Repairs and Tires	____/____	____/____	____/____	____/____
Car Insurance	____/____	____/____	____/____	____/____
License and Taxes	____/____	____/____	____/____	____/____
Car Replacement	____/____	____/____	____/____	____/____
***CLOTHING**				
*Children	____/____	____/____	____/____	____/____
*Adults	____/____	____/____	____/____	____/____
*Cleaning/Laundry	____/____	____/____	____/____	____/____
MEDICAL/HEALTH				
Disability Insurance	____/____	____/____	____/____	____/____
Health Insurance	____/____	____/____	____/____	____/____
Doctor	____/____	____/____	____/____	____/____
Dentist	____/____	____/____	____/____	____/____
Optometrist	____/____	____/____	____/____	____/____
Medications	____/____	____/____	____/____	____/____
PERSONAL				
Life Insurance	____/____	____/____	____/____	____/____
Child Care	____/____	____/____	____/____	____/____
*Babysitter	____/____	____/____	____/____	____/____
*Toiletries	____/____	____/____	____/____	____/____
*Cosmetics	____/____	____/____	____/____	____/____
*Hair Care	____/____	____/____	____/____	____/____
Education/Adult	____/____	____/____	____/____	____/____
School Tuition	____/____	____/____	____/____	____/____
School Supplies	____/____	____/____	____/____	____/____
Child Support	____/____	____/____	____/____	____/____

Allocated Spending Plan *(Continued)*

Alimony	____/____	____/____	____/____	____/____
Subscriptions	____/____	____/____	____/____	____/____
Organization Dues	____/____	____/____	____/____	____/____
Gifts (including Christmas)	____/____	____/____	____/____	____/____
Miscellaneous	____/____	____/____	____/____	____/____
***BLOW MONEY**	____/____	____/____	____/____	____/____
RECREATION				
*Entertainment	____/____	____/____	____/____	____/____
Vacation	____/____	____/____	____/____	____/____
DEBTS (Hopefully None)				
Visa 1	____/____	____/____	____/____	____/____
Visa 2	____/____	____/____	____/____	____/____
MasterCard 1	____/____	____/____	____/____	____/____
MasterCard 2	____/____	____/____	____/____	____/____
American Express	____/____	____/____	____/____	____/____
Discover Card	____/____	____/____	____/____	____/____
Gas Card 1	____/____	____/____	____/____	____/____
Gas Card 2	____/____	____/____	____/____	____/____
Dept. Store Card 1	____/____	____/____	____/____	____/____
Dept. Store Card 2	____/____	____/____	____/____	____/____
Finance Co. 1	____/____	____/____	____/____	____/____
Finance Co. 2	____/____	____/____	____/____	____/____
Credit Line	____/____	____/____	____/____	____/____
Student Loan 1	____/____	____/____	____/____	____/____
Student Loan 2	____/____	____/____	____/____	____/____
Other ________	____/____	____/____	____/____	____/____
Other ________	____/____	____/____	____/____	____/____

Irregular Income Planning

Many people have an "irregular" income, which simply means that their compensation fluctuates from month to month. This is especially common for the self-employed, as well as commission-based salespeople. While this makes it more difficult to predict your income, you are still responsible for doing a monthly budget!

The "Monthly Cash Flow Plan" should remain a crucial part of your plan, as it lays out exactly how much money you need to bring home each month to survive and prosper. However, instead of doing the "Allocated Spending Plan," you will use this "Irregular Income Planning" sheet.

On this form, simply look at the individual items from your "Monthly Cash Flow Plan" sheet and prioritize them by importance. Ask yourself, "If I only have enough money to pay one thing, what would that be?" Put that at the top of your list. Then, ask yourself, "If I only have enough money to pay one more thing, what would that be?" That's number two. Keep this up all the way down the list.

With your list in place, you're ready to get paid. If you get a $1,500 paycheck, you will spend that $1,500 right down the list until it is gone, recording the cumulative amount spent in the "Cumulative Amount" column. At that point, you're finished spending, no matter what remains unpaid on the list. That's why the most important things are at the top of the list, right?

Be prepared to stand your ground. Things usually have a way of seeming important when they are only urgent. For example, a once-in-a-lifetime opportunity to see your favorite band perform live may seem important, but in reality, it is only urgent, meaning that it is time-sensitive. Urgency alone should not move an item to the top of this list!

ITEM	AMOUNT	CUMULATIVE AMOUNT
______________________	____________	____________
______________________	____________	____________
______________________	____________	____________
______________________	____________	____________
______________________	____________	____________

SAMPLE CREDITOR LETTER

(Date) ______________________________

From: ______________________________

____

____

To: ______________________________

____

____

RE: ______________________________

Dear ______________________________,

I am writing to formally request that, in accordance with the 1977 Federal Fair Debt Collection Practices Act, your firm (or agency hired by your firm) no longer contact me at my place of employment, ______________________.

Please take note that this letter was mailed certified mail, return receipt requested, so that I will have proof that you are in receipt of this letter should legal action against you become necessary.

I am willing to pay the debt I owe you, and I will be in touch with you soon to work out arrangements.

Feel free to contact me at my home between _____ AM and _____ PM at the following number: ______________, or by mail at my home address: ____.

Please give this matter your immediate attention.

Sincerely,

(Signature) ______________________________

Breakdown of Savings

After you have fully funded your emergency fund, you can start to save for other items, such as furniture, car replacement, home maintenance or a vacation. This sheet will remind you that every dollar in your savings account is already committed to something. For example, it's a bad idea to take money away from car repairs to pay for an impulse Hawaiian vacation, even if you pay cash for it. What would you do if the car broke down the week you got back home? However, it can be okay to re-assign the dollars to another category, as long as you do it on purpose and it doesn't put you in a pinch in another category. Keep up with your breakdown of savings every month.

ITEM	**BALANCE BY MONTH**		
	________	________	________
Emergency Fund (1) $1,000	________	________	________
Emergency Fund (2) 3–6 months	________	________	________
Retirement Fund	________	________	________
College Fund	________	________	________
Real Estate Taxes	________	________	________
Homeowner's Insurance	________	________	________
Repairs or Mn. Fee	________	________	________
Replace Furniture	________	________	________
Car Insurance	________	________	________
Car Replacement	________	________	________
Disability Insurance	________	________	________
Health Insurance	________	________	________
Doctor	________	________	________
Dentist	________	________	________
Optometrist	________	________	________
Life Insurance	________	________	________
School Tuition	________	________	________
School Supplies	________	________	________
Gifts (incl. Christmas)	________	________	________
Vacation	________	________	________
Other ____________________	________	________	________
Other ____________________	________	________	________
TOTAL	________	________	________

Debt Snowball

Now it's time to knock out that debt! List your debts in order, from the smallest balance to the largest. Don't be concerned with interest rates, unless two debts have a similar payoff balance. In that case, list the one with the higher interest rate first. As you start eliminating debts, you'll start to build some serious momentum. These quick wins will keep you motivated, so you'll be able to stay on track.

The idea of the snowball is simple: pay minimum payments on all your debts except for the smallest one. Then, attack that one with gazelle intensity! Every extra dollar you can get your hands on should be thrown at the smallest debt until it is gone. Then, you attack the second one. Every time you pay off a debt, you add its old minimum payment to your next debt payment. So, as the snowball rolls over, it picks up more snow. Get it?

Redo this sheet every time you pay off a debt so that you can see how close you're getting to total debt freedom. The "New Payment" is the total of the previous debt's payment PLUS the current debt's minimum. As these payments compound, you'll start making huge payments as you work down the list.

ITEM	TOTAL PAYOFF	MINIMUM PAYMENT	NEW PAYMENT

Pro Rata Debt List

"Pro rata" means the fair share, or the percent of your total debt each creditor represents. This will determine how much you should send them when you cannot make the minimum payments. Even if you cannot pay your creditors what they request, you should pay everyone as much as you can. Send the check for their pro rata share, along with a copy of your budget and this form, every month. Do this even if the creditor says they will not accept it.

Do You Need to Use a Pro Rata Plan?

First, determine your total disposable income by looking over your monthly cash flow plan. Simply write down your income on the line at the top of the form. Then write down the total you spend on necessities (not including consumer debt) each month. Subtract the necessity expense from the income, and you are left with your disposable income. This is the money you have to put toward your debts.

Second, add up your total amount of debt, not including your home, and write that in the blank provided. Below that, write in the total of the minimum monthly payments on all your debts. If the total of your minimum payments is greater than your total disposable income, you need to use the pro rata plan.

For example, Jake and Whitney have a total debt of $2,000, with a combined total minimum payment of $310. However, they only have $200 in disposable income each month, which means they do not have enough money to make the minimum payments. So, they will use the pro rata plan to give each creditor their fair share of the couple's $200.

How to Use This Form

This form has six columns:

1. **ITEM:** the name and type of the account

2. **TOTAL PAYOFF:** the total amount due on the account

3. **TOTAL DEBT:** the combined total of all your debts

4. **PERCENT:** the portion of the total debt load that each account represents. You can calculate this by simply dividing the Total Payoff by the Total Debt for each line.

5. **DISPOSABLE INCOME:** the amount of money you have left after paying necessities

6. **NEW PAYMENT:** the amount you will now send to each creditor. You calculate this by multiplying the numbers in each line's Percent and Disposable Income Columns.

The pro rata plan helps you to meet your obligations to the best of your ability. Of course, your creditors will not like receiving less than their required minimum payments. However, if you keep sending checks, they'll most likely keep cashing them.

Pro Rata Debt List

Income ____________

Necessity Expense – ____________

Disposable Income = ____________

Total Debt: __________

Total Monthly Payments: __________

ITEM	TOTAL PAYOFF		TOTAL DEBT		PERCENT		DISPOSABLE INCOME		NEW PAYMENT
		/		=		X		=	
		/		=		X		=	
		/		=		X		=	
		/		=		X		=	
		/		=		X		=	
		/		=		X		=	
		/		=		X		=	
		/		=		X		=	
		/		=		X		=	
		/		=		X		=	
		/		=		X		=	
		/		=		X		=	
		/		=		X		=	
		/		=		X		=	
		/		=		X		=	
		/		=		X		=	
		/		=		X		=	

Monthly Retirement Planning

Too many people use the READY-FIRE-AIM approach to retirement planning. That's a bad plan. You need to aim first. Your assignment is to determine how much per month you should be saving at 12% interest in order to retire at 65 with the amount you need.

If you save at 12% and inflation is at 4%, then you are moving ahead of inflation at a net of 8% per year. If you invest your nest egg at retirement at 12% and want to break even with 4% inflation, you will be living on 8% income.

Step 1: Annual income (today) you wish to retire on: ______________

Divide by .08

(Nest egg needed) equals: ______________

Step 2: To achieve that nest egg you will save at 12%, netting 8% after inflation. So, we will target that nest egg using 8%.

Nest Egg Needed $ ______________

Multiply by 8% Factor X ______________

Monthly Savings Needed = ______________

Note:
Be sure to try one or two examples if you wait 5 or 10 years to start.

8% Factors
(select the one that matches your age)

Your Age	Years to Save	Factor
15	50	.000126
20	45	.000190
25	40	.000286
30	35	.000436
35	30	.000671
40	25	.001051
45	20	.001698
50	15	.002890
55	10	.005466
60	5	.013610

Monthly College Planning

In order to have enough for college, you must aim at something. Your assignment is to determine how much per month you should be saving at 12% interest in order to have enough for college.

If you save at 12% and inflation is at 4%, then you are moving ahead of inflation at a net of 8% per year.

Step 1: In today's dollars, the annual cost of the college of your choice is:

Amount per year $ ______________

X 4 years = $ ______________

(Hint: $15,000 to $25,000 annually)

Step 2: To achieve that savings you will save at 12%, netting 8% after inflation. So, we will target that by using 8%.

College Savings Needed $ ______________

Multiply by 8% Factor X ______________

Monthly Savings Needed = ______________

Note:
Be sure to try one or two examples if you wait 5 or 10 years to start.

8% Factors
(select the one that matches your child's age)

Child's Age	Years to Save	Factor
0	18	.002083
2	16	.002583
4	14	.003287
6	12	.004158
8	10	.005466
10	8	.007470
12	6	.010867
14	4	.017746

Credit Card History

CARD NAME	NUMBER	ADDRESS	PHONE #	CLOSED	WRITTEN CONFIRMATION REQUESTED	WRITTEN CONFIRMATION RECEIVED
Visa	1234 567989 12	1234 Poplar Grove, suite 130	123-456-1890	09/21/06	09/21/06	11/21/06

Insurance Coverage Recap

TYPE	COMPANY	PLAN ID#	POLICY #	AMOUNT	AGENT	PHONE #
Term life	ABC Insurance	1234 567989 12	1234 567989 12	$450,000	John Smith	456-7890

SAMPLE CEASE & DESIST LETTER

(Date) ______________________________

From: ______________________________

____

____

VIA: Certified Mail, Return Receipt Requested

To: ______________________________

____

____

RE: ______________________________

Dear ________________________,

You are hereby notified under provisions of Public Law 95-109, Section 805-C, the FAIR DEBT COLLECTION PRACTICES ACT to CEASE AND DESIST in any and all attempts to collect the above debt.

Your failure to do so WILL result in charges being filed against you with the state and federal regulatory agencies empowered with enforcement.

Please be further warned that if ANY derogatory information is placed on any credit reports after receipt of this notice, that too will result in action being taken against you.

Please give this matter your immediate attention.

Sincerely,

(Signature) ______________________________

SAMPLE CREDIT BUREAU LETTER

(Date) ______________________

From: ______________________

____

____

To: ______________________

____

____

RE: ______________________

In reviewing the attached credit bureau report issued by your agency, I have detected an error. The following account(s) is/are reported inaccurately:

Company Name:______________________________

Account Number: ____________________________

Under the provisions of the 1977 Federal Fair Credit Reporting Act, I hereby request that your agency prove to me in writing the accuracy of the reporting of this account. Under the terms of the Act and succeeding court cases, you have 30 days to prove such accuracy or remove the account entirely from my report. I ask that you do so.

This letter was sent certified mail, return receipt requested. I expect a response within the 30-day period. Should I not hear promptly from you, I will follow up with whatever action necessary to cause my report to be corrected.

Please feel free to call me if you have any questions. My home phone number is ______________, and my office number is ______________.

Sincerely,

(Signature) ______________________

Glossary

401(k): defined contribution plan offered by a corporation to its employees, which allows employees to set aside tax-deferred income for retirement purposes; in some cases, employers will match their contributions.

403(b): retirement plan similar to a 401(k) plan, but one that is offered by non-profit organizations (rather than corporations); employees invest tax-deferred dollars.

457 plan: non-qualified, deferred compensation plan established by state and local governments for tax-exempt government agencies and tax exempt employers; eligible employees are allowed to make salary deferral contributions to the 457 plan; earnings grow on a tax-deferred basis and contributions are not taxed until the assets are distributed from the plan.

529 plan: college savings plan that allows individuals to save on a tax-deferred basis in order to fund future college and graduate school expenses of a child or beneficiary; generally sponsored by a state, these are professionally managed investments.

12b-1 Fee: An annual fee that some mutual funds charge to pay for marketing and distribution activities.

Accountability: the quality or state of being accountable, liable or answerable.

Accelerated Payment: bi-weekly mortgage payments that allow for additional payment on your mortgage annually.

Active: money is very active...it is always moving and can be utilized in many ways.

Adjustable Rate Mortgage (ARM): mortgage in which the interest rate changes periodically (i.e. annually); a way for banks to transfer the risk of higher interest rates to the consumer.

Aggressive Growth Stock Mutual Fund: fund that seeks to provide maximum long-term capital growth from stocks of primarily smaller companies; the most volatile fund; also referred to as a "small-cap" fund.

Allowance: money given to a child, typically on a weekly basis.

Ambition: one's goals and desires in life (i.e., career goals).

Amoral: lacking morals; neither good nor bad.

Amortization Table: breakdown showing how much of each regular payment will be applied toward principal and how much toward interest over the life of a loan; also shows the gradual decrease of the loan balance until it reaches zero.

Annuity: contract sold by an insurance company, designed to provide payments to the holder at specified intervals, usually after retirement; the holder is taxed at the time of distribution or withdrawal, making this a tax-deferred arrangement.

Annual Fee: fee charged by a credit card company for the use of their credit card.

Annual Percentage Rate (APR): cost of borrowing money on an annual basis; takes into account the interest rate and other related fees on a loan.

Appraisal: an opinion of value.

Appreciation: an increase in value.

Asset: anything that is owned by an individual; with respect to saving and investing, assets are generally categorized as liquid (cash) and capital (investment) assets.

Asset Allocation: the process of deciding how investment dollars will be apportioned among various classes of financial assets, such as stocks, bonds and cash investments.

Asset Classes: major categories of financial assets or securities. The three primary classes are common stocks, bonds and cash investments.

ATM card: automated teller card which allows you to make transactions in automated teller machines.

Auction: a public sale in which property or items of merchandise are sold to the highest bidder.

Auto Insurance: insurance to protect a car owner in the event of an accident or damage to a vehicle.

Average Annual Return: the rate of return on investments averaged over a specific period of time. It is determined by adding together the rates of return for each year and dividing by the number of years in the calculation.

B

Baby Steps: the seven steps to a healthy financial plan.

Back-End Load: sales commission paid when the investor sells mutual fund shares; sometimes phased out over several years; also called redemption fee or contingent-deferred sales charge.

Balanced Fund: mutual fund that invests in more than one type of financial asset: stocks, bonds, and in some cases, cash investments.

Balloon Mortgage: home loan in which the sum of the monthly payments is insufficient to repay the entire loan; a final payment comes due, which is a lump sum of the remaining principal balance.

Bankruptcy: legal procedure for dealing with debt problems of individuals and businesses.

Bargain: deals obtained when negotiating and paying a lesser price than asked for an item.

Beneficiary: the recipient of assets passed on from the death of a friend or relative.

Bond: debt tool where an issuer, such as a corporation, municipality or government agency owes you money; a form of I.O.U.; the issuer makes regular interest payments on the bond and promises to pay back or redeem the face value of the bond at a specified point in the future (the maturity date).

Bond Mutual Fund: mutual funds that buy bonds.

Brand Recognition: consumer awareness that a particular brand exists.

Break-Even Analysis: method used to evaluate the wisdom of a financial decision by determining the length of time it will take for the cost of the decision to be recouped.

Budget: written cash flow plan; assigns every dollar to a specific category/expense at the beginning of each month.

Buyer's Remorse: regretting a purchase soon after making it.

C

Capital Gain: a positive difference between an asset's price when bought and its price when sold; the opposite of capital loss.

Capital Gains Distribution: payment to mutual fund shareholders of any gains realized during the year on securities that have been sold at a profit. Capital gains are distributed on a "net" basis after subtracting any capital losses for the year. When losses exceed gains for the year, the difference may be carried forward and subtracted from future gains.

Capital Loss: a negative difference between an asset's price when bought and its price when sold; the opposite of capital gain.

Carbon Check: a copy of each check you write; the check has a piece of carbon paper underneath that duplicates it.

Career: your line of work.

Cash Investments: investments in interest-bearing bank deposits, money market instruments and U.S. Treasury Bills or notes.

Cash Value Insurance: also known as whole life, universal life, variable life or permanent life insurance; premiums include a death benefit and a plan to build savings within the policy; significantly more expensive than term life insurance.

Caveat Emptor: Latin term for "buyer beware."

Certificate of Deposit (C.D.): usually at a bank; savings account with a slightly higher interest rate because of a longer savings commitment (i.e. six months, one year, etc.).

Chapter 7 Bankruptcy: chapter of the Bankruptcy Code providing for liquidation of the debtor's assets in order to repay the creditors; certain assets or aggregate value of assets of the debtor may be exempt based on state law.

Chapter 11 Bankruptcy: reorganization bankruptcy, usually involving a corporation or partnership; generally includes a plan of reorganization to keep a business alive and pay creditors over time.

Chapter 13 Bankruptcy: chapter of the Bankruptcy Code providing for an individual to repay debts over time, usually three to five years; debtor makes periodic payments to the bankruptcy trustee, who in turn pays the creditors; sometimes includes adjustments to debt balances within the bankruptcy.

Checking Account: account set up to maintain daily financial activities. Users can draft checks for payment, issue deposits into their accounts, and keep track of their debit card transactions through their checking account.

Claim: paperwork filed with an insurance company in order to get them to cover a loss.

Co-Insurance: in a health insurance policy, after you pay the deductible the insurance company pays a percentage and you pay a percentage; 80/20—insurance pays 80% and you pay 20%.

Collision: portion of auto insurance that covers losses due to vehicle damage in an accident.

Commission: money paid for providing a service.

Commodity: a food, metal, or fixed physical substance that investors buy or sell, usually via future contracts.

Compensation: the total wage or salary and benefits that an employee receives.

Compound Interest: interest paid on interest previously earned; credited daily, monthly, quarterly, semi-annually or annually on both principal and previously credited interest.

Comprehensive: pays for damage to your car that is not a result of an accident.

Consignment Shop: retail store where people sell items and the owner of the shop gets a percentage of the sale.

Consumer: person who buys and/or uses a product.

Contact Letter: a letter informing a prospective employer that you are interested in working for their company.

Contents Insurance: insurance policy that covers personal possessions in a home or apartment.

Conventional Loan: mortgage obtained through the Federal National Mortgage Association (FNMA), which insures against default; generally includes a down payment of 5–20% or more.

Copay: in regards to health insurance, paying a set amount per medical visit.

Cover Letter: similar to a contact letter but is used to inform the prospective employer of your interest and capabilities as they relate to a specific employment opportunity; always accompanied by a resume.

Coverage: applies to the amount of protection you have through an insurance company in the event of a loss.

Co-signing: offering to guarantee someone else'sloan; becoming responsible for loan repayment ifthe borrower defaults.

Credit: an amount of money placed at a person's disposal by a bank; money owed.

Credit Bureau: an agency which collects the credit history of consumers so that creditors can make decisions about granting loans.

Credit Card: type of card issued by a bank that allows users to finance a purchase.

Credit Disability: insurance that pays for financed items or purchases if you become disabled and are unable to earn an income.

Credit Laws:

- **Fair Credit Reporting Act (1971):** federal law governing the reporting of debt repayment information; establishes when a credit reporting agency may provide a report to someone; states that obsolete information must be taken off (seven to 10 years); gives consumers the right to know what is in their credit report; requires that both a credit bureau and information provider (i.e. department store) have an obligation to correct wrong information; gives consumers the right to dispute inaccurate information and add a 100-word statement to their report to explain accurate negative information; gives consumers the right to know what credit bureau provided the report when they are turned down for credit.

- **Fair Credit Billing Act (1975):** federal law that covers credit card billing problems and applies to all open-end credit accounts (i.e. credit cards and overdraft checking); states that consumers should send a written billing error notice to the creditor within 60 days (after receipt of first bill containing an error), which the creditor must acknowledge in 30 days; requires the creditor to investigate and prohibits them from damaging a consumer's credit rating while a dispute is pending.

- **Fair Debt Collection Practices Act (1978):** federal law that prohibits debt collectors from engaging in unfair, deceptive, or abusive practices when collecting debts; requires collectors to send a written notice stating the name of the creditor and the amount owed; prohibits contacting the consumer if he or she disputes the debt in writing within 30 days (unless collector furnishes proof of the debt); requires collectors to identify themselves on the phone and limits calls to between 8:00 a.m. and 9:00 p.m. unless the consumer agrees to another time; prohibits calling the consumer at work if requested.

Credit Laws: *(Continued)*

- **Equal Credit Opportunity Act (1975):** federal law that ensures consumers are given an equal chance to receive credit; prohibits discrimination on the basis of gender, race, marital status, religion, national origin, age or receipt of public assistance; prohibits lenders from asking about plans to have children, or refusing to consider consistently received alimony or child support payments as income; grants the consumer legal rights to know why he or she was denied credit.

- **Truth in Lending Act (1969):** federal law that mandates disclosure of information about the cost of credit; mandates that the finance charge (i.e. all charges to borrow money, including interest) and the annual percentage rate (APR) must be displayed prominently on forms and statements used by creditors; provides criminal penalties for willful violators, as well as civil remedies; protects against unauthorized use of one's credit card, limiting personal loss to $50 if the card is lost or stolen.

- **Fair Credit and Charge Card Disclosure Act (1989):** portion of the Truth in Lending Act that mandates a section on credit card applications that describes key features and cost (i.e. APR, grace period for purchases, minimum finance charge, balance calculation method, annual fees, transaction fees for cash advances, and penalty fees such as over-the limit fees and late payment fees).

Credit Life: insurance that pays for financed items or purchases in the event of your death.

Credit Report: a document showing your credit history, credit inquiries and facts about any accounts you have opened with individual credit lines and on-time or late payment activities.

Credit Score: a calculated score that measures an individual's creditworthiness; the two main types of credit score are the
FICO score and the VantageScore.

Credit Union: not-for-profit cooperatives of members with some type of common bond (i.e., employer) that provide a wide array of financial services, often at a lower cost than banks.

Curb Appeal: the appearance of a home from the street.

Currency: money.

Custodian: one who is responsible for an account listed in someone else's name.

D

Day Trading: establishing and liquidating the same position or positions within one day's trading.

Debit Card: a card that often bears the seal of a major credit card company, issued by a bank and used to make purchases; unlike a credit card, the money comes directly out of a checking account; also called check card.

Debt Consolidation: act of combining all debts into one monthly payment, typically extending the terms and the length of time required to repay the debt.

Debt Snowball: preferred method of debt repayment; includes a list of all debts organized from smallest to largest balance; minimum payments are made to all debts except for the smallest, which is attacked with the largest possible payments.

Deductible: amount you have to pay out-of-pocket for expenses before the insurance company will begin to cover all or a portion of the remaining costs.

Deduction: an amount subtracted from something especially as an allowance against tax.

Deed: the legal document conveying title to a property.

Deflation: a broad, overall drop in the price of goods and services; the opposite of inflation.

Delinquency: broadly refers to not being current on your payments.

Depreciation: a decline in the value of property; the opposite of appreciation.

Direct Deposit Service: a service that electronically transfers all or part of any recurring payment, including dividends, paychecks, pensions and Social Security payments directly to a shareholder's account.

Direct Transfer: movement of tax-deferred retirement plan money from one qualified plan or custodian to another; results in no immediate tax liabilities or penalties, but requires IRS reporting.

Disability Insurance: policy that insures a worker in the event of an occupational mishap resulting in disability; compensates the injured worker for lost pay.

DISC Personality Profile: a behavior profile test that yields insights into how you process decisions and what your natural tendencies may be.

Discipline: self-control used in directing behavior; the key to wealth building is being consistent over time.

Discount Points: used in the mortgage industry in reference to government loans, meaning FHA and VA loans. Discount points refer to any "points" paid in addition to the one percent loan origination fee. A"point" is one percent of the loan amount.

Disposable Income: amount of money left over after all necessities and expenses are paid.

Dividend Distribution: payment of income to mutual fund shareholders from interest or dividends generated by the fund's investments.

Diversification: to spread around one's investment dollars among several different classes of financial assets and among the securities of many issuers; results in lowered risk.

Dividend: distribution of a portion of a company's earnings, decided by the board of directors, to a class of its shareholders; generally distributed in the form of cash or stock.

Down Payment: the part of the purchase price of a property that the buyer pays in cash and does not finance with a mortgage.

Duplicate Checks: type of checks that make duplicate copies as you write them out.

Earned Income: payment received for work, such as wages, salaries, commissions and tips.

Educational Savings Account (ESA): after-tax college fund that grows tax-free for educational uses; eligibility based on parents' annual income.

Elimination Period: amount of time that lapses after a disabling event before the insurance company begins to pay benefits.

Emergency Fund: three to six months of expenses in readily available cash to be used only in the event of an emergency; Baby Step 1 begins the process, and Baby Step 3 is the completed amount.

Employee Benefit: something of value that an employee receives in addition to a wage or salary. Examples include health insurance, disability insurance, discounted childcare, etc.

Employer-Sponsored Retirement Savings Program: tax-deferred savings plans offered by employers that provide a federal tax deduction, tax deferral of contributions and earnings, and in some cases employer matching. They include 401(k) plans for corporate employees, 403(b) plans for employees of schools and nonprofit organizations, and Section 457 plans for state and local government employees.

Empowerment: to gain strength emotionally or spiritually.

Entrepreneur: a person who starts a business.

Envelope System: series of envelopes that are divided into categories (food, entertainment, gas, etc.) and are used to store cash for planned monthly expenses.

Equity: the value of a piece of property over and above any mortgage or liabilities related to it.

Estate Sale: type of yard sales with more items, usually the entire contents of a household.

Exchange Privilege: the right to exchange shares in one fund for shares in another fund within the same fund family; typically at no charge or for a nominal fee.

Excise Tax: a tax levied on the purchase of certain non-essential consumer goods such as tobacco, airline tickets, etc.

Expense: the cost of goods or services.

Expense Ratio: the percentage of a fund's average net assets used to pay annual fund expenses. The expense ratio takes into account management fees, administrative fees, and any 12b-1 marketing fees.

Extended Replacement Cost: part of homeowner's insurance policy that pays a percentage beyond the insured price of the home for purposes of rebuilding it in the event of a catastrophic loss. If you do not update this, it will not cover the appreciation of your home (e.g. house is insured for $200,000, but the value goes up to $300,000, you are covered for the $200,000 plus whatever the coverage states).

Federal Deposit Insurance Corporation (FDIC): a federal institution that insures bank deposits.

Federal Fair Credit Reporting Act: federal law that regulates the collection, distribution and use of consumer information, including consumer credit information.

Federal Fair Debt Collection Practices Act: federal law that prohibits unfair debt collection practices, such as lying, harassing, misleading and otherwise abusing debtors, by debt collectors working for collection agencies.

Federal Housing Administration (FHA): federally sponsored agency chartered in 1934 whose stock is currently owned by savings institutions across the United States. The agency buys residential mortgages that meet certain requirements, sells these mortgages in packages, and insures the lenders against loss.

Federal Housing Administration (FHA) Loan: type of loan that is issued by the Federal Housing Authority; geared toward providing a mortgage to moderate-and low-income families that would not otherwise be able to afford a mortgage.

Federal Insurance Contributions Act (FICA): government legislation that funds Social Security.

Federal Reserve System: the monetary authority of the United States, established in 1913, and governed by the Federal Reserve Board located in Washington D.C. The system includes 12 Federal Reserve Banks and is authorized to regulate monetary policy as well as to supervise Federal Reserve member banks, bank holding companies, international operations of US banks, and US operations of foreign banks.

Fee Table: a table, placed near the front of a mutual fund's prospectus, disclosing and illustrating the expenses and fees a shareholder will incur.

Financial Goals: short-, immediate-, and long-term goals that require money and guide a person's future plans and savings decisions.

Financial Plan: a plan of action that allows a person to meet not only the immediate needs but also their long-term goals.

Financial Resources: financial assets that can be accessed when necessary.

Financing: to buy an item with credit; paying over time.

Finite: having a beginning and an end.

Fiscal: having to do with money.

Fiscal Year: accounting period covering 12 consecutive months over which a company determines earnings and profits. The fiscal year serves as a period of reference for the company and does not necessarily correspond to the calendar year.

Fixed Annuity: type of annuity that guarantees a certain rate of return; see annuity.

Fixed Income Securities: investments, such as bonds, which provide current income from a fixed schedule of interest payments. While the level of income offered by these securities is predetermined and usually stable, their market value may fluctuate.

Fixed Rate: an interest rate that does not change over time.

Floor Plan: the basic layout of a home.

Forbearance: agreement of a lender to suspend foreclosure proceedings and allow a debtor to "catch up" a past due account over a specified period of time; lender grants a postponement of loan payments for a set period of time, giving the borrower time to make up for overdue payments.

Foreclosure: the process by which the holder of a mortgage sells the property of a homeowner who has not made interest and/or principal payments on time as stipulated in the mortgage contract.

Fraud: a seller's intentional deception of a buyer, which is illegal.

Free Application for Federal Student Aid (FAFSA): a form that is completed annually by current and prospective college students to determine their eligibility for financial aid.

Free Spirit: a person who thinks that everything will work out fine; typically hates to deal with numbers.

Front-End Load: sales commission that is paid upfront when shares of a mutual fund are purchased.

Fund Family: a group of mutual funds sponsored by the same organization, often offering exchange privileges between funds and combined account statements for multiple funds.

Futures: a term used to designate all contracts covering the sale of financial instruments or physical commodities for future delivery on a commodity exchange.

Garnishment: a court-ordered attachment that allows a lender to take monies owed directly from a borrower's paycheck; only allowed as part of a court judgment.

Grace Period: time period during which a borrower can pay the full balance of credit due with no finance charges.

Grant: a form of federal or state financial aid that does not need to be repaid; usually given to students who demonstrate financial need.

Gratuity: an amount paid beyond what is required usually to express satisfaction with service quality; also known as a tip.

Gross Income: a person's total income prior to withholdings and deductions.

Gross National Product (GNP): measures an economy's total income. It is equal to Gross Domestic Product, plus the income abroad accruing to domestic residents, minus income generated in domestic market accruing to non-residents.

Growth and Income Mutual Fund: fund comprised of large, well-established companies; also called a "large-cap" fund.

Growth Stock Mutual Fund: fund that buys stock in medium-sized companies that have experienced some growth and are still expanding; also called a mid-cap fund.

Guaranteed Renewable: if you have a 20-year policy, the insurance has to provide coverage after 20 years regardless of health; it will only be more expensive because you are older.

Guaranteed Replacement Cost: part of homeowner's insurance policy that pays for the full cost of replacing damaged property without a deduction for depreciation and without a dollar limit.

Health Insurance: covers you in the event of illness or injury.

Health Savings Account (HSA): a health insurance plan for self-employed people containing a large deductible. Money saved in this account grows tax deferred. It can be used for medical care with no penalties and no taxes, and may be kept if unused.

Home Equity Loan (HEL): credit line offered by mortgage lenders that allows a homeowner to borrow money against the equity in their home.

Home Inspector: an individual who inspects homes for defects prior to the closing of a home sale to protect the buyer or lender's investment.

Home Warranty: an agreement that ensures the structural soundness of a home.

Homeowner's Insurance: policy that covers a loss due to damage, theft, or injury within one's home.

House Poor: a condition of having a disproportionately high house payment that limits one's ability to maintain the home and/or meet necessities.

Impulse Purchase: to buy an item without carefully weighing the consequences.

Income: earnings from work or investment.

Income Fund: a mutual fund that invests in bonds and stocks with higher than average dividends.

Income Risk: the possibility that income from a mutual fund or other investment will decline either as a fund's assets are reinvested or when a fixed income investment matures and is replaced with a lower-yielding investment.

Income Tax: a progressive tax on the financial income of individuals, companies, deceased estates, and certain bankrupt estates paid to the government.

Index: a statistical benchmark designed to reflect changes in financial markets or the economy. In investing, indexes are used to measure changes in segments of the stock and bond markets and as standards against which fund managers and investors can measure the performance of their investment portfolios.

Index Fund: a mutual fund that seeks to match the performance of a predetermined market benchmark or index.

Individual Retirement Arrangement (IRA): tax-deferred arrangement for individuals with earned income and their non-income-producing spouses; growth is not taxed until money is withdrawn; contributions to an IRA are often tax-deductible.

Inflation: rate at which the general level of prices for goods and services rise.

Inflation Hedge: an asset rising in value, which helps one to keep up with the rising cost of inflation; real estate can be a great inflation hedge.

Integrity: having to do with a person's honesty and moral attributes.

Interest: 1) charge for borrowed money generally defined as a percentage. 2) money paid to savers and investors by financial institutions, governments, or corporations for the use of their money (such as a 2% return on money held in a savings account).

Interest Only Loan: a mortgage where you only pay the interest.

Interest Rate: percentage paid to a lender for the use of borrowed money.

Interest Rate Risk: the risk that a security or mutual fund will decline in price because of changes in market interest rates.

Internal Revenue Service (IRS): federal agency responsible for the collection of federal taxes, including personal and corporate, Social Security, and excise and gift taxes.

International Stock Mutual Fund: fund that contains international or overseas companies.

Introductory Rate: an interest rate charged to a customer during the early stages of a loan; the rate often goes up after a specified period of time.

Investment: account or arrangement in which one would put their money for long-term growth; should not be withdrawn for a suggested minimum of five years.

Investment Advisor/Manager: the individual who manages a portfolio of investments. Also called a portfolio manager or a money manager.

Investment Objective: a mutual fund's performance goal, such as long-term capital appreciation, high current income, or tax exempt income.

Investors: people investing in securities, such as stocks and bonds, or other investments, to achieve long-term financial goals.

Interview: a meeting between an employer and an applicant; the employer asks the applicant questions to assess whether he or she has the right social skills and intelligence suitable for the workplace.

J

Job: a regular activity performed in exchange for payment, especially as one's trade, occupation, or profession.

L

Land Survey: a survey that shows where one's property lines begin and end.

Large-Cap Fund: funds comprised of large, well established companies.

Lease: a long-term rental agreement, and a form of secured long-term debt.

Level Term: this means you pay the same amount for the entire term of the policy.

Liability: the state or quality of being obligated according to law or equity.

Liability Insurance: policy that protects an individual in the event of a lawsuit due to injury on one's personal property or as the result of an automobile accident.

Life Insurance: type of insurance designed to replace income lost due to death; traditionally two types: term and cash value.

Liquidity: quality of an asset that permits it to be converted quickly into cash without loss of value; availability of money; when there is more liquidity, there is typically less return.

Loan: temporary borrowing of a sum of money.

Loan Term: time frame that a loan agreement is in force, and before or at the end of which the loan should either be repaid or renegotiated for another term.

Load Fund: mutual fund that sells shares with a sales charge of typically 2-6% of the net amount sold; some no-load funds also levy distribution fees permitted by Article 12b-1 of the Investment Company Act. These are typically 0.25%; a true noload fund has no sales charge.

Loan To Value (LTV): value of a property versus the amount borrowed against it; Example: a 70/30 LTV means that the property owner owes 70% of the item's worth and owns 30% of the item's worth.

Long-Term Care Insurance: policy that covers the cost of nursing home or in-home care; recommended for everyone over age 60.

Long Term Coverage: coverage for an extended period of time.

Long Term Disability: disability insurance designed to replace lost income for a period of five years or greater.

Loss: the negative difference between total revenue from a business or investment minus total expense.

Low-Load Fund: mutual fund that charges a sales commission equal to 3% or less of the amount invested.

Lump Sum Savings: saving money specifically for a purchase such as vacations or replacing cars.

M

Management Fee: the fee paid by a mutual fund to its investment advisor.

Market Risk: the possibility that an investment will fall in value due to a general decline in financial markets.

Mark-Up: the difference between the wholesale price and retail price.

Maximum Payment: the amount an insurance company will pay before you are dropped from coverage (with health insurance keep at least a one million dollar maximum pay).

Medicare: federal government program that pays for certain health care expenses for citizens 65 or older; managed by the Social Security Administration.

Mid-Cap Fund: mutual fund containing a group of medium-sized companies that are growing.

Money: currency and coin that are guaranteed as legal tender by the government.

Money Market Fund: mutual fund that seeks to maintain a stable share price and to earn current income by investing in interest-bearing instruments with short-term (usually 90 days or less) maturities.

Money Order: a financial instrument backed by a deposit at a certain firm, such as a bank, that can be easily converted to cash.

Mortgage: loan secured by the collateral of real estate property, which obligates the borrower to make a predetermined series of payments. Mortgage Life Insurance: insurance policy that pays off the remaining balance of the insured person's mortgage at death.

Motivation: a feeling of enthusiasm, interest, or commitment that makes somebody want to do something.

Multiple Listings Service (MLS): computer program used by realtors to search frequently updated listings of available properties in order to find prospective homes for their clients.

Murphy's Law: anything that can happen will happen.

Mutual Fund: pool of money managed by an investment company and invested in multiple companies, bonds, etc.; offers investors a variety of goals depending on the fund and its investment charter; often used to generate income on a regular basis or to preserve an investor's money; sometimes used to invest in companies that are growing at a rapid pace.

Myth: information that has been passed on but is not true.

N

Necessities: something that is necessary; a requirement or need for something.

Need: economic goods and services that are basic for living such as food, clothing, and shelter.

Negotiating: to bargain for a lower price.

Nerd: one who is picky about budgeting and numbers.

Nest Egg: sum of money earmarked for ongoing living expenses at retirement or when employment income otherwise stops.

Net Asset Value (NAV): the market value of a mutual fund's total assets, less its liabilities, divided by the number of outstanding shares.

No-Load Mutual Fund: open-ended investment company whose shares are sold without a sales charge; might include other distribution charges, such as Article 12b-1 fees, but a true no-load fund has neither a sales charge nor a distribution fee.

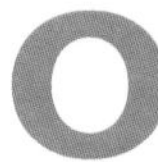

Objective: a goal or plan.

Occupational Disability: type of insurance that provides an income in case the insured becomes unable to perform the job he/she was educated or trained to do.

Opportunity Cost: the true cost of something in terms of what you have to give up to get the item; the benefits you would have received by taking the other action.

Out-of-Pocket Expense: a specific amount of money that you are required to pay.

Owner Financing: type of mortgage in which the existing owner acts as the mortgage holder; payments are made to the owner rather than to a mortgage company or bank.

Paradigm: your belief system; the way you see or perceive things.

Patience: the ability to wait or delay an action without becoming upset or annoyed.

Pawn Shop: retail establishment selling items that have been traded as security for a cash loan.

Payroll Deduction: amount subtracted from a paycheck, either by government requirement (mandatory taxes, Social Security, etc.) or at the employee's request (health insurance, retirement plan, etc.).

Permanent Disability: disabilities that are ongoing and are not expected to end.

Policy: describes the type of coverage in an insurance agreement.

Portfolio: a list of your investments.

Portfolio Transaction Costs: the costs associated with buying and selling securities, including commissions on trades, dealer mark-ups on bonds, bid-asking spreads, and any other miscellaneous expenses. These costs are not included in the expense ratio.

Pre-Authorized Checking (PAC): system of automatic payment processing by which bills, deposits, and payments are handled electronically and at regular intervals or on a predetermined schedule.

Pre-Paid Tuition: paying for college ahead of time by accumulating units of tuition.

Pre-Tax Retirement Plan: a type of retirement plan where you put money in before taxes have been taken out, but must pay taxes on the money at the time of withdrawal.

Premium: amount you pay monthly, quarterly, semiannually or annually to purchase different types of insurance.

Principal: original amount of money invested, excluding any interest or dividends; also called the face value of a loan.

Priority: level of high importance or great urgency.

Private Mortgage Insurance (PMI): policy paid by the mortgage borrower that protects the lender against loss resulting from default on a mortgage loan.

Pro-Active: to have a strong initiative; when one happens "to" things.

Procrastinating: to put off until later; waiting until the last minute.

Profit: the positive difference between total revenue from a business or investment minus total expense.

Pro Rata: debt repayment plan by which the borrower repays each lender a fair percentage of the total debt owed when one cannot make the minimum payments on one's debt.

Prospectus: official document that contains information required by the Securities and Exchange Commission to describe an investment.

Rate of Return: return on an investment expressed as a percentage of its cost; also called yield.

Real Estage Agent: a real estate professional who receives a commission for arranging and facilitating the sale of a property for a buyer or a seller. Also referred to as a real estate broker.

Reconcile: to match your bank statement with your checkbook, preferably within 72 hours of receiving the statement.

Redemption Fee: fee charged by some mutual funds for selling (redeeming) shares.

Refunding: sending in proofs of purchase to receive cash back or free gifts.

Re-investment: use of investment income or dividends to buy additional shares.

Rent: periodic fee for the use of property.

Rental Real Estate: buying real estate to rent out as an investment.

Renter's Insurance: type of insurance that provides coverage for accidents, damages and losses in a rental (apartment or house) or dormitory.

Replacement Cost: insurance that pays the actual cost of replacing your home and its contents after a catastrophic event.

Repo Lot: a place where items that have been repossessed are offered for sale.

Restoration Services: part of identity theft insurance that assigns a counselor to clean up the mess made when your identity was stolen.

Résumé: personal and work history used for gaining employment.

Retailer: one who buys a product to re-sell.

Reverse Mortgage: used to release the home equity in a property. The home owner either makes no payments and the interest is added to the lien of the property, or the homeowner receives monthly payments there by increasing the debt each month.

Risk: degree of uncertainty of return on an asset; in business, the likelihood of loss or reduced profit.

Risk-Return Ratio: relationship of substantial reward in comparison to the amount of risk taken.

Rollover: movement of funds from a tax-deferred retirement plan from one qualified plan or custodian to another; incurs no immediate tax liabilities or penalties, but requires IRS reporting.

Roth IRA: retirement account funded with after-tax dollars that subsequently grows tax free.

Roth 401(k): a retirement plan similar to a 401(k) that has after-tax contribution benefits.

Rule of 72: a quick way to calculate the length of time it will take to double a sum of money. Divide 72 by the expected interest rate to determine the number of years (72 divided by 8% = 9 years).

Rule of 78: prepayment penalty in a financing contract; the portion of a 90-days same-as-cash agreement that states that the entire loan amount plus the interest accumulated over the first 90 days becomes due immediately.

Salary: payment for work, usually calculated in periods of a week or longer. Salary is usually tied to the completion of specific duties over a minimum, but not maximum, number of hours; also see wage.

Sales Tax: a tax levied on the sales of goods and services. It is collected by the retailer and given to the state.

Saving: the process of setting aside money until a future date instead of spending it today. The goal is to provide for emergencies, short term goals, and investments.

Savings Account: accounts at financial institutions that allow regular deposits and withdrawals; the minimum required deposit, fees charged, and interest rate paid varies among providers.

Savings Bond: certificate representing a debt; example: U.S. savings bond is a loan to the government in which the government agrees to repay to the bondholder the amount borrowed, with interest; government bonds are issued in face value denominations from $50 to $10,000, with local and state tax-free interest and semi-annually adjusted interest rates.

Savings & Loan Associations (S&Ls): financial institutions that provide loans and interest bearing accounts which are federally insured.

Scholarship: a form of financial aid that does not need to be repaid; usually awarded on the basis of academic, athletic or other achievements.

Sector Fund: a mutual fund that invests its shareholders' money in a relatively narrow market sector, e.g. technology, energy, the internet, or banking.

Self-Esteem: one's attitude about themselves.

Self-Insured: condition of wealth at which time one no longer needs an outside insurance policy to cover a loss.

Share: piece of ownership in a company or mutual fund.

Short-Term Disability: minimal period of incapacitation; often used to describe an insurance policy that insures one's income for the immediate future following an incapacitating event.

Short-Term Policy: insurance policy that only covers a minimal period of time.

Significant Purchase: an amount of money you spend, usually $300 or more, that causes some pain to part with.

Simple Interest: interest credited daily, monthly, quarterly, semi-annually, or annually on principal only, not previously credited interest.

Simple IRA: salary deduction plan for retirement benefits provided by some small companies with fewer than 100 employees.

Simplified Employee Pension Plan (SEPP): pension plan in which both the employee and the employer contribute to an individual retirement account.

Single Stocks: an investment in one particular stock only.

Sinking Fund: saving money for a specific purpose to allow interest to work for you rather than against you.

Small-Cap Fund: mutual fund that invests in companies whose market value is less than $1 billion; largely consists of smaller, more volatile companies; also called aggressive growth stock mutual fund.

Social Security: federal government program of transfer payments for retirement, disability, or the loss of income from a parent or guardian; funds come from a tax on income, which is a payroll deduction labeled FICA.

Speculative: purchasing risky investments that present the possibility of large profits, but also post a higher-than-average possibility of loss.

Stock Markets:

- **National Association of Securities Dealers Automated Quotation System (NASDAQ):** the electronic stock exchange run by the National Association of Securities Dealers for over the counter trading. Established in 1971, it is America's fastest growing stock market and aleader in trading foreign securities and technology shares. The NASDAQ uses market makers who trade for their own account and profit on the spread between bid and ask prices. Although once the province of smaller companies, NASDAQ today is where many leading companies are traded.
- **New York Stock Exchange (NYSE):** the NYSE traces its origins back more that 200 years to the signing of the Buttonwood Agreement by 24 New York City stockbrokers and merchants in 1792. The NYSE utilizes a trading floor for traditional exchanges where buyers and sellers meet directly—that is, brokers representing investors on each side of the transaction come together on a price.

Stocks: securities that represent part ownership or equity in a corporation, wherein each share is a claim on its proportionate stake in the corporation's assets and profits, some of which may be paid out as dividends.

Stop-Loss: total out-of-pocket expense for health insurance; once reached, insurance company will pay 100%.

Take-Home Pay: the amount of money one has available after taxes have been taken out of their pay. Total wage, salary, commissions, and/or bonuses minus payroll deductions.

Tax: a government fee on business and individual income, activities, products, or services.

Tax Credit: an amount that a taxpayer who meets certain criteria can subtract from tax owed.

Tax Deduction: expense that a taxpayer is allowed to deduct from taxable income; examples include money paid as home mortgage interest and charitable donations.

Tax Deductible: the effect of a tax deduction, such as charitable contributions and mortgage interest.

Tax-Deferred Income: dividends, interest, and unrealized capital gains on investments in a qualified account, such as a retirement plan, in which income is not subject to taxation until a withdrawal is made.

Tax Exempt: investments whose earnings are free from tax liability.

Tax Exemptions: amount that a taxpayer who meets certain criteria can subtract from a taxable income; see tax credit and tax deduction.

Tax-Favored Dollars: money that is working for you, either tax-deferred or tax-free, within a retirement plan.

Taxable Income: income subject to tax; total income adjusted for deductions, exemptions and credits.

Term Insurance: life insurance coverage for a specified period of time.

Timeshare: vacation property in which a company sells a small segment of time to a customer; the costs of running the property are shared among all of the owners who bought into the time share.

Time Poverty: a situation in which a person is lacking time, which leads to stress.

Time Value of Money: money at the present time is worth more than the same amount in the future.

Title Insurance: coverage that protects a policyholder from future challenges to the title of a property that may result in loss of the property.

Total Return: the change in percentage over a particular period in the value of an investment; including any income from the investment and any change in its market value.

Track Record: the past history of something; with investments, look at the five or ten year record.

Turnover Rate: a measure of a mutual fund's trading activity. Turnover is calculated by taking the lesser of the fund's total purchases or total sales of securities (not counting securities with maturities under one year) and dividing by the average monthly assets. A turnover rate of 50% means that during a year, a fund has sold and replaced securities with a value equal to 50% of the fund's average net assets.

Umbrella Liability Insurance: high-limit insurance policy that acts as a protective covering over your home and car insurance against liability caused by an accident.

Underwriter: a firm that buys an issue of securities from a company and resells it to investors. In general, a party that guarantees the proceeds to the firm from a security sale, thereby in effect taking ownership of the securities.

Unearned Income: money received for which no exchange was made, such as a gift.

Uniform Gifts to Minors Act (UGMA): legislation that provides a tax-effective manner of transferring property to minors without the complications of trusts or guardianship restrictions.

Uniform Transfers to Minors Act (UTMA): law similar to the Uniform Gifts to Minors Act (UGMA) that extends the definition of gifts to include real estate, paintings, royalties, and patents.

Universal Life: type of life insurance policy, similar to cash value, but with better projected returns.

Unrealized Capital Gain/Loss: an increase/decrease in the value of a stock or security (mutual fund) that is not "realized" because the security has not yet been sold for a gain or a loss.

Veterans Administration (VA) Loan: type of mortgage loan designed to benefit veterans that allows for a true zero-down mortgage; generally more expensive than a conventional mortgage.

Value Fund: mutual fund that emphasizes stocks of companies whose growth prospects are generally regarded as sub-par by the market, resulting in stocks typically priced below average based on such factors as revenue, earnings, book value, and dividends.

Value System: a person's priorities, beliefs and standards that affect how he or she views the world.

Variable Annuity: annuity that has a varying rate of return based on the mutual funds in which one has invested; also see annuity.

Variable Life: type of life insurance that is similar to cash value, but buys into mutual funds to project better returns.

Viatical: contractual arrangement in which a business buys life insurance policies from terminally ill patients for a percentage of the face value.

Vocation: the work in which an individual is employed; your calling as a career.

Volatility: fluctuations in market value of a mutual fund or other security; the greater a fund's volatility, the wider the fluctuations between high and low prices.

W-4: a federal tax form filled out by an employee to indicate the amount that should be withheld from his/her paycheck for taxes.

Wage: payment for work, usually calculated in periods of an hour rather than longer; also see salary.

Walkaway Power: the ability to walk away from a purchase when negotiating.

Wants: desires for economic goods or services not necessary in order to survive.

Wealth: accumulating assets such as money and possessions, often as a result of saving or investing.

Win-Win Deal: a negotiation where both parties benefit.

Withholding: a portion of employee's wages or salary deducted for taxes.

Whole Life Insurance: type of insurance that contains a low-yield savings plan within the insurance policy; more expensive than term life insurance.

Work Ethic: how motivated, loyal and honest you are in your work.

Work Study: a program that allows students to work part time while continuing their studies.

Yield: the annualized rate at which an investment earns income, expressed as a percentage of the investment's current price.

Z

Zero-Based Budget: cash flow plan that assigns an expense to every dollar of one's income, wherein the total income minus the total expenses equals zero.